MANCHESTER
MEDIEVAL
LITERATURE
AND CULTURE

The gift of narrative in medieval England

MANCHESTER
1824

Manchester University Press

Series editors: Anke Bernau, David Matthews and James Paz

Series founded by: J. J. Anderson and Gail Ashton

Advisory board: Ruth Evans, Patricia C. Ingham, Andrew James Johnston, Chris Jones, Catherine Karkov, Nicola McDonald, Haruko Momma, Susan Phillips, Sarah Salih, Larry Scanlon, Stephanie Trigg and Matthew Vernon

MANCHESTER
MEDIEVAL
LITERATURE
AND CULTURE

Manchester Medieval Literature and Culture publishes monographs and essay collections comprising new research informed by current critical methodologies on the literary cultures of the Middle Ages. We are interested in all periods, from the early Middle Ages through to the late, and we include post-medieval engagements with and representations of the medieval period (or 'medievalism'). 'Literature' is taken in a broad sense, to include the many different medieval genres: imaginative, historical, political, scientific, religious. While we welcome contributions on the diverse cultures of medieval Britain and are happy to receive submissions on Anglo-Norman, Anglo-Latin and Celtic writings, we are also open to work on the Middle Ages in Europe more widely, and beyond.

Titles available in the series

The gift of narrative in medieval England

Nicholas Perkins

MANCHESTER UNIVERSITY PRESS

The right of Nicholas Perkins to be identified as the author of this work
has been asserted by him in accordance with the Copyright, Designs and
Patents Act 1988.

Published by Manchester University Press
Altrincham Street, Manchester M1 7JA

www.manchesteruniversitypress.co.uk

British Library Cataloguing-in-Publication Data
A catalogue record for this book is available from the British Library

ISBN   978 1 5261 3991 7   hardback

First published 2021

The publisher has no responsibility for the persistence or accuracy of
URLs for any external or third-party internet websites referred to in this
book, and does not guarantee that any content on such websites is, or
will remain, accurate or appropriate.

Typeset
by New Best-set Typesetters Ltd

For my family,
and for Polly: BWV 1043

Contents

Figures

Figures 2–4 are reproduced by kind permission of the John Rylands Library, and are copyright of the University of Manchester.

Acknowledgements

In a book about gifts and exchange, the acknowledgements take on an especially telling role. I owe a huge amount to many people and institutions: debts, exchanges, obligations and friendships that have developed over the nearly twenty years since I first started thinking about this topic. First I should like to thank Girton College, Cambridge, St Hugh's College, Oxford, and the English Faculties at the Universities of Cambridge and Oxford for providing the environment in which this work took place, including financial support, fantastic libraries and librarians, supportive and inspiring colleagues, and thoughtful students – from first-year undergraduates to doctoral researchers. A particular mention goes to the Girton students I taught for the 'Courts and Courtliness' option so long ago. I owe a great deal to the Leverhulme Trust for awarding me a research fellowship in 2018–19. This paid for replacement teaching (ably taken on by Ayoush Lazikani), and without the fellowship it would have been very difficult to bring the book together. At Manchester University Press I am very grateful to Meredith Carroll and her colleagues, along with the series editors and anonymous readers, for backing the project and improving it through their helpful comments. At the latter stages of preparing the typescript, I had excellent assistance from Niall Summers and Rebecca Menmuir.

I first started talking publicly about some of the ideas in the book in 2006, at the Romance in Medieval Britain conference in York and the New Chaucer Society Congress in New York. These and other conferences have provided a particularly helpful way to discuss developing thoughts, learn from others, meet and make friends; thanks, then, to the conference organizers who make that happen, and to everyone taking part in Romance in Medieval Britain at

St Hugh's in 2012. I have also benefited greatly from discussion with seminar and lecture audiences, including in Bern, Boulder, Cambridge, Leicester, Lausanne, London, Odense and Oxford.

At Girton College, I was surrounded by people whose intellectual energy and openness left a mark on me, including Marilyn Strathern and Sarah Kay (both of whom gave me ideas and reading about gifts), Juliet Dusinberre, Anne Fernihough, Jill Mann and Deana Rankin. After moving to St Hugh's College, I have benefited hugely from the exchange of ideas with my colleagues in English there, including Hugh Gazzard, Rosie Lavan, Rhodri Lewis, Eleanor Lybeck, David Taylor and Abigail Williams. In particular, Peter McDonald has been a brilliant colleague, interlocutor and friend. I also owe thanks to many others across the College, including Elish Angiolini, Vicki Stott, Roy Westbrook, Nora Khayi, Thea Crapper, and all the people with whom I worked as Dean. Many colleagues and friends have invited me to give a talk, commented on draft materials, supported grant applications, answered questions, bought the drinks, or just tried to help me think better (sometimes a lost cause). This will be an incomplete list, but thanks to Alastair Bennett, Jessica Brantley, Helen Cooper, Robert Epstein, Laura Feldt, Rosalind Field, Vincent Gillespie, Alfred Hiatt, Simon Horobin, Hsin-yu Hu, Chris Jones, Martin Kauffmann, Elliot Kendall, Annette Kern-Stähler, Philip Knox, Katie Little, Sally Mapstone, Nicola McDonald, Deborah McGrady, Jenni Nuttall, Heather O'Donoghue, Denis Renevey, Maddy Slaven, Tony Spearing, Paul Strohm, Helen Swift, Marion Turner, Daniel Wakelin, Judy Weiss, and Alison Wiggins. I especially want to thank four very generous people who have, at just the right times, helped me remember or forget that I was working on this book: Jenny Adams, Helen Barr, Morgan Dickson and Annie Sutherland. Finally, James Simpson has been crucial, from conversations over lunch in Girton to incisive commentary on draft chapters, and in providing a model of generosity in and beyond academic life: *grazie mille*.

Many other friends and their families have helped me, especially at the points when writing a book seemed like the last thing I was ever likely to do again. Profound thanks to Susan Barton, Sally Burlington, Sarah Coatsworth, Sue and Scott Dickinson, Andrew and Catherine Dilnot, Kate Elliott, Jim Harris, Diane Leblond, Jacqui Lewis, Patrick Mulcare, Paul Oliver, Senia Paseta (YNWA), Solomon and Naomi Pomerantz, Owen Rees, Gary Snapper, Mark Thompson and Jane Blumberg, Diana and Nick Walton, and Wes Williams. The dedication of the book expresses my love and gratitude to my family, especially Mum and Peter; Caroline, Jonathan and their families; and of course, Imogen and Guy. It's a small way, too, of saying a great big thank you to Polly Walton.

Oxford
September 2019

Abbreviations

AND	*Anglo-Norman Dictionary*
ANTS	Anglo-Norman Text Society
DIMEV	*Digital Index of Middle English Verse*
EETS e.s.	Early English Text Society, extra series
EETS o.s.	Early English Text Society, original series
MED	*Middle English Dictionary*
NIMEV	*New Index of Middle English Verse*
ODNB	*Oxford Dictionary of National Biography*
OED	*Oxford English Dictionary*
PMLA	*Publications of the Modern Language Association of America*
SAC	*Studies in the Age of Chaucer*
TEAMS	Consortium for the Teaching of the Middle Ages

Introduction

Some years ago, my mother gave me a flattish black box. It was leather-covered, like an old book, with an embossed gold line framing a hinged lid, secured by a spring push button. Nestled in the box was a set of six silver spoons, a bit bigger than teaspoons. They were delicately patterned at the handle. I knew these spoons: in my childhood they'd been in a drawer with things that were kept for best. They were a pleasure to use, fitting comfortably into the hand and the mouth. Along with the spoons, my mother wrote me a note about them. They had been a wedding present to her in 1964 from an elderly lady (someone referred to in the family as 'Old Miss Sprake'), the sister of a man in whose small law firm my grandfather's father had worked his way up from clerk to partner. Along with her note, my mother included the letter that Miss Sprake had written to accompany the spoons, while declining the wedding invitation. The letter is addressed to my grandfather: the invitations had been sent out by the bride's parents, as was customary, and Miss Sprake was invited as an important connection, though she barely knew my mother. Miss Sprake was an old lady in 1964, and had not been well. In her letter, she tells my grandfather that the spoons were made by the firm of McFarlane in Glasgow in 1842 (though those details are not quite borne out by the hallmarks). She notes that they are unused, and somewhat archly expresses the hope that 'your daughter likes <u>some</u> old-fashioned things!' – a topic perhaps on the mind of a Victorian lady who had lived through two world wars, contemplating the young generation of the 1960s. Perhaps the spoons had themselves been a present to Miss Sprake at a much earlier point in her life, but this is pure speculation. In her own note to me, my mother jokes that I might be interested in their provenance because of my research on gifts. I sometimes use the spoons when I have family or friends over. Their monetary value is not great, but they are beautiful and well-designed. More than that, they carry with them a set of connections and a story: one sometimes retold when they are used. Many families have objects with equivalent stories, often far more dramatic or romantic than this. I keep the two letters – from Miss Sprake to my grandfather, and from my mother to me – in the box. Perhaps one day I will give the spoons to one of my children, and include another note.

These spoons are a small example of how gifts connect people, often renewing or complicating those connections over many years and generations. Gifts both represent and embody mutual obligations: in this case, between families who were linked professionally but for whom those relations extended into a social and personal sphere, particularly at significant events such as a wedding. They tell a story about changing perceptions of duty and gendered roles over the last hundred and more years. They can establish both generosity and hierarchy (or, in some circumstances, threat). The energy they bring to interpersonal relations is not used up in the moment of their being given, but is stored and then renewed at certain key moments in their continuing journey, or in acts of conservation within a family or community. In the words of Margaret Atwood, 'every time a gift is given it is enlivened and regenerated through the new spiritual life it engenders both in the giver and in the receiver'.[1] Gifts themselves have a trajectory that can be traced and told. They provoke explanation and reflection: in other words, they give rise to stories. We could say that they materialize narratives, sometimes through their form, history and human connections; sometimes in readable signs, such as the Glasgow assay marks on my spoons, and the accompanying letters. Many of these attributes of gifts we implicitly understand and are attuned to, subtly adjusting our habits and expectations depending on whom we are with, where we travel, and what our own circumstances are, even if we do not know or care about the ways in which anthropologists and theorists might describe those habits.

In this book, I will read narrative texts from the Insular Middle Ages in the light of debates about gifts and objects. Most of the texts I focus on are romances, or are connected to the broad genre of romance, and they range in date from the twelfth-century *Romance of Horn* by an author named Thomas, to the fifteenth-century *Troy Book* by John Lydgate. The texts exist in manuscript books that themselves were commissioned, given, sold, and then preserved. The given-ness of manuscripts is a valuable area of study in itself, and I engage with it explicitly in Chapter 5, but my main focus is on how acts of giving and receiving are embedded and described in these texts, tracing, deepening or constraining relations between their protagonists; how persons may themselves become given objects; and how gifts in these narratives are intimately linked to the telling of stories: the gift of narrative.

The gift is a subject that has received enormous amounts of attention, particularly following the work of Marcel Mauss and Bronislaw Malinowski in the 1920s.[2] It would not be an exaggeration to say that it is a foundational subject for the field of Anthropology. To take one example, Karen Sykes chooses the gift as a pathway into Anthropology for a 2005 introductory book because of its fundamental role in societies and in the discipline. Echoing Mauss, she describes gift exchange as 'a total social fact that concentrates and condenses social processes and thereby provides anthropologists with the descriptive and explanatory means to discuss how people live in the round'.[3]

Anthropological debates about the gift have had an impact on literary scholarship and critical theory at many levels. While learning from these debates, I am conscious of the risks in comparing medieval Western with recent or contemporary non-European cultures, where much of the core fieldwork on gifts and exchange has taken place. These cultures are not an image of Europe or 'the West' at an earlier stage of development, notwithstanding a tradition of reading them as such that is deeply embedded in Western politics and scholarship; nor are they simply 'gift societies' as opposed to Northern/Western 'commodity societies'.[4] Thinking, however, about how a variety of cultures approach questions of, for example, reciprocity and generosity can help generate more reflective readings of medieval texts. For that reason, my engagement with anthropological debate is intended to generate tools for thinking rather than direct comparison, and my approach is designedly eclectic and open to question (in several senses). Each chapter takes a distinct but overlapping approach to the issues, and in a moment I shall summarize them.

First, though, I want to say more about the questions provoked by placing gifts and narrative texts together. One of the best-known attempts to introduce theories of the gift to a broader audience and relate them to the process of literary and artistic creation is Lewis Hyde's *The Gift*, first published in 1979. Hyde argues for the value that gifts bring to social life and the imagination. He identifies traditional stories and fairy tales as particularly powerful descriptions of the gift in operation, creating long-term bonds between people, returning in unexpected or transformational ways, and providing a challenge to traditional economic understandings of commodity exchange. Hyde additionally finds the generative capacity of the gift in artists' understanding of inspiration, especially in Walt Whitman's stance that the artist's self 'becomes the gifted self ... [a]nd the work of the artist can only come to its powers in the world when it moves beyond the self as a gift'.[5] Hyde's work has brought concepts of gift and commodity into many people's understanding of what it means to be an artist, and of how the gift of art might be reconciled with the commerce of the market.[6] At the same time, however, the ability of the gift to open up social relations or to maintain its distinction in the economic sphere has regularly been challenged, to the point where the possibility of pure, altruistic gifts has been questioned, and instead the gift's embeddedness within structures of hierarchy and economic calculation foregrounded. Jacques Derrida, for example, describes this idea of the pure gift as '[no]t impossible but *the* impossible. The very figure of the impossible'; yet it is, for him, necessarily thinkable: 'For finally, if the gift is another name of the impossible, we still think it, we name it, we desire it. We intend it.'[7] Can generosity survive the drag of obligation that it imposes on the receiver? How can individual acts of giving be understood in relation to the 'système des prestations totales' [system of total prestations; or system of overall obligations] that Mauss posited, within whose balancing structures an individual, asymmetrical act of generosity takes place?[8] Equally, how do literary texts represent those moments of giving amongst networks of power, identity and affinity? And how does the exchange of objects, people or promises relate to acts of telling? In short, is storytelling itself a form of giving?

These are some of the questions at the heart of this book. My interest in using romance as a grounding genre for discussion stems from romances' foregrounding of narrative events and objects to carry meaning; their traditional structures within which shifts of generosity and obligation may be played out;[9] and the importance of acts of telling, in and outside the narrative. Romances both absorb and think through dilemmas contemporary to their initial audiences, but they also frequently create other, mythistorical worlds in which to test those dilemmas, exploring the consequences of decisions, actions and speech acts.[10] In this respect, they practise what we might call a speculative Anthropology of their own: representing the lives of others in order to learn more about the range of human experience, its bonds, emotional heft and social interplay. This engages the pleasures of shock, suspense and recognition, playing with alternative pasts and extreme scenarios that prompt their audiences to reflect on and debate their eventual outcomes, however much those outcomes seem to accord with socially convenient expectations, such as marriage and the safeguarding of lineage.[11] The five chapters of this book discuss how gift and exchange work as part of this dynamic relationship between story and audience, inside and beyond the texts.

In Chapter 1, I take *The Romance of Horn* – one of the earliest romances to survive from Britain – as the grounding point for exploring how romance narratives are patterned with the dynamics of gift exchange and reciprocity. I read the text's eponymous hero as himself a gift: arriving as if unmotivated, before our accruing knowledge of his past and his actions reveals the narrative's commitments, debts and patterns of reward and revenge. In *The Romance of Horn*, the act of storytelling, both in the text and of the text, also shares these attributes of a gift, and this interplay between objects and people who are exchanged, and acts of telling as exchange, is something to which I return in subsequent chapters. Chapter 1 takes Mauss's discussion of the *hau* of the gift from his reading of Maori practice as a point of entry for longstanding arguments about what surplus or yield a gift might bring to a relationship, or in its continuing journey; and what kind of altruism, if any, may motivate giving: in other words, where do gifts come from, and how do they operate in time? Pierre Bourdieu's work on time and reciprocity is valuable here, in particular how he characterizes reciprocal relations as setting up expectations that can be varied by individual choices and performances.[12] In this spirit I conclude the chapter by examining two other performances of the Horn legend: *King Horn* and *Horn*

Childe and Maiden Rimnild, asking how they reshape patterns of reciprocity according to their styles and changing audience(s).

In Chapter 2, *Horn Childe* acts as a bridge into a book containing one of the major surviving collections of romances in English: the Auchinleck Manuscript (Edinburgh, National Library of Scotland, Advocates MS 19.2.1). I ask what role the itineraries of objects as gifts play in a number of the Auchinleck romances, counterpointing these written texts with a particularly resonant object from medieval England – the Savernake Horn – as an instance of something made, given, used and told over time as an object and event. My reading of the Auchinleck *Amis and Amiloun*, *Tristrem* and *Orfeo* focuses on how keeping as well as giving is an important marker of status, loyalty and continuity. Here I draw on Annette Weiner's work for understanding how layers of obligation, contests of possession and circulation, and gendered roles play a part in the complex movement and stasis of objects and people in narratives.[13] These movements might be read across texts as well as within them, with a manuscript collection itself forming a system of overall obligations, in which individual texts have both debts and investments. Finally, I turn to *Sir Gawain and the Green Knight* to explore how Gawain himself functions as possession, gift, object, narrative and teller, the energies of the gift flowing through him as well as being harnessed by him.

Chapter 3 pursues the idea that persons may at various times be givers, receivers and given objects in patterns of reciprocal relations. I focus here on prisoners and on gendered exchange in Chaucer's *The Knight's Tale* and *Troilus and Criseyde*, reading them through debates over the 'traffic in women', and through the complex, reflective work of Marilyn Strathern on gender and the gift.[14] How does Chaucer represent these texts' protagonists as both given objects and desiring subjects? Strathern's interest in 'partible' persons, and her attention to the way that people's agency is expressed through the obligations in which they are bound, prompt a reading of Chaucer's poems as a network of obligations, forces and gendered performances, embedded in which are ideas of what it means to have agency, to give, and to be given.

Up to this point, my readings have focused on objects that are given; on people who give, receive and themselves circulate; on the notion that protagonists may act as gifts to a narrative; and on the idea that telling may also be a form of giving. In Chapter 4 I move more specifically to analyse a verbal aspect of exchange: the giving and receiving of promises and speech acts. Reading *The Franklin's Tale* and *The Manciple's Tale* from *The Canterbury Tales* through this lens, I ask what kinds of generosity are engaged by promising and other performatives, and how both gender and genre make a difference to the effects of these linguistic acts. These two Canterbury tales extend the generic range of the book from romance to the (closely related) Breton *lai* and (more distant) Ovidian fable, and one of the questions they pose is how genre also influences expectations of generosity and reciprocity in narrative. *The Franklin's Tale's* potential sex triangle is resolved through the protagonists' generosities of body, word and coin, which aligns with the way that the *lai* foregrounds the power of transformative language. In *The Manciple's Tale*, by contrast, a generic affiliation to the fable helps create a darker narrative patterning whose reciprocal gestures are destructive, and whose final warnings are of the dangers of giving and telling. Both tales represent the spoken or written word as an unpredictable object, whose meanings and return value may be initiated but not finally contained by its speaker or author.

The final chapter explores the persistence and ambivalence of narrative exchange through John Lydgate's *Troy Book* – a retelling of the Trojan story encompassing epic, moral history and romance. I show how Lydgate's poem is inevitably patterned by the repeated exchanges of words, acts of violence, gifts and thefts, and the movement of bodies in and out of the besieged city. A particular focus is the apparent power of objects to combat or execute the workings of reciprocity and of fortune: for example, the ingeniously preserved body of Hector; the sacred Palladium; and one of the best-known gifts in Western culture: the Trojan Horse itself. I discuss these in the context of theories of materiality, the vibrancy of matter and networks of agency, though with a sceptical lens that sees Lydgate struggling to manage the contradictions of human agency, Classical narrative and Christian ethics. One lesson of studying gift exchange is that context and performance matters. In this chapter, my reading of the *Troy Book* is focused through a particular performance of the *Troy Book*, in Manchester, John Rylands Library MS English 1. This magnificently illustrated copy, itself both a gift book and containing the recursive histories of Trojan exchange, provides an arena for exploring how the reciprocities that I discuss in each of the chapters here are not limited to the narrative structures of a particular literary text, but are embedded in relations between source and poem, author and patron, and a book and its owners or audiences.

While this book is not a cultural history of gift-giving in medieval Britain nor a study of economic relations *per se* in literary texts, it inevitably draws on work in these and related areas. Gift-giving was integral to royal courts, noble and gentry households, trading relationships, urban and village communities throughout the Middle Ages.[15] Practices of giving and exchanging were likewise embedded at all levels of religious practice, including monastic foundations, parishes, and between the living and the dead.[16] In the index to his illuminating edition of medieval household accounts, C.M. Woolgar lists dozens of different items given as gifts, payments or rewards, including greyhounds, falcons, wine and New Year's gifts.[17] It is noteworthy, though, that the vocabulary of giving (including *dona*) does not clearly separate what we might call gifts from other forms of payments, and that this linguistic context matches the plural and overlapping forms of medieval exchange. Woolgar makes the important observation that 'context is everything ... we need to understand the nuances of occasion in order to interpret [gift-giving]'.[18] And while Diana Wood characterizes the late-medieval period as developing a monetized economy, 'herald[ing] a transition to secular values' in which '[e]verything came to have its price', Martha C. Howell stresses the interdependence of gifts with other forms of exchange, and the value placed on them precisely as commercial ideas of value developed: '[i]n effect, the quantification of value produced its cultural opposite'.[19] The range of meanings that gift-giving could have, including its being embedded in commercial environments, does not invalidate gifts or simply absorb them into the market; instead they played important functions alongside market transactions, for example in establishing reputation and status for commercial agents, public authorities and religious patrons, as well as circulating at many levels of society to secure and maintain bonds. However, they could also mark a turn away from (or at least a deferral or misrecognition of) the reckoning of immediate value. The act of giving can employ a subtle palette of meanings that different performances highlight and different audiences can observe; as Valentin Groebner suggests: '[t]he offering always takes place before an audience that must be regarded not simply as a mute backdrop but as a participating factor'.[20] Studies of gift books, for example, describe some of these tonal effects in royal and gentry environments,[21] and there has also been growing interest in the intimate connections between medieval imaginative texts and household practices. Vance Smith's *Arts of Possession* in particular places the challenges of surplus and lack, of possession and economic (etymologically, household) management as integral to fourteenth-century romance telling: 'The romance is the space in which the *oikos* is transgressed, crossed over, in search of the limitless regions of the otherworld of possession, where things can be totally, unproblematically, and cannily, possessed.'[22] Smith's thoughtful readings of household and (other) imaginative texts are influential on my own work here, and they join numerous studies that have helped shape or provide points of reference for this book, from a classic discussion of *Sir Gawain and the Green Knight* by Jill Mann, to an essay on *Sir Amadace* by Ad Putter which insightfully probes some ethical and narrative consequences of imagining gift and commodity exchange in romance.[23] Two books, published late in the process of constructing this one, exemplify how debates surrounding gifts and exchanging are continuing to generate new discussion in the field: Robert Epstein's *Chaucer's Gifts*, and Walter Wadiak's *Savage Economy*. Epstein focuses on *The Canterbury Tales* and a crucial question about the possibility of reading gifts not as disguised commodities nor unrealistic fantasies. Citing neo-Maussian scholars such as Alain Caillé, and influenced by the work of David Graeber on value and debt, Epstein resists the collapse of our ideas of gift and exchange into a shadow form of commercial transaction or commodity exchange, arguing that 'the social relations of capitalism and the free market are not the original, natural, exclusive and inevitable organizing principles of society'; instead, gift exchange 'operates under its own logic' that promotes social interaction rather than commercial profit itself: 'exchanges cannot always be reduced to the desire for economic profit, nor to the desire for symbolic profit … at the same time, they are not the same as simple generosity or charity'.[24] By contrast, Wadiak proposes a dark power in the inter-relation of the gift with violence in romance, in which the knight's ability to be generous is predicated on the threat of bloodshed that maintains his rank and power. The aristocratic right to wield violence is a gift 'that underwrites and reaffirms the feudal power of a privileged group'. For Wadiak, the survival of romance as a genre too is intimately linked to its repeated turn to violence. Alongside this, he also acknowledges the possibility of another kind of book 'that saw the gift work of romance not as an attempt at asymmetrical violence, but rather a way of imagining the gift as a truly radical gesture, along the lines of calls for us to "think the gift" as a means of going beyond our own restrictive economic and political regimes'.[25]

My work differs from both Epstein and Wadiak in its focus on how acts of telling themselves participate in the interplay of giving and receiving, whether that interplay is coercive, generous, constrained or potentially radical. Nevertheless, my readings of romance and related texts are in some senses a version of Wadiak's 'other kind of book', and my position vis-à-vis the possibility of generosity and the value of giving aside from already constructed hierarchies is closer to that of Epstein. But I do not believe that the differences here are zero-sum. This book explores a network of messages in romance suggesting how generosity, though always at interplay with dynamics of power and conflict, may open the self to the other, whether within established groups or across divides of rank, belief and gender; and how a turn away from generosity may have short-term benefits, but will also close ethical, social and narrative possibilities. That exploration starts with the twelfth-century *Romance of Horn*, finding that some of the strongest characteristics of romance and its relation with time, narrative and (re)telling, are also those bound up with giving, receiving and reciprocating.[26]

Notes

1 Margaret Atwood, 'Introduction', in Lewis Hyde, *The Gift: How the Creative Spirit Transforms the World* (Edinburgh: Canongate, 2012), pp. vii–xi, at p. vii.

2 Marcel Mauss, *Essai sur le don: Forme et raison de l'échange dans les sociétés archaïques* (Paris: Quadrige/Presses Universitaires de France, 2007; first published in the journal *L'Année Sociologique* in 1925 (for 1923/4)); *The Gift: Expanded Edition*, ed. and trans. Jane I. Guyer (Chicago, IL: Hau Books, 2016). Quotations and translations will be from these editions. Much previous English-language discussion relies on *The Gift: The Form and Reason for Exchange in Archaic Societies*,

trans. W.D. Halls (London: Routledge, 1990). Bronislaw Malinowski, *Argonauts of the Western Pacific: An Account of the Native Enterprise and Adventure in the Archipelagoes of Melanesian New Guinea* (London: Routledge, 1922, reprinted 2002).

3 Karen Sykes, *Arguing with Anthropology: An Introduction to Critical Theories of the Gift* (London: Routledge, 2005), p. 12. Other valuable guides or critical interventions include Chris Gregory, *Gifts and Commodities* (New York: Academic Press, 1982); Arjun Appadurai (ed.), *The Social Life of Things: Commodities in Cultural Perspective* (Cambridge: Cambridge University Press, 1986); Alan D. Schrift (ed.), *The Logic of the Gift: Toward an Ethic of Generosity* (London: Routledge, 1997); Hirokazu Miyazaki, 'Gifts and exchange', in Dan Hicks and Mary C. Beaudry (eds), *The Oxford Handbook of Material Culture Studies* (Oxford: Oxford University Press, 2010), pp. 246–64.

4 Mauss prefaces *The Gift* with an extract from the Old Norse *Hávamál*, including 'A gift given always expects a gift in return', and embeds discussion of medieval texts alongside more recent ethnographic material, but the claim that he had a nostalgic desire to turn the clock back and reject modern market systems is not really accurate: see Keith Hart, 'Marcel Mauss: in pursuit of the whole. A review essay', *Comparative Studies in Society and History* 49 (2007), 473–85, esp. pp. 481–4. For the tendency to elide the medieval past with the present of other cultures, see e.g. Ananya Jahanara Kabir, 'Analogy in translation: imperial Rome, medieval England, and British India', in Ananya Jahanara Kabir and Deanne Williams (eds), *Postcolonial Approaches to the European Middle Ages: Translating Cultures* (Cambridge: Cambridge University Press, 2005), pp. 183–204.

5 Hyde, *The Gift*, p. 205.

6 Ibid., esp. pp. 276–83.

7 Jacques Derrida, *Given Time I: Counterfeit Money*, trans. Peggy Kamuf (Chicago, IL: University of Chicago Press, 1992), pp. 7, 29. See also Mary Douglas, 'Foreword: No free gifts', in Mauss, *The Gift*, pp. vi–xviii, and discussion in Simon Jarvis, 'The gift in theory', *Dionysius* 17 (1999), 201–22, esp. pp. 211–16. I discuss this further in Ch. 1, along with other challenges to, and readings of, Mauss; and see also below, note 24. For a useful summary of the debate in the context of Chaucer studies, see Robert Epstein, *Chaucer's Gifts: Exchange and Value in the 'Canterbury Tales'* (Cardiff: University of Wales Press, 2018), pp. 1–8.

8 Mauss, *Essai sur le don*, p. 71 (original emphasis); *The Gift*, p. 61. See Guyer's discussion of the meanings of *don*, *cadeau*, *present* and *prestation*: *The Gift*, pp. 12–19.

9 For romances as traditional stories, see Derek Brewer, *Symbolic Stories: Traditional Narratives of the Family Drama in English Literature* (Harlow: Longman, 1980), esp. chs 3–5. In Vladimir Propp's *Morphology of the Folktale*, trans. Laurence Scott, ed. Louis A. Wagner, 2nd edn (Austin: University of Texas Press, 1968), e.g. pp. 39–50, one of the key folk-story protagonists is termed the 'donor' (or 'provider' of a magical agent), and Propp attempts to map out their role in structural terms, but the systematization of his approach is limiting.

10 I borrow the term 'mythistory' from John D. Niles, 'Myth and history', in Robert E. Bjork and John D. Niles (eds), *A 'Beowulf' Handbook* (Exeter: University of Exeter Press, 1997), pp. 213–32.

11 On romances' incorporation of the extreme, see e.g. Nicola McDonald, 'A polemical introduction', in Nicola McDonald (ed.), *Pulp Fictions of Medieval England: Essays in Popular Romance* (Manchester: Manchester University Press, 2004), pp. 1–21; and James Simpson, 'Unthinking thought: romance's wisdom', in Katherine C. Little and Nicola McDonald (eds), *Thinking Medieval Romance* (Oxford: Oxford University Press, 2018), pp. 36–51: 'the civilized order, however we define it, is not a unitary order; for that order to maintain its balance, it must have commerce with, and enter into, everything that threatens it' (p. 51).

12 While I have largely resisted introducing a further methodological perspective, that of narratology, this is an area where theories of gift, time and reciprocity may be brought into conversation with theories of narrative and time, including Paul Ricœur, *Time and Narrative*, 3 vols (Chicago, IL: University of Chicago Press, 1984–88). See e.g. I.57: 'If, in fact, human action can be narrated, it is because it is always already articulated by signs, rules, and norms. It is always already symbolically mediated.'

13 Annette B. Weiner, *Inalienable Possessions: The Paradox of Keeping-While-Giving* (Berkeley: University of California Press, 1992).

14 Especially her *The Gender of the Gift: Problems with Women and Problems with Society in Melanesia* (Berkeley: University of California Press, 1988).

15 For contexts and developing vocabularies of exchange, see Esther Cohen and Mayke B. de Jong (eds), *Medieval Transformations: Texts, Power, and Gifts in Context* (Leiden: Brill, 2001); Gadi Algazi et al. (eds), *Negotiating the Gift: Pre-Modern Figurations of Exchange* (Göttingen: Vandenhoeck & Ruprecht, 2003); Wendy Davies and Paul Fouracre (eds), *The Languages of Gift in the Early Middle Ages* (Cambridge: Cambridge University Press, 2010); Andrew Galloway, 'The making of a social ethic in late-medieval England: from *gratitudo* to "kyndnesse"', *Journal of*

the History of Ideas 55 (1994), 365–83; Felicity Heal, 'Reciprocity and exchange in the late medieval household', in Barbara A. Hanawalt and David Wallace (eds), *Bodies and Disciplines: Intersections of Literature and History in Fifteenth-Century England* (Minneapolis: University of Minnesota Press, 1996), pp. 179–98; Diana Wood, *Medieval Economic Thought* (Cambridge: Cambridge University Press, 2002).

16 Evidence of donation and patronage abounds in late-medieval parish churches in England. For an emblematic example, see Eamon Duffy, 'Late medieval religion', in Richard Marks and Paul Williamson (eds), *Gothic: Art for England, 1400–1547* (London: V&A Publications, 2003), pp. 56–67, at pp. 56–9; and for the larger relationship between parish churches and gentry patrons, Nigel Saul, *Lordship and Faith: The English Gentry and the Parish Church in the Middle Ages* (Oxford: Oxford University Press, 2017). A theoretically alert study of gift relationships in the Low Countries, including religious institutions, is Arnoud-Jan A. Bijsterveld, *Do ut Des: Gift-Giving, 'Memoria', and Conflict Management in the Medieval Low Countries* (Hilversum: Uitgeverij Verloren, 2007); and see Stephen D. White, *Custom, Kinship, and Gifts to Saints: The 'Laudatio Parentum' in Western France, 1050–1150* (Chapel Hill: University of North Carolina Press, 1988), and the important article by Ilana F. Silber, 'Gift-giving in the great traditions: the case of donations to monasteries in the medieval West', *Archives européenes de sociologie* 36 (1995), 209–43. For the living and dead, see Patrick J. Geary, 'Exchange and interaction between the living and the dead in early medieval society', in his *Living with the Dead in the Middle Ages* (Ithaca, NY: Cornell University Press, 1994), pp. 77–92. On economic ideas in religious texts, see e.g. James Simpson, 'Spirituality and economics in passus 1–7 of the B text', *Yearbook of Langland Studies* 1 (1987), 83–103; D. Vance Smith, *Arts of Possession: The Middle English Household Imaginary* (Minneapolis: University of Minnesota Press, 2003), ch. 4.

17 C.M. Woolgar, *Household Accounts from Medieval England*, 2 vols (Oxford: Oxford University Press, 1992).

18 C.M. Woolgar, 'Gifts of food in late medieval England', *Journal of Medieval History* 37 (2011), 6–18, at p. 7.

19 Wood, *Medieval Economic Thought*, p. 206; Martha C. Howell, *Commerce before Capitalism in Europe, 1300–1600* (Cambridge: Cambridge University Press, 2010), p. 201. For early modern cultures of the gift, see esp. Natalie Zemon Davis, *The Gift in Sixteenth-Century France* (Oxford: Oxford University Press, 2000); Jason Scott-Warren, *Sir John Harington and the Book as Gift* (Oxford: Oxford University Press, 2001); Felicity Heal, *The Power of Gifts: Gift Exchange in Early Modern England* (Oxford: Oxford University Press, 2014).

20 Valentin Groebner, *Liquid Assets, Dangerous Gifts: Presents and Politics at the end of the Middle Ages*, trans. Pamela E. Selwyn (Philadelphia: University of Pennsylvania Press, 2002), p. 12.

21 To take only a few examples: André Michel Bossy, 'Arms and the bride: Christine de Pizan's military treatise as a wedding gift for Margaret of Anjou', in Marilynn Desmond (ed.), *Christine De Pizan and the Categories of Difference* (Minneapolis: University of Minnesota Press, 1998), pp. 236–56; Jenny Stratford, 'Royal books', in Richard Marks and Paul Williamson (eds), *Gothic: Art for England 1400–1547* (London: V&A Publications, 2013), pp. 180–6; Corine Schleif, 'Gifts and givers that keep on giving: pictured presentations in early medieval manuscripts', in Georgiana Donavin and Anita Obermeier (eds), *Romance and Rhetoric: Essays in Honour of Dhira B. Mahoney* (Turnhout: Brepols, 2010), pp. 51–71; Nicholas Perkins, 'Introduction: the materiality of medieval romance and *The Erle of Tolouse*', in Nicholas Perkins (ed.), *Medieval Romance and Material Culture* (Cambridge: Brewer, 2015), pp. 1–22; Deborah McGrady, *The Writer's Gift or the Patron's Pleasure? The Literary Economy in Late Medieval France* (Toronto: University of Toronto Press, 2019).

22 Smith, *Arts of Possession*, p. xvii. For the context of the household, and gentry readers, see also Elliot Kendall, *Lordship and Literature: John Gower and the Politics of the Great Household* (Oxford: Oxford University Press, 2008); Michael Johnston, *Romance and the Gentry in Late Medieval England* (Oxford: Oxford University Press, 2014). Roger A. Ladd perceptively identifies varieties of giving and the messages embedded in exchange to read passages of Gower's *Confessio amantis*: 'Gower's Gifts', in Ana Sáez-Hidalgo and R.F. Yeager (eds), *John Gower in England and Iberia: Manuscripts, Influences, Reception* (Cambridge: Brewer), pp. 229–39.

23 Jill Mann, 'Price and value in *Sir Gawain and the Green Knight*', *Essays in Criticism* 36 (1986), 294–318; Ad Putter, 'Gifts and commodities in *Sir Amadace*', *Review of English Studies* 51 (2000), 371–94.

24 Epstein, *Chaucer's Gifts*, p. 8. See also Jonathan Parry and Maurice Bloch, 'Introduction: money and the morality of exchange', in Jonathan Parry and Maurice Bloch (eds), *Money and the Morality of Exchange* (Cambridge: Cambridge University Press, 1989), pp. 1–32.

25 Walter Wadiak, *Savage Economy: The Returns of Middle English Romance* (Notre Dame, IN: University of Notre Dame Press, 2017), pp. viii, ix. The phrase 'think the gift' comes from Derrida, *Given Time I*, pp. 28–9.

26 Mauss, *The Gift*, p. 73: 'total prestation does not bring with it only the obligation to return the gifts [*cadeaux*] received; it presupposes two

others, of equal importance: the obligation to give them, on the one hand, and the obligation to receive them, on the other'. For a critique of this general statement in the context of the history of economic theory, see David Graeber, *Toward an Anthropological Theory of Value: The False Coin of our Own Dreams* (New York: Palgrave, 2001), e.g. pp. 209–21. Graeber's argument, that gifts do not always need to be repaid, leads back into the question of what total prestations are – especially if they are obligations that are not crystallized as objects, or continue as apparent indebtedness over long periods.

1

The gift of narrative in the romances of Horn

Discussions of twelfth-century Insular writing have long emphasized its engagement with questions of identity (race, nation, language, region, gender), devotion, personal loyalties and collective beliefs that were at issue in the post-Conquest period, whether that is through history and chronicle, life writing, theology, geography and travel writing, political treatises, or fictional narrative.[1] This chapter concentrates on a strikingly ambitious twelfth-century text – *The Romance of Horn* – which certainly probes these questions, while its generic affiliations allow for connections with other forms of writing and thinking. I shall return to some of those generic links and pressing questions, but my focus will be on gifts at various levels – linguistic, structural, thematic, ethical – in relation to some core debates about the gift in Anthropology and theory. Later, I will ask how the operation of the gift is engaged in two other Insular versions of the Horn story: *King Horn* and *Horn Childe and Maiden Rimnild*.

The Romance of Horn is one of the earliest and greatest of Insular romances. Its ambitious scope and commanding style appear both to celebrate and scrutinize aristocratic values, but also to focus them on pious belief in a providential God, active in the world. It was probably composed around 1170: Dominica Legge and subsequently Judy Weiss have suggested that a likely occasion for its commissioning and performance was the visit of Henry II to Dublin in 1171–2.[2] The Angevin court of this period was both a military institution and an arena of burgeoning artistic production and imagination. Ian Short has commented that 'there can be no doubt that the environment of the itinerant Angevin court was particularly propitious to literature'; the virtuosic treatment of its narrative certainly shows an artist confident of the value of his work and its ability to speak to a receptive audience.[3] The poem is written in French by someone calling himself 'Mestre Thomas' – Master Thomas – and who shows some knowledge of England and perhaps Ireland. Mildred Pope postulated that Thomas could have been the son of immigrants to England from the Loire valley, judging from continental influence on the morphology, phonology and vocabulary of the poem, while '[t]he Anglo-Norman element is curiously patchy: strong in syntax and appreciable in vocabulary, but almost non-existent in morphology, and in phonology striking only where it is supported by the usage of the South-Western region'.[4] While *The Romance of Horn* itself is dated to around 1170, versions or elements of the story were undoubtedly circulating well before this, perhaps in the late eleventh century.[5] It is composed in rhymed laisses of Alexandrine lines. Pope discusses the relationship of its form to that of chansons de geste such as the *Song of Roland* as part of her detailed study of its language, and also notes that the 'unusual cut of the line' helps suggest composition 'at an experimental stage in the metrical develop-ments of the later twelfth century'.[6] Five manuscripts survive contain-ing parts of *The Romance of Horn*, and Pope bases her edition on Cambridge, University Library MS Ff. 6. 17, which has the most complete text.[7]

Beginnings

Before outlining the narrative shape of *The Romance of Horn*, I shall start at the beginning of the poem – though any account of 'the beginning' is precisely at issue in discussions of the gift:

> Seignurs, oi avez le[s] vers del parchemin,
> Cum li bers Aaluf est venuz a sa fin.
> Mestre Thomas ne volt k'il seit mis a declin
> K'il ne die de Horn, le vaillant orphanin,
> Cum puis l'unt treit li felun sarasin.
> Un en i ot, guaigna[rt], del lignage Chain –
> En language alfrican l'apelent Malbroin.
> Ci[l] trova primes Horn repuns enz un gardin,
> Od lui xv valez ki erent de sun lin –
> N'[en] i ot ne fust fiz de bon palain:

Cume seignur serveint tuit Horn, le meschin.
Chascun aveit vestu bliaut ynde u purprin
E Hor[n] ert conréét d'un paile alexandrin.
Oilz aveit vers e clers e le vis ot rosin,
Gente façun aveit, bien semblot angelin;
Cum esteile jornals, quan lievet al matin,
Sur les altres reluist, ki li sunt pres veisin,
Sur tuz ses cumpaignu[n]s resplent Horn [li meschin].

Malbroïn al requei ad les enfanz trovez,
Ki erent pur l'esfrei la tuit xv muscez;
Il les ad pris trestuz, ad les xv liez,
Mes a Horn ne fist mal, kar ne fud destinez;
Si lui ot Deus dune par ses digne buntez
Un eür: k'i ne fust pur nul hom esgardez,
Ki sempres n'en eüst e merciz e pitiez. (1–25)

[You will have heard, my lords, from the verses in the parchment, how the noble Aalof came to his end. Master Thomas does not want to end his own life without telling the story of Horn, fatherless and brave, and his fate at the hands of the wicked Saracens. One of them, a scoundrel descended from Cain, was called 'Malbroin' in the African language. He was the first to find Horn hidden in a garden, with fifteen other boys of his race; all good counts' sons, they acknowledged the young Horn as their lord. Each wore a crimson or blue tunic, while Horn was clad in Alexandrian brocade. His eyes were clear and bright, his face rosy, his bearing noble. He looked like an angel. Like the day-star, rising in the morning, Horn shone brighter than his nearest companions: the boy surpassed all his friends in splendour.

Malbroin found the children in their refuge where all fifteen had hidden themselves from fear. He took them all and bound them, but did no harm to Horn, as fate intended. Out of His great kindness, God gave Horn this good fortune, that all seeing him would at once pity and have mercy on him.][8]

These opening lines worry almost obsessively at the question of origins. First, there is the parallel drawn between Horn's father Aalof, and Thomas as poet-narrator.[9] Aalof's death is a story that the audience are assumed or imagined to have encountered, while Thomas 'ne volt k'il seit mis a declin' (3) [does not wish to bring himself to an end] before relating the story of Horn. Judy Weiss translates one sense of this – 'does not want to end his own life' – but the meaning of 'does not want to finish writing' – is, I believe, also lurking here. Given the way that Thomas's presence is embedded in his poem, these two meanings are close to being co-extensive. *The Romance of Horn*, then, is also a last testament from a fictionally dying author, whose life stretches as far as the reach of his own poem, and of whose mortality we are reminded in its closing lines. The story of Aalof, which Thomas says that his audience will have heard from a written account ('le[s] vers del parchemin' (1)), may have existed as a partner text to *The Romance of Horn*; Maldwyn Mills has discussed the possible influence of an Anglo-Norman **Aalof* on later versions of the Horn legend.[10] At this point in *The Romance of Horn*, however, Aalof is summoned and dispatched in one line, and Thomas the author-progenitor faces his own 'declin' (3), leaving Horn fatherless: 'le vaillant orphanin' (4). By contrast, Malbroin's background is all too familiar: 'del lignage Chain' (6) [descended from Cain]. Malbroin's link with Cain immediately reinforces the poem's religious and racial yoking of 'Saracens' with a larger struggle of good against evil, and here there is relatively little differentiation in the treatment of Saracen others: they are mostly homogenous, all wicked. Such a fundamental conflict provides a framing narrative for the poem, and also allows other, more local or personal contests, conflicts or relations to nestle inside its capacious structure.[11]

In direct apposition to this monstrous or diabolical figure, Horn is quickly described as like an angel, or like the day-star rising: a kind of unfallen Lucifer. In addition, he and his companions are found in a garden, yet another originary or pre-lapsarian situation. But far from being a helpless infant, the focus here is on Horn as already a fully-formed leader, not as Aalof's son. His familial connections – 'son lin' – are, as it were, beneath him or horizontal to him, rather than something from which he is descended, and instead these fifteen boys who share Horn's line of verse look up to him as leader.[12] Horn is also a figure of immediate and notable value: his eyes bright and clear, and his face rosy. While the others wear tunics of red or blue, Horn's clothing is distinguished both by its costly fabric and Eastern origin: a silk, perhaps brocade robe ('paile' (13)) from Alexandria. Recent work on French romance in particular has drawn attention to the network of orientalist fantasies that such fabrics could evoke.[13] Here, Horn is both familiarized as a member of an aristocratic elite through his looks and clothing, but he is also set apart through the outstanding quality and far-fetched origin of his clothes. Wrapped up in this physical value is the 'eür' (24: literally 'possession'; Weiss translates 'fortune', but she has told me that she might now translate it as 'gift') given to him by God, that anyone looking at him will have mercy on him.[14]

The opening of the poem, then, insists on Horn as a one-off, not textually inheriting or growing into his identity, but instead discovered and without immediate ties to his father's narrative, despite the reference to Aalof at the very start. Instead, the poem presents us with a number of telling originary motifs, including Eden, Cain and Lucifer, with Horn's value guaranteed by the gift of God. This kind of 'discovered self' is, of course, a familiar element in romance, especially romances that use the motif of *le bel inconnu*.[15] While Horn is not unknown at the start of the text, he is almost immediately detached from his surroundings and his progress in the story is powered again by qualities of givenness and unexpected arrival. Several times in *The Romance of Horn*, such apparent new beginnings are attempted or proffered, only for their previous entanglements to be subsequently revealed, to the story's protagonists and to us as its audience. That relationship between ostensibly untied or unmotivated initiatives and their underlying or hidden motivations has certain connections with anthropological and critical accounts of gift-giving and exchange.

Before discussing these, however, I shall briefly summarize *The Romance of Horn*'s story, since its narrative shape is itself party to the dynamics that I am concerned with:

> Horn, after being discovered by Malbroin, is taken with his fellows to the Saracen king Rodmund, who pities them too much to kill them immediately. Instead, he has them placed in a boat and cast out to sea. They are towed from Suddene, Horn's homeland,[16] and left to drift. God ensures that they wash up on the coast of Brittany. The good seneschal Herland finds the boys and takes them to King Hunlaf. Horn reveals his parentage to the King, and Hunlaf arranges for the boys to be fostered by his followers, promising that he will help Horn to regain his lost kingdom. Horn duly grows up to be an outstanding young man, and the King's daughter, Rigmel, falls passionately in love with him – even before she has seen him. She arranges for him to be brought to her chamber and declares her love, offering him a ring, but Horn refuses it until he has proved himself and become a knight. The opportunity for this soon arises in the form of an invading pagan army, and once Horn has killed many Saracens,

he does take the ring, and promises loyalty and love to Rigmel. They are betrayed by Horn's disgruntled cousin, Wikele, who falsely tells King Hunlaf that the couple have already had sex, and provokes the king to banish Horn.

Horn goes to Ireland, changing his name to Gudmod. He becomes a favourite of the Irish King Gudreche, whose daughter Lenburc falls in love with him. A messenger arrives from Brittany, telling Horn that the treacherous Wikele is now seneschal, and has arranged for Rigmel to be married against her will to another king. Horn returns and rescues Rigmel, marries her and is prevailed upon to pardon Wikele. He then sets off for Suddene to reclaim his own kingdom from the pagan Rodmund, and after dispatching the Saracens, is reunited with his mother. Meanwhile, back in Brittany, Wikele has betrayed Horn again, seizing Rigmel for himself. Horn has a foreboding dream about this, and rushes back, eventually killing Wikele, securing a marriage between his kinsman Modin and the Irish princess Lenburc, and living a long and happy life with Rigmel.

The narrative, then, moves in a pattern of expulsion, establishment of prowess, and return, and in *The Romance of Horn* that pattern is repeated, with two exiles – in Brittany and then Ireland – and two rescues (Figure 1). Judy Weiss has traced some of these plot elements and suggested how they might have come to be incorporated into the romance as we have it, and Susan Crane has also remarked on the notable 'doubled pattern of expulsion and return' in *The Romance of Horn*, aligning this with the search for origins that she posits as a core feature of Insular romance narrative in the wake of the Norman Conquest of England:

> Each narrative element in the work's doubled pattern of expulsion and return echoes and expands a previous element in an even progression toward the achievement of land, power, and stability. Each stage in the story's progress marks, both in itself and in its echoing of a previous stage, the steady movement from deprivation to reacquisition and from moral wrong to right.[17]

Crane lists a number of elements that are echoed or answered later in the poem, including Horn's service in his first and second exiles (in Brittany and Ireland), being wooed by Rigmel and then the Irish princess Lenburc, and returning in disguise twice to rescue Rigmel. Crane suggests that the poet Thomas's attraction to doubled plot elements at various levels of structure are tied into 'the theme of a family's renewal and extension, generation by generation, of its

Suddene (South-West England?)	Brittany	Westir (Ireland)
[Aalof killed]		
Horn found by Malbroin and taken to Rodmund		
cast adrift		
	Horn found by Herland and taken to Hunlaf	
	fostered by Herland	
	loved by Rigmel	
	fights pagans; saves Herland's life	
	accepts Rigmel's ring	
	betrayed by Wikele	
	goes to Ireland	
		calls himself Gudmod
		serves King Gudreche
		loved by Lenburc
		fights pagans (brothers of Rodmund)
		refuses to marry Lenburc
		called back by Herland's son
	returns to Brittany	
	enters wedding celebrations disguised as a pilgrim	
	defeats Wikele's plan to marry Rigmel to Modin	
	rescues and marries Rigmel	
	pardons Wikele	
	restores Herland as seneschal	
returns to Suddene		
meets Hardré, Aalof's seneschal (now Rodmund's)		
Rodmund has foreboding dream		
Hardré betrays Rodmund		
Horn defeats pagans		
reunited with his mother, Samburc		
foreboding dream about Wikele		
sets off for Brittany	enters city disguised as musician	
	rescues Rigmel, kills Wikele	
	goes to Ireland	
		gives Lenburc to Modin; finds a wife for Haderof
	returns to Brittany	
returns to Suddene		
has a valiant son, Hadermod		

Figure 1 narrative diagram of *The Romance of Horn*

vitality and its rights'.[18] Crane's valuable reading of *The Romance of Horn* helps identify a prominent feature of its structuring. I will suggest that an equally important kind of structure, at a range of levels, can be found by reading the poem alongside accounts of the gift and its power to engage relationships and demand returns.

Early in the poem, when the good seneschal Herland spots Horn
and the other boys who have been wrecked on the Brittany coast,
he immediately talks of them as valuable objects, which can be
exchanged for favours at court:

'Veëz, mi cumpaignun,   Deu vus doinst beneiçon!
Dites si·s conoissez;   ki sunt cil valletun?
Unc ne vi gencesors   par ma salvatïun.
Joe savrai ki il sunt,   de quel avoeisun.
Bien semble k'(e)il seient   fiz de gentil baron.
Si'l vindrent par werek,   grant pru i averon;
Bien purrum al rei faire   [la] presentatïon.
Unkes mais ne li vint   [ne] si gent ne si bun.
Plus en iert honuréé   tote sa regïon.'

* * *

'Par Deu, sire Herland,'   diënt li chevalier,
'Ci ad mut gent werec   e bien fait a preisier.
Bien les porrum lo rei   noblement presenter.' (145–53; 176–8)

['Bless you, my friends, look! Who are these boys? Speak, if you
know them. By God my Saviour, I never saw handsomer ones! I shall
discover who they are and of what allegiance. They certainly seem
to be noble barons' sons. If they are shipwrecked, we shall greatly
profit from it: we can offer them to the king. No finer or nobler
beings have ever yet come his way. His whole realm will be held in
greater honour.' ... 'By God, my lord Herland!' said the knights, 'this
is very fine wreckage, much to be prized. We can certainly present
them to the king with honour.' (7, p. 4; 9, p. 5)]

Herland and his fellows then take their finds to King Hunlaf, and
Thomas here blends free indirect discourse with an authenticating
voice that assimilates their speculation about the value of their gifts:
'Ja li front tiel present   k'unc mais ne reçut tal' (210) [Now they
would make him a gift such as he had never received before. (10,
p. 6)]. Herland addresses Hunlaf, reminding him that the boys are
a gift to the king, but that Hunlaf can, if he wishes, realize their
immediate value and sell them as slaves:

'quant savrez qu'il sunt,   si vus en cunseillez
Quels ert vostre plaisir: si nurrir les vulez,
U si·s f(e)rez veneter   e aveir en prendrez.
Des or mes sunt il voz;   faites en [les] vos grez.' (234–7)

['When you know who they are, take counsel on what it will please you to do, whether you want to bring them up, or sell them and profit by it. Henceforth they are yours: do what you want with them.' (11, p. 6)]

Herland's speech stresses the power that Hunlaf has over the boys, expressed through variation on the language of pleasure, ownership and will: 'vostre plaisir'; 'vulez'; 'sunt il voz'; 'faites en [les] grez'. Equally, Herland is embedding in the moment of giving an expectation that the king will take counsel; Herland's speech thus becomes a self-descriptive artefact – a verbal gift that also prescribes the appropriate way to handle the present of the boys, and by implication figures future advice-giving as a form of gift exchange.

King Hunlaf must thus decide whether to treat the boys as a commodity – to sell them and make a profit – or whether to nurture them himself. One of factors in his decision is Horn's own declaration of his lineage:

> 'Mis peres fud uns bers   vaillant hom durement,
> Aäluf ad a nun,   si ma geste ne ment;
> En Suddene fud nez,   si la tint longement;
> Reis Silauf le trova,   si·l norrit bonement.
> Apres, fu koneü   par Deu comandement
> Qu'(il)iert de geste real   descendu veirement.
>
> *   *   *
>
> 'Quant çoe fud koneü   ke Aalof fud bien né
> Qu'il fu nefs Baderof,   le bon e l'alosé,
> Ki iert sur Alemauns   enperere clamé,
> Dunc li ad reis Silaus   par grant amur doné
> Une fille qu'il out   – le vis out coluré –
> E ovoc li dona   apres sei sun regné.' (250–5; 262–7)

['My father was a very noble, valiant man, of the name of Aalof, if my lineage does not lie. He was born in Suddene and ruled it a long while. He was a foundling of King Silauf's, who brought him up kindly. Later, by God's command, it became known that he was really of royal descent ... 'When it was discovered that Aalof was well-born, grandson of Baderof, the good and renowned Emperor of the Germans, then King Silauf, out of great affection, gave him his rosy-cheeked daughter and his kingdom too when his own reign was over.' (12–13, pp. 6–7)]

This embedded romance narrative rewards the listener with a history and context for Horn that the text's opening in large part withheld. It is also, of course, proleptic of his own story (and this self-referential quality is perhaps indicated by punning on the word 'geste' (251), meaning lineage, but also story). Hunlaf responds to Horn's genealogy/ story by entering an ongoing relationship of gift-exchange with him in two ways: he promises to help Horn recover his lost kingdom, and he places Horn and his companions with foster-families at his own court. Horn goes to the household of Herland the seneschal, and the bond created there is repaid later in the romance, when Horn saves Herland's life, and afterwards is sought out by Herland's son to ask him to return from Ireland. King Hunlaf later calls to mind Horn's family history when he decides to give him arms and let him fight the pagan invaders:

> De Aalof li membra   od la fiere façon,
> Cum delivra Silauf,   ki fud sun norriçon,
> Des paiens, des feluns,   lui e sa regïon.
> Fiaunce ot en cestui –   e si ot grant reisun –
> Qu'il feïst autretel   e traisist a nacion. (1387–91)

[He remembered Aalof the fierce and how he had saved Silauf, his foster-father, from heathen wretches, him and his realm. He had faith – and he was right – that this man would do the same and be true to his birth. (70, p. 33)]

Early in this story, then, the narrative energy of the romance is charged by the sudden and unmotivated arrival of a precious object at court, in the form of Horn, who then reveals the story of his life and involves Hunlaf in what turns out to be an already existing network of exchange, exile and revenge.

The surplus of the gift in *The Romance of Horn*

What does that phrase 'narrative energy' mean in the context of *The Romance of Horn*'s structure of obligations, debts, gifts and repayments? The significance of gift and exchange has, of course, long been an important part of anthropological and critical enquiry, especially since Marcel Mauss's *Essai sur le don*. Mauss described the gift neither as an anomalous or purely disinterested transaction, nor as an exchange whose obligations are immediately discharged, but as part of a 'système des prestations totales' [system of total prestations, or, of overall obligations]: a mutually supportive and regulatory web of interests which helped to structure social relations in the cultures he studied.[19] This system could initiate and also exemplify contestive or rivalrous displays of wealth and power, for example through the destruction of goods in the 'potlach', to which I shall return in Chapter 3. For now, I will focus on Mauss's much-debated discussion of the *hau* of the gift – a Maori concept describing the power that a gift generates in being passed on, and what we might call the gift's homing instinct, bringing a return to the giver. This is how Mauss reports the *hau* (which he compares to the Latin *spiritus* as 'wind and soul'):

> With respect to the *hau*, the spirit of things and particularly of the forest, and the game within it, Tamati Ranaipiri, one of Elsdon Best's best Maori informants, gives us quite by chance, and without bias, the key to the problem:
>
> … Suppose that you possess a certain article, and you give that article to me, without price. We make no bargain about it. Now, I give that article to a third person, who, after some time has elapsed, decides to make some return for it (*utu*), and so he makes me a present of some article (*taonga*). Now, that article (*taonga*) that he gives to me is the *hau* of the article I first received from you and then gave to him. The goods (*taonga*) that I received for that item I must hand over to you. It would not be right for me to keep such goods for myself … I must hand them over to you, because they are a *hau* of the article (*taonga*) you gave me. Were I to keep such equivalent for myself, then some serious evil would befall me, even death. Such is the *hau*, the *hau* of personal property, or the forest *hau*. *Kati ena.* (Enough on these points.)
>
> … The gift (*cadeau*) received and exchanged is binding as the thing received is not inert. Even abandoned by the giver, it is still something of his.[20]

Mauss's version of Elsdon Best's information from Tamati Ranaipiri (this chain of retelling is itself significant) has been much debated in the decades since *Essai sur le don* was published. I cite it at length (itself in translation) because it is so influential and productive of argument. However, numerous later commentators have critiqued or modified Mauss's discussion. Some have seen Mauss's perspective as generated by his placement in a tradition of Western philosophy that foregrounds human reciprocity.[21] Others have argued that Mauss tends to mystify the relationships and encourages a religious aura to surround the continuing journey of exchange, where senses of ownership, value and obligation are sufficient.[22] Marshall Sahlins retranslates *hau* and embeds it in a larger context of Maori exchange, suggesting that the relationships at work are less spiritual and more practical and social: 'The meaning of *hau* one disengages from the exchange of *taonga* is as secular as the exchange itself. If the second gift is the *hau* of the first, then the *hau* of a good is its yield.' Later, Sahlins discusses the meaning of the verb *hau* as 'to exceed, be in excess', and *hau* as a substantive meaning 'excess, parts, fraction over and complete measurement', and 'property, spoils'. In his version of the description above, *hau* becomes not 'spirit' of the gift, but 'product of', 'return on' the gift.[23] When two or three anthropologists are gathered together, they will debate the meaning and context of *hau*. Sahlins's approach is in turn modified by Maurice Godelier, who draws back from the connotations of profit that he sees in Sahlins's demystifying interpretation. Godelier reviews how Mauss saw a system of total services to operate, and defends him to an extent against those who regard his work as naïve or nostalgic. In Godelier's account, a renewed reading of Mauss allows us to see that different societies embed gift-giving and exchange in different ways depending on the balance of their commodity and gift relationships; that certain goods are exempted from exchange and thus provide fixed points in their understanding of value; and that gift-giving allows us also to examine relationships and hierarchies before, during and after an act of exchange: 'By its very nature, gift-giving is an ambivalent practice which brings together or is capable of bringing together opposing emotions and forces.'[24]

I believe that this more open and ambivalent account of the gift and the *hau* is productive for reading the gifts and verbal or physical transactions at play in a text such as *The Romance of Horn*; noticing 'yield' and 'excess' at different levels of the text, for example. Another approach would be to study in more detail the Angevin court's practices of gift exchange, and to compare those with *The Romance of Horn*. This could have value as a historicist enterprise, and as an investigation of what the poem might be saying in its rhetorical moment, but it too would have limitations. Here I am working with a looser sense of the poem's textual environment, and focusing more on the text as itself a system of prestations.[25] This will not be a complete system without acknowledging the text's prior commitments and its links with contexts of performance and transmission – the very ways in which its fictional claims to completeness are in fact permeable – but it will focus our attention on how it imagines itself as a world of its own, while giving us some directions to follow those links beyond its fictional boundaries. In such a reading, the concept of the active gift – one that grows and yields something more – is a powerful one. We might connect this understanding of the gift in/as narrative with the idea of the text's surplus. It resonates in interconnected ways through Horn's revelation to Hunlaf about his parentage, the story of Aalof's life before him, and the 'making good' of the orphan through adoption, service and marriage. One instance of this is the way that Aalof's career demonstrates the accruing power of generosity. King Silauf's generous action in taking Aalof in ('Reis Silauf le trova,   si·l norrit bonement' (253)) is repaid when Aalof saved Silauf from his enemies (Hunlaf remembered how Aalof 'delivra Silauf ... Des paiens' (1388–9)). To use Tamati Ranaipiri's terms, Aalof's aid to Silauf is the *hau* (the yield; the surplus) of Silauf's earlier gift of nurture, carried out 'bonement' ('kindly', and closely linked of course to *bon*, 'good, true, kind' as an adjective; 'good fortune, fine possession, good deed' as a noun).[26] This might seem obvious or trivial: of course, Aalof helps Silauf, both from the perspective of noble duty, and from the narrative perspective of a satisfying denouement. But I think it is worth extending the observation further. Horn's retelling of his father's story is all the more powerful because of Aalof's initial status as a foundling, and Silauf's generous *noriture*. Its stored energy – that of the return gift – is brought into operation not only within the embedded narrative of Aalof and Silauf, but in relation to Horn's narrative too. Aalof's history is both *analogous* or *parallel* to that of Horn, and becomes a *direct cause* of Horn's fostering by Hunlaf, triggering his sense of returning obligations. In addition, and as important, the story of Aalof is also a *mise en abîme* for the romance narrative we are in. By this, I mean that the embedded story is also a figure for the production of romance narrative itself as a form of gift-giving, which passes on the uncalculating pleasure of a good tale told, but also places its listeners under certain obligations of interest and return.[27] Arriving as if afresh on the shore of Brittany, Horn is a precious gift object that solidifies the ongoing exchanges between Herland and his lord Hunlaf. Horn then recalls a previous gift relationship between Aalof and Silauf, to which Hunlaf is intimately bound by his own connection to Silauf ('sun norriçon' (1388): cf. 'norrit' (253)). This in turn clarifies Hunlaf's decision: to act generously to Horn. But Horn is not only a gift object; his own storytelling is a gift, both to Hunlaf and to *The Romance of Horn*'s audience. At each of these levels, the story seeds obligations whose interconnecting root system, at times unseen, sustains and thickens the narrative.

It might be objected that the relationships at play in the poem between Silauf, Aalof, Hunlaf, Herland and Horn are not truly generous ones, but to a greater or lesser extent are self-interested or calculating, and that this should puncture the dreamy picture of aristocratic generosity that I seem to have proposed. After all, we are dealing with a militaristic culture in which binding obligations between powerful men were part and parcel of social life, and hardly without the anticipation of mutual advantage. As with debates over the *hau*, the question of whether a gift can really be 'free' is one that has exercised anthropologists and other readers of the work of Mauss and his great contemporary Bronislaw Malinowski for decades. Malinowski, in his *Argonauts of the Western Pacific*, posited a range or spectrum of exchange in the cultures that he studied, from 'pure gifts' to 'trade, pure and simple'.[28] Later Malinowski emphasized the calculation at work even in exchanges that seemed to be closer to the 'free gift' end of the spectrum. In an important article, Jonathan Parry summarizes the effects of this shift in Malinowski's approach:

> The various elements in this model – the tendency to see exchanges as essentially *dyadic* transactions between *self-interested individuals*, and as premised on some kind of *balance*; the tendency to play down *supernatural* sanctions, and the total contempt for questions of *origin* – all these constituted an important legacy of Malinowski's teaching, and directly or indirectly exercised a major influence over much of the subsequent literature.[29]

Some readers of Mauss and Malinowski have wanted to 'toughen up' the concept of the gift, querying the notion that it is really separable from or has some additional power to that of barter, in the sense that Hyde describes: '[w]hen we barter we make deals, and if someone defaults we go after him, but the gift must be a gift. It is as if you give a part of your substance to your gift partner and then wait in silence until he gives you a part of his'.[30] Likewise, a sceptical reader of *The Romance of Horn* might wish to downplay the generosity of Silauf and then Hunlaf, and instead argue for an underlying social and literary structure more like the *quid pro quo* advised towards the start of *Beowulf*:

> Swa sceal ge(ong) guma   gode gewyrcean,
> fromum feogiftum   on fæder (bea)rme,
> þæt hine on ylde   eft gewunigen
> wilgesiþas,   þonne wig cume,
> leode gelæsten.[31]

[So must a young man bring it about by liberal deeds, by generous gifts while in his father's ambit, that in turn ready companions will stand by him later, men be loyal when war comes.]

I am not seeking to ignore the ideological force of *The Romance of Horn*'s narrative, which privileges the return of Horn's property and rightful possessions because of his lineage and destiny.[32] However, I believe that the representation of Horn as orphan and then foundling, the invocation of generosity via the story of Silauf and Aalof, and the way in which this then unlocks Herland and Hunlaf's generous treatment of Horn is more than a convenient narrative ploy or sleight of hand. Withholding or for a time forgetting the prior obligations of the story and its protagonists allows that yield of generosity to be evoked as a narrative structuring – something that I think Thomas the poet implies does have a spiritual dimension: initiated by God's favour to Horn, and then acting through Horn's surplus value. Once this surplus – the *hau* of Silauf's *noriture*, the *hau* of the story told and received – has been infused into the text, its overall balancing system of prestations is able to be revealed without damaging that gift of an opening.[33]

The Romance of Horn, then, can be read as itself an exercise in what we might call speculative Anthropology. It explores another culture (a mythistorical one), both creating and mediating for its audience the structures that hold that culture together; the forces that threaten it; and the systems of belief and exchange that drive its narratives forward, all the while suggesting that these structures, forces and systems have a bearing on how the members of its audience relate to their own contemporary culture. In that context, I hope that my reading of *The Romance of Horn* is not, then, merely dreamily optimistic, but can open a space to explore the narrative effect of the hero as gift object, and of the gift as story. It is a narrative that might tell us something about aristocratic cultures of giving in the twelfth century, but whose imaginative reach is not limited to those practices. Tellingly in the context of hero and/as object, Parry's review of the anthropological debate brings to the fore the question of how persons and things are interrelated in Mauss's work: 'The general principle – of which this and the Maori *hau* are only two amongst a whole battery of *illustrations* – is the absence of an absolute distinction between persons and things'.[34] This is an idea that will return in different forms and from different critical directions a number of times in the following pages.

Reciprocity and/as story

Further questions, especially about time and origin, will emerge later in the chapter, but first I shall fill out our picture of *The Romance of Horn* as a narrative structured around, and containing, many layers of reciprocal exchange and obligation. As we have seen, one way of reading Hunlaf's treatment of Horn is as a decision not to regard the beautiful foundling and his companions as commodities that can be immediately traded, but instead to regard them as gifts.[35] In doing so, Hunlaf will receive much more than their monetary value later, by Horn's unmatched prowess in battle. In turn (though this high-level summary again privileges the total system over the series of individual exchanges themselves), Horn gains the hand of Rigmel – the closest and most permanent bond between parties in this romance environment: both between the man and woman who marry, and the hero and father-in-law whose relationship is cemented by the marriage to/gift of the woman.

The Romance of Horn contains many examples of how the obligations accrued by the gift (and by revenge) are nurtured, passed on and returned, through the multiplying sets of interests that Horn develops. As I suggested above, this does not mean that we need to ascribe the poem's patterning to an abstract, mystified *hau* or 'spirit of the gift'. Instead it is to note the complexity of mutual obligations working in an overall system, both at the level of the plot, and at the level of poetic artifice. The poem makes claims about that system (for example, figuring God as its guarantor and only begetter), but we do not have to accept that ideology to perceive how it gives the poem structuring patterns. These patterns show that *The Romance of Horn* does not only work with simple or abstracted models of exchange, but that different kinds of giving and taking are scrutinized at many levels of its intricate structure, and that they sometimes misfire or are shown to be illegitimate. In one of the best-known episodes of the poem, Rigmel, King Hunlaf's daughter, attempts to persuade Herland the seneschal to bring Horn to her own chamber by offering him an ever-increasing list of gifts:

> Al premier ad doné   a Herland un anel,
> Gros, d'or quit melekin: des le tens Danïel
> Fud forgié, si·l forga   li orfievre Marcel.
> Un tiel saphir i mist   ki bien vaut un chastel.
> Pus apela a sei   un soen fraunc jovencel,
> Ki iert sun buteiller;   hom l'apele Rabel.
> 'Di va,' fait la gentil,   'siez tu pur quei t'apel?
> Fai m'aporter le vin,   del mieuz qu'as en tonel,
> En ma grant cope d'or,   entaillé a cisel
> Del oevre Salemun,   ki fud rei d'Israhel,
> Ke mis peres, li reis,   me dona a Burdel.' (559–69)

[First she gave Herland a big ring, of pure, refined gold. It was crafted in Daniel's time, by Marcel the goldsmith. Then she called one of her free-born youths to her, her cup-bearer, named Rabel. 'Listen,' said the princess, 'do you know why I have sent for you? Have the wine, the best you have in the cask, brought to me in my great golden cup, carved and richly chased in Solomon's style, king of Israel, which the king my father gave me in Bordeaux.' (29, pp. 13–14)]

This is followed by a peerless horse, named Blanchard, two grey-hounds ('white as swans and fast as falcons'), and to cap it all, a fine goshawk (raising the question of how poor old Herland will shepherd this menagerie home). Of the hawk, the poet says:

> Ne·l donast en nul sen   pur argent në or mer.
> Dunc ne siet il cumment   le puisse mercïer,
> Mes cele ki est cointe   descovre sun penser.
> 'Bien me purrez,' fait ele,   'mes duns guerredoner,

Si vus vient a talant,   seneschal dreiturer.
Ne quer fors vëeir Horn,   le truvé el graver
Ki fud fiz Aaluf   de Suddene, le fier,
Kar vus l'avez nurri,   si l'avez a garder.
Celui m'amenez ça,   kar autre rien ne quier.'
'Dame,' [li] fet Herlaund,   'bien fait a otrïer.' (641–50)

[[Herland] would have exchanged it for nothing, neither silver nor pure gold. Then he did not know how he could easily requite her, but she cleverly discerned his thoughts. 'You can easily reward me for my gifts,' she said, 'if it pleases you, honest seneschal. I only ask to see Horn, the foundling on the shore, son of Aalof the proud of Suddene, for you have nurtured and cared for him.' 'My lady,' said Herland, 'agreed!' (33, pp. 15–16)]

Rigmel's lavish gifts are a paradox, signalling both her elevated status and her desperate love and thus lack of control.[36] They physicalize the material imagery and associations applied elsewhere to Horn: he is like a lion in battle, but also accomplished in courtly arts, beautiful in the way he wears costly clothes and armour, and outstanding in his skill as a craftsman.[37] In calling to mind Horn's value as a luxury good, Rigmel also initially refers to him as a discovered object: 'le truvé el graver' (646) – not so much 'hero on the beach' as flotsam on the shoreline. Could there be a punning reference here to Horn's invented status as a literary figure too, with an established meaning of *trover* being to compose a text, and 'graver' as 'beach' punning on the verb *graver*: 'engrave, incise in letters, inscribe'?[38] Horn certainly is a character engraved in literary writing, just as his father was in the opening lines of Thomas's poem.[39] Rigmel's description of Horn here miniaturizes the narrative process that the poem has followed: focusing first on Horn's status as a foundling; then on filling in his family context; and after that his fostering by Herland. In this passage of the poem, where Horn's virtues and beauty are being evaluated by a woman who has never seen him, Thomas in some ways replicates the process of poetic making – Rigmel's fantasy of Horn's attributes, described in poetic language, is itself a figure for the power of poetic making too, for an audience who has also never seen Horn in the flesh, except perhaps that of the 'parchemin' (1), if they are reading rather than listening. He exists at a juncture between person, object, desire and trope.

This verbal encounter, however, also presents an attempt at exchange by someone who does not have authority to act in the matter. This is not only because the nature of the exchange is much more of a short-term barter than a long-term or sublimated gift relationship. In addition, Rigmel is in some ways her father's property.[40] She is a gift-in-waiting for the King to dispense. Rigmel's attempt to establish her own economic relationship with Herland and through him with Horn is, then, problematic amidst the masculine hierarchy of the poem's world. Herland initially breaks his agreement with Rigmel by bringing Horn's right-hand man Haderof instead, and Rigmel is fooled until her nurse comes in with the gossip from the hall, and recognizes Haderof. Rigmel's anger is only soothed by the promise that Horn really will come next time. This comic episode ratchets up the anticipation of Horn's appearance in Rigmel's chamber, emphasizes his value over and above even the best of his companions, and also lays the ground for what kind of exchange will take place when Rigmel finally does encounter Horn. She offers him a ring, along with her body:

> 'Ja vus met joe mun cors,   mun aveir en present.
> Pernez en a pleisir   solunc vostre talent,
> K'a dependre en aiez,   quant voldrez, largement.' (1182–4)

> ['Now, I make you a present of my body and my possessions. Take them as you will, whenever you desire, so that you have them to spend, lavishly, when you wish.' (60, p. 28)]

Even the syntax of line 1182 embeds Rigmel's self, body and goods ('joe'; 'mun cors'; 'mun aveir') within the act of giving to Horn ('vus met … en present'), annealing those categories into the property that Horn can enjoy and spend in the future. Horn refuses, saying that he has not yet proved himself worthy of her, and he tells her that some emperor's son will come and claim her before that. This makes sense for the unfolding plot, since Horn's military obligations will press into the story soon. It confirms his moral purity. But it also signals a caution about establishing a relationship of exchange with someone who herself is an exchangeable object. In fact Horn ticks her off for apparently pricing herself too low:

> 'Ne vus frai nul covent,   danzelë, a cest tur
> Devant ke seit seü   cum avrai de valur. …

> La grant beauté de vus   ne turnez a folur.' (1203–4; 1218)

['I will promise you nothing now, my lady, until it is known what I am worth ... Do not wantonly bestow your great beauty.' (61, pp. 28–9)]

Though the romance exemplifies what Judy Weiss has called a 'wooing woman', then, it also shows the marginality of the female sphere of action, physically removed from the hall and at the edge of its power structures, and it figures the female body as a precious possession for Horn to receive. Horn's loyalty and service to Rigmel, with his awareness of his (at that point) lesser rank, does not overthrow that larger gendered dynamic but enables the poem to reflect on love as gift exchange between the protagonists. Their bond is established by statements of desire, by the gift of Rigmel's ring, and by the promises made to return or wait, projecting the movement of the given objects into the future and across physical space. The ring and Horn/a horn will indeed return much later in the narrative, as objects that interlace the lovers with these gifts and the unfolding of the narrative in time.

These gift relationships draw forth subtle negotiations around status and personhood beyond the two main protagonists. For example, once Horn has won his spurs from Hunlaf and accepted Rigmel's ring (though not, we are assured, her body), Wikele, Horn's treacherous kinsman, approaches him:

'Un dun kar me donez,   ke ne facez ore al
Ke vus ne·l me doingez: çoe est le blanc cheval,
Ke vus donand l'autrier   Herland le seneschal.'
'Wikele,' çoe dist Horn,   'cest don fust vergundal.
Doné l'ai Haderof   des le jor de noal,
E un bon brand ovoc,   li pont est de cristal.
Mes un autrë avrez,   ki iert plus principal.'

* * *

'Or vei bien,' dist Wikele,   'ke cest don n'avrai mie.
De poi me pus fier   en vostre druërie.
Autre part, si joe pus,   querrai avoërie,
De qui aië beaus dons   e al bosoing aïe.
N'est pas sage, m'est vis,   ki trop en vus se fie.
Quant purrai, si vus iert   la demande merie
Dont joe n'avrai or nent.   Fous est ki vus en prie!' (1846–52; 1859–65)

['Now grant me a gift, pray don't refrain from giving it me: it is the white horse which Herland the steward gave you the other day.' 'Wikele,' said Horn, 'that would be a shameful gift. I gave it to Haderof on Christmas Day, and a good sword too, with a pommel of crystal. But you shall have another, more splendid.' ... 'Now I see very well,' said Wikele, 'that I shan't get this gift. I don't have much confidence in your friendship. I will look for a lord to serve somewhere else, if I can, who can give me fine presents and aid, if necessary. I think whoever puts too much trust in you is foolish. I will pay you back for my unanswered request, when I'm able. He is mad who asks you for anything!' (90, p. 43; 91, p. 43)]

Once again, a crucial point in the narrative revolves around the discussion of a gift, here an impertinent request by Wikele. Feudal relationships are often explicitly figured as exchanges of goods for service; does Wikele's conversation with Horn really, then, come under the aegis of gift-giving?[41] To ask that question is to focus on the system or relationship at the macrocosmic level, seeing the *quid pro quo* at work synchronically. At the moment of exchange, however, it is still possible, even socially *necessary*, for a gift or service to retain (or for an artistic work to represent it as retaining) its own integrity as freely given and not visibly repaid. A twelfth-century audience could both acknowledge that the total system implied give and take in appropriate rewards for service, but also abhor instances where that overall balance of values was blatantly reckoned up at the time of exchange itself. Here, that embargo on valuing the exchange in the moment is broken. The repetition of 'dun'; 'donez'; 'doingez'; 'donand'; 'don'; 'doné' focuses our attention on what constitutes a legitimate gift, and what becomes a shameful one ('vergundal' (1849)). In this case, Horn's objection to Wikele is not on the grounds of value, which would commodify his affection for Haderof vis-à-vis Wikele: indeed, he says that he will give him something 'plus principal' (1852). Rather, the already-given horse and sword now carry with them a *hau* that strengthens his relationship with Haderof, and whose retraction or misuse would poison that virtuous circle of exchange with his right-hand man. Wikele's response exemplifies his rejection of these virtuous cycles, and turns a gift relationship into its symbiotic shadow, the feud. Wikele's summary of the feudal (patron–client) relationship is etymologically and, to a twelfth-century audience, ethically preposterous, based as it seems to be on what he can gain from having a patron ('De qui aië beaus dons e al bosoing aïe' (1861*a*)) rather than what he might offer in service. The destructive cycle at work in his relationship with Horn is emphasized too by the vocabulary of repayment in his threat: 'Quant purrai, si vus iert la demande merie' (1863).[42]

One way to read these moments is to view them as assessing, like a mirror for princes, the minutely calibrated set of verbal and physical relationships that constitute the economics of the feudal system (remembering the Greek origin of the term as regulating the household: *oikonomos*). This testing of relationships through imagined scenarios and debates is also reminiscent (though in a very different genre) of the roughly contemporary *De amore* by Andreas Capellanus, with its series of graded and ironic love-dialogues whose focus is regularly on the reckoning of love as service or payment, and on modelling modes of behaviour and speech in imaginary or even parodic scenarios.[43]

Beyond these examples of how gift relationships power the action of *The Romance of Horn*, paying, repaying, exchanging, valuing and measuring are a major currency of the romance. When Horn is helping King Hunlaf against the pagans, he comes across the enemy King Eglaf, and the poem notes with irony that he 'made him a present of his sword' (80, p. 38) ('li fist de sun brand un present' (1632)). Relative values are constantly being judged, again sometimes comically or ironically:

> Horn brandist sun espié, dunt l'enseigne traïne,
> Si ferit un paien, Turlin de Tabarine ...
>
> Que l'escu ne li vaut l'ele d'une geline
> Ne l'auberc dublentin la pel d'une hermine,
> Qu'il li trencha le piz, le feie e la corine. (1663–4; 1666–8)

> [Horn brandished his spear, with its trailing pennon, and struck a pagan, Turlin of Tabarine ... so hard that his shield was not worth a chicken's wing, nor his double-meshed hauberk a weasel's skin, for he cut through his breast, liver and entrails. (81, p. 39)]

Horn's own comments in battle mingle religious identity with the refusal of tribute. Gibelin, a prominent pagan warrior, is picked out from the crowd by the narrative voice: 'he sat well-armed on an Arab steed and poured out threats against our people' (82, p. 39).

Haderof kills him, prompting Horn to say: 'Bien aiez, Haderof! vengé sui del mastin! / Par cestui ne vendra   nostre lei mes a fin, / Ne ne rendrum treü   mes a utre marin' (1688–90) ['Bless you, Haderof! I'm avenged on the cur! He'll never destroy our creed, nor shall we ever pay tribute to foreigners!' (82, p. 39)]. This little episode itself pays attention both to the status and material value of Gibelin with his Arab horse and fine arms, and to the acts of exchange or repayment that revenge and tribute constitute. Immediately afterwards, Horn has the opportunity to help King Hunlaf's seneschal Herland, who brought Horn up. This vignette echoes Haderof's loyal service to Horn, and binds the Christian warriors together with mutual and overlapping sets of obligations. The poem continues to couch these explicitly as forms of debt and repayment: 'Ja·l me lerrez, musart! / Joe li dei bien eidier,   il me nurri tusart, / Si l'en dei guerredun   a certes nun endart' (1701–3) ['Villain, don't touch him! I owe him my help: he brought me up as a lad and indeed I owe him a recompense, no question about it' (83, p. 40)]. After the fighting, Horn plunders the pagans' ships, making sure to distribute the gold and pay the King his due. In this episode, Horn is shown at a moment of transition, acquiring attributes of lordship. The old King Hunlaf passes authority over to him, and the economic exchanges are clearly imbricated with the establishment of Horn's identity as ruler. The proper management of treasure in relationships with allies and with enemies is both an element of practical statecraft for a twelfth-century military narrative, and a figure for Horn's own value as protagonist, reinforcing his position in the layers of exchange constituting the romance's feudal world. Descriptions of battle are also descriptions of networks of payment and repayment, or the refusal of exchange, and a commentary on those networks is constituted by an economy of language, via promises, thanks, threats and proverbs. Likewise, this passage is the fruition of predictions made earlier in the text about Horn himself, and via the recessed narrative of Horn's father Aalof: it is a moment of narrative payback.

I should like to examine one more section of the poem where these connections between what seems the obviously exchange-related culture *in* the poem, and the exchange-related dynamic *of* the poem, are at work together. Horn's second exile is to Westir – the old name for Ireland, as the poem tells us. We have already seen how the Westir episodes are a doubled narrative unit. But it would be an attenuated reading of the poem merely to see the Westir section as doubling. Repetition itself provokes comparison, reflection and the calibration of difference. Some valuable readings of *The Romance of Horn* have recognized the importance of its second exile to the shape or texture of the narrative.[44] Here I want to focus on how story and voice work as part of the narrative exchange system I have already discussed.

The Westir scenes are linked to the previous narrative, of course, by Horn himself, whose body is the exchangeable object setting out afresh. Horn, indeed, takes passage on a merchant ship. The mariner praises Westir because of King Gudreche's power, but also his sons' generosity: 'Dous fiz ad chevaliers   de mut grant largeté: / Chevaliers ki la vunt,   bien i sunt soudéé' (2147–8) ['He has two sons, knights of great liberality. Knights who go there are well paid' (104, p. 50)]. Horn's decision to change his name likewise assimilates him to the ship's cargo, at the intersection of noble aspiration and economic transaction:

> Ki Gudmod des or mes   sera il apelé:
> Pur çoe turna sun num,   dunt ainz esteit nomé,
> Qu'il ne fust koneü   en estrange regné
> Desque pruesce oust fait   dunt doust ester preisié. (2160–3)

[He will now be called Gudmod. He changed his name from what it was at first, so that he should not be recognized in a foreign land until he had performed valiant deeds that deserved praise. 104, p. 50]

Having arrived in Ireland, Gudmod is scrutinized in detail by ladies in the port, by the King's sons Guffer and Egfer, and then at Gudreche's court. Careful attention is paid to his physical attributes and their imagined value in bed or in battle: 'E si dient plusur   ke bor fu cele néé / Ki·n oust fait sun pleisir   e de lui fust privéé: / Tant cum l'en sovendreit   de mal n'avreit haschéé' (2189–91) ['Many said it would be a lucky woman who could intimately enjoy him and the memory of it would put all later suffering out of her mind.' (106, p. 51)].

Gudmod enters the service of the King's younger son Egfer, and his reception at Gudreche's court is a repetition and variation of that at King Hunlaf's court as a boy. The potential energy of the unknown arrival is engaged once more, with Gudreche also revealing a connection to Aalof of Suddene:

> 'Bien conois le païs –   en Suddene fui ja –
> E bien conui Aaluf,   le bon rei k'(i)i regna:

> Prist mei a cumpaignun,   sun aveir me(n) dona;
> Un fiz petit qu'il out,   ilokes me mustra.
> Unkes hoem en cest mund   autre plus ne sembla,
> Ke vus faites celui   ki joe dunkes vi la,
> Si joe·l tenisse ci,   par celi qui·l cria,
> Rendreïë lui le bien   ke Aalof cummença.' (2361–8)

['I was in Suddene once – and knew Aalof well, the good king reigning there: he made me his comrade-in-arms and gave me gifts. He had a little son, whom he showed me there. No man on earth ever resembled another as much as you do the child I saw then. If I had him here, by God who made him, I would repay him for Aalof's kindness.' (114, p. 55)]

The French text's structure is even more insistently balanced than perhaps the translation allows for. It is the benefit (yield, *hau*) 'ke Aalof cummença' – 'that Aalof initiated' – that Gudreche wishes to pay back to Aalof's son. This time, the narrative of exchange – both the remembered exchanges of Gudreche and Aalof; the apparently new relationship with Gudmod; and the gifts of narrative in the king's and Gudmod's storytelling speeches – is inflected with a comic element of (mis)recognition:

> 'Sire,' çoe dit Gudmod,   'meinte feiz avendra
> K'un povre valletun   (al) riche resemblera
> Mes de mei e d'iceus   parentage n'i a,
> Dunt parlastes a mei: de noauz m'en esta.' (2369–72)

['Sire,' said Gudmod, 'it will often happen that a poor lad resembles a rich one, but there is no connection between me and the boy you speak of: I have no such luck.' (114, p. 55)]

Gudmod's life story is bound up in his physical value so intimately (his life history is in a sense written on his body), that despite this denial, he is an inscribed object continually being read or admired by those around him. As with his arrival in Brittany, the holding back of motivation or connection allows the story to proceed 'as if' Gudmod were a gift to Ireland and the poem; but the unveiling of Gudreche's links with Aalof then deepens the pattern of relations, the total system of exchanges, with which *The Romance of Horn* is so concerned. The persona of Gudmod also provokes some questions about luck and fate. While publicly resisting the connection between his looks, his birth and his luck, Gudmod's

actual identity as Horn proves the opposite, and his invocation of
God at this moment brings divine providence back into the story in
a relatively lighthearted but deeply meant way, once again identify-
ing Horn's beauty with a God-given gift that will produce worldly
success:

> 'Peise mei, bien siet Deus!   De mei [seit] k'il vudra!'
> 'Amis, mult dites bien;   cum il veut, si serra:
> Si sun pleisir i est   tost vus enrichera.
> N'iert pas povre del tut   ki tiel beauté avra.' (2373–6)

'It irks me, God knows! [i.e. Gudmod's supposed poverty] May His
will be done!' 'My friend, you say well: as He wishes, so shall it be.
If it please him, you shall soon grow rich. Whoever owns such beauty
will not be altogether poor.' (114, p. 55)]

In this exchange with Gudreche, the relationship between valuable goods, speaking or acting well, and the external beauty that
signals true worth are subtly woven together, with Horn's new name
Gudmod likewise binding him into that circuit of value, and the
community of the Irish court.[45] The Irish King's daughter Lenburc
attempts to woo Gudmod in ways similar to Rigmel in Brittany.
She sends a youth called Guidhere (himself due to be betrothed
to her) to Gudmod with a message and a fine goblet, asking him
to share the drink and keep the vessel. Courteously but firmly
rebuffed, she then offers rewards to a boy to bring Gudmod to see
her. This attempt at exchange by the King's daughter is a variation
on the theme of Rigmel's gifts to Herland, but modulated into a
lighthearted key: Gudmod never has any intention of accepting
her love, and so the poet explores tropes of love-longing through
Lenburc's desires, and the friendly interactions of Lenburc and her
brothers.[46]

Rosalind Field has explored the differences between court cultures
represented by the poem, persuasively arguing that the more relaxed
environment of the Irish court is part of a fine-grained analysis of
social mores and courtly culture: 'This portrait of a family at the
centre of the society, both parents living, with two sons and two
lively daughters all interacting with convincing humour, impatience,
tension and affection is remarkable.'[47] On another level, the repeated
pattern of proffered gift exchange is itself a form of narrative
rebalancing – a repayment or echo of the previous element, giving

the audience a return on their investment of attention to the richness of the text. That richness – the layered quality – of the romance is signalled through a song performed by Lenburc. Her brothers ask her to take up her harp and she plays beautifully, before telling them that she knows the first half of a song composed by Rigmel's brother Baltof, about Rigmel and Horn:

> Mut en avez oï   parler en cest regné
> E de l'amur de Horn   ke ele ad taunt amé –
> Si ad dreit, kar n'est hom   qui taunt eit de bunté,
> Cum cil Horn ad en sei;   bien m'a esté nuncié. (2795–8)

[You've heard much talk of her in this kingdom, and of Horn's love, whom she held so dear – and she was right, for there's no man who is as good as Horn: indeed that's what I've heard tell. (135, p. 65)]

Lenburc's singing of the first part of the lay prompts Gudmod to a complete performance. The lay not only tells the story of Horn and Rigmel (though it is not quoted), but its transmission is also analogous to Horn/Gudmod's own journey from Brittany to Ireland. Its use here is both narratively effective and self-consciously reflective. Gudmod's skilful performance furthers his relationships of exchange with Gudreche's children; it allows the protagonists and Gudmod to reflect on the central power of the Horn–Rigmel relationship at this moment, despite Rigmel's distance; and it shows poetic retelling as a form of gift exchange in aristocratic circles, as a figure for *The Romance of Horn* as a whole. That last dynamic is reminiscent of Marie de France's playful embedding of narrative, composition and performance in her *Lais*, as for example in *Chevrefoil*, where Tristan composes the lay of 'Chevrefoil' which both gives rise to, and is embedded within, Marie's own performance in a complex mirroring pattern.[48] Subtly, Thomas has Lenburc validate Horn/Gudmod's relationship with Rigmel by singing their lay and praising it. This has the effect of neutralizing the potentially disruptive effect of Lenburc as an alternative object of desire for Horn, and also shows her, too, participating in the creation and transmission of desiring narratives.

This episode reinforces the inevitable movement of Horn as narrative object within and beyond this particular moment of performance, and offers a reminder to the audience of the paradox of Horn both as a desirable, exchangeable object, and as something

that interrupts exchange, something beyond ordinary value and
outside normal explanatory narratives:

> 'Çoe est Horn, cum joe crei,   dunt l'en sout taunt parler – ...
> U n'est pas hom mortel: nul ne·l poet resembler:
> Del ciel est descendu   pur la gent espïer.
> Frere, kar li preiez   qu'il me deigt enseigner
> Cest lai k'oï avez: j'en ai grant desirer.
> Joe l'en dorrai asez   e argent e or mer:
> Asez prenge del mien,   asez ai ke doner.' (2852; 2855–60)

[It must be Horn, I believe ... or else it's no mortal man. No one
resembles him; he has come down from heaven to look at mankind.
My brothers, beg him deign to teach me this lay we heard: I want it
so. I will give him much, both silver and pure gold. Let him take
many of my possessions, I have plenty to give.' (137, p. 66)]

Lenburc's speech enters into this complex play with layers of narration
and of gift exchange. Echoing the opening of the poem, she compares
Gudmod to an angel in a way that short-circuits normal equivalence
and even hyperbole. At the same time, she expresses her desire through
the wish to give money and precious objects. The poem toys with
these incompatible systems of valuation, at times equating them,
and at times refusing their relationship. Since of course both kinds
of value system are constituted here by language, they are inevitably
drawn into the same sphere of calculation and comparison, for all
that describing the hero as an angel might claim to set him apart.
Meanwhile, Thomas as poet is insinuating the power of song itself
not only to represent but to foster desire through its creation and
exchange, as Lenburc's reactions show. The Irish section of the
poem deepens the narrative not simply through repetition, then,
but by the way that not-quite-repetition becomes reflection: both
on the conduct of Gudmod and the Irish court, and on narrative,
poetics and other kinds of circulation that take place in this finely
crafted story.[49]

Time and the gift, *if there is any*

The episodes I have discussed above could be multiplied, but I hope
are sufficient to show how an awareness of the gift in benign and

destructive forms works its way into the descriptive texture of the poem, providing the impetus for vital moments of the narrative, and also binding the larger structures of *The Romance of Horn* together: thus Horn's outward trajectory is governed by exile (whose return is restitution and revenge), within which are set the bonds of love and loyalty, which demand both a physical and emotional return from him. Romance as a genre is known for tying up those loose ends, reckoning those repayments and returns: its detractors have argued that its drive to do this, sometimes after extended digressions, risks parody or artificiality. But just as a too hasty discharging of a debt tends to commodify and so depersonalize the transaction, so in a romance, it is frequently in the very delay or frustration of the return, in the gift's continuing journey, that narrative suspense and pleasure – the *jouissance* engendered by the gift's interruptive power – is contained.[50] That is not to argue that an episodic structure *per se* creates the kind of complex relationships we see in *Horn* (episodic can just mean rambling), but that romances' attention to long-lost connections and far-fetched treasures can potentially develop their own accrued power, enriching the narrative's final return to its tonic key by the interrupted cadences and development of motifs along the way.

Processes of time like this are intimately connected both to the experience of narrative and that of the gift. As we saw earlier, pioneering anthropological work on the gift formulated the distinction between gift and commodity exchange as being partly one of time. Pierre Bourdieu emphasizes time's work as crucial to the performance of the gift relationship:

> It is all a matter of style, which means in this case timing and choice of occasions; the same act – giving, giving in return, offering one's services, paying a visit, etc. – can have completely different meanings at different times, coming as it may at the right or wrong moment, opportunely or inopportunely.[51]

Bourdieu's recognition of uncertainty in reciprocity – the way that human actors can behave in unpredictable or minutely variable ways – works both as a critique of more mechanistic models of exchange (his specific target here is Claude Lévi-Strauss), and as a reminder that even within boundaries of expectation (what we could call 'genre'), choices can be made (Bourdieu's 'style') that change the dynamics of the performance. In this context, we might read the expectations of a return on narrative investment in a medieval romance in a similar way to Bourdieu's set of practices, whose variations of timing and style create a richer, experiential understanding of the gift of narrative, the gift *as* narrative. Romance as a genre typically presents itself as an interruption or freezing of social activity such as feasting, for example, in order to satisfy, paradoxically, the demand for another kind of shared social experience. It is an interruption, the romance narrator claims, that will repay the attention that it is given:

> Alle beon he blithe
> That to my song lythe!
> A sang ich schal you singe
> Of Murry the Kinge.

> If ye wil lysten this laye   bot on little while,
> I schal telle hit as tite,   as I in toun herde.[52]

In these two Middle English examples, the narrating voice inserts itself into the social interactions of court or hall, but also initiates an exchange between teller and audience based on time and attention, with an eventual return of pleasure and profit. The narrative choices or style, and the audience's response, will create the complex engagement of practice that Bourdieu envisages in gift exchange. Nevertheless, that characteristic initiating moment of a romance – an unexplained entrance or irruption that breaks the temporal flow and operates apparently unmotivated – is both integral to romance narrative structures and embedded in the dynamics of the gift.

People's practices of exchange, then, themselves construct narrative in real time and space. While set in Insular mythistory, *The Romance of Horn* also acts as a series of decisions about giving and receiving that can be understood by its audience from the perspectives of the 'theoretical matrix' and the 'practical matrix'.[53] The former provides a framework for Horn to achieve glory, be an agent of divine power, and embody ideological messages about land, lineage and rulership. The latter allows for disaster, love-longing, the threat of death, and the danger of temptation to be experienced as part of the practice of the story, notwithstanding its larger framework, its system of total prestations. Romance as a genre is particularly apt to show this kind of relationship between different strata of logic and practice.

The fact that *The Romance of Horn* foregrounds acts of gift and exchange in its story and its figurative language makes it a particularly telling arena for investigating these relationships.

While keeping in mind Bourdieu's analysis of time, exchange and practice, I should like briefly to address the challenge to gift–time relations that Jacques Derrida sets out in *Given Time 1: Counterfeit Money*, a meditation on time, value and gift. Derrida describes what he terms a 'double bind' of the concept of pure gift. The gift, in order fully to live up to its name, must, he proposes, be *un*motivated by any thoughts of recompense, not accepted in the spirit of repayment – in fact, the very opposite of the economic circle that Derrida takes Mauss's 'système des prestations totales' to represent:

> Now the gift, *if there is any*, would no doubt be related to economy. One cannot treat the gift, this goes without saying, without treating this relation to economy, even to the money economy. But is not the gift, if there is any, also that which interrupts economy? That which, in suspending economic calculation, no longer gives rise to exchange? ... It must not circulate, it must not be exchanged, it must not in any case be exhausted, as a gift, by the process of exchange, by the movement of circulation of the circle in the form of return to the point of departure. If the figure of the circle is essential to economics, the gift must remain *aneconomic*.[54]

The true gift would thus stand alone, an *ur*-gift without prior history and thus outside time. In order to operate as a gift, its motivation (in other words its genealogy) would have to be erased, or at least go unrecognized. Elsewhere Derrida says: 'If the gift is calculated, if you know what you are going to give to whom, if you know what you want to give, for what reason, to whom, in view of what, etc., there is no longer any gift.'[55] The passage quoted above from *Given Time* characteristically postulates the *non plus ultra* of a proposition (the gift must not demand a return), perceives its impossibility (there is no pure gift since every gift implies an already-existing relationship or an expectation of return), and then opens the door just a crack to let a chink of refracted light show through ('it must not in any case be exhausted'). For Derrida, the gift, *if there is any*, becomes an interruption, a tear in the fabric of time, taking the 'circle' both as a social/spacial and temporal phenomenon.[56] While Derrida's initial objection to Mauss's gift as never-a-real-gift and so theoretically invalid is itself questionable, he does raise probing questions involving motivation, circularity and time as problematic features of the very idea of the gift.[57] Positing the gift as an interruption of time, but then placing it in time as its inevitable dimension, holds, I think, a powerful relation to the engendering of narrative:

> For finally, the overrunning of the circle by the gift, if there is any, does not lead to a simple, ineffable exteriority that would be transcendent and without relation. It is this exteriority that sets the circle going, it is this exteriority that puts the economy in motion. It is this exteriority that engages the circle and makes it turn. If one must render an account (to science, to reason, to philosophy, to the economy of meaning) of the circle effects in which a gift gets annulled, this account-rendering requires that one take into account that which, while not simply belonging to the circle, engages in it and sets off its motion. What is the gift as the first mover of the circle? And how does it contract itself into a circular contract? And from what place? Since when? From whom?[58]

It may already have struck medievalist readers how close is Derrida's description of the gift to the characteristics of many romance heroes: always-already charged with recursive, recompensing and/or revenging power, they nevertheless enter into a situation that does not (yet) recognize their narrative trajectory.[59] The question that Derrida poses here of exteriority, of an appeal to an outside force or environment that can regulate, energize or define the field of action bears affinity to his larger scepticism about structures of thinking that make claims to naturalism or objectivity but are in fact ideological and constructed. Derrida's thinking-through of origins and the gift echoes the problem of narrative beginning faced by any author. Reflecting on the need for all stories to employ 'the make believe of a beginning', George Eliot writes in *Daniel Deronda*, her own romance of origins and the search for national and personal identities: 'No retrospect will take us to the true beginning; and whether our prologue be in heaven or on earth, it is but a fraction of that all-presupposing fact with which our story sets out.'[60] Both Derrida's questions 'Since when? From whom?' and Eliot's acknowledgement of the 'all-presupposing fact' that allows stories to begin at some beginning, bear relevance for post-Conquest Insular texts, which reimagine origins and continuities in the face of historical rupture and subsequent entanglements of peoples, power and politics.

How does *The Romance of Horn* encounter these problems of beginning, and does its idea of the gift, *if there is any*, survive Derrida's challenge? Here I think that Derrida's phrase 'render an account' is a valuable way into the process by which *The Romance of Horn*, and other romances, overcome the potential impasse. As a form of narrative beginning, the romance text and its audience collaborate in an act of misrecognition or 'forging': the unknown hero is granted the energy of an originary gift, and his or her prior commitments are, for the time being, set aside. This then allows for the narrative to be charged with the power of the gift; for protagonists also to act as gifts to the story; and for the circle to turn. Eventually, these stories do 'render an account' in an economic sense, by balancing the debts and repayments set in motion by and through the text. But their way of rendering an account – by telling a story – is not contained only within economic calculations of balancing, and even a temporary suspension of those valuations allows the story to begin. We might, then, look back to the opening of *The Romance of Horn*, which strives to show Horn operating as a gift to the narrative. He is virtually begotten, not made (he's an angel, a day-star, found in an Edenic garden). But the story cannot long avoid the recursive force of genealogy and history; it is always under pressure to find a prior originary moment. Malbroin has a genealogy stretching back to Cain; Aalof's story is later revealed, and he too was a foundling; Hunlaf knew Aalof of old; and in an equivalent moment in Ireland, we learn that the Irish King Gudreche saw Horn as a child. The give and take of good and evil, exchange and revenge, has been established long before this narrative takes place, and the potential for further multiplication is always there. For Thomas as narrating figure, Horn is fundamentally God's gift to the story, and receiver of gifts ('eür' (24)). God's arbitrating presence provides for Thomas that validating and initiating force which, prior to any other story, has set the circle in motion.

There is one more important scene in *The Romance of Horn* that we might read in the light of these connections. It is in many ways the climactic moment of the story. Horn has returned to Brittany from Ireland disguised as a pilgrim, just in time to see the wedding feast of Rigmel and King Modin, with Wikele stage-managing events. As is the custom, Rigmel must serve wine to the assembled company, carrying a ceremonial drinking vessel of ox-horn. The pilgrim chides her for not serving the poor down at the foot of the table, and so she fetches a magnificent gilded cup and offers it to him. He ignores it, much to her consternation, and she asks why:

'Or me dites, bea[u] chier,
Quant beivre ne volez,   ke deit le demander?
Dous feiz l'ai aporté,   n'en vousistes guster:
Al semblant que joe vei   le corage avez fier.'
Dunc respundi si Horn – ne se pout plus celer –
'Bele, sacez de fi,   joe fui ja costumier
Ke plus riches vesseaus   me seut hom aporter.
Mes "corn" apelent "horn"   li engleis latimier,
Si vus pur sue amur,   ki si se fait nomer,
Icel corn plein de vin   me vollez bailler,
Ke vus vi des orainz   a vostre ami doner,
D'icel beivrë od vus   si serai meiteier.'

* * *

Tiel doel out en sun quoer,   pur poi ke ne pasma.
Quant revint, s'arestut   e si se purpensa.
Ke il fust messager   de part Horn, çoe quida:
Ke il meismes le fust   entercier ne l'osa. (4199–210; 4215–8)

['Now tell me, my fair friend, if you don't want to drink, why ask for it? I've brought it you twice and you wouldn't taste it: as far as I can see, you have a proud heart.' Then Horn replied thus – he could hide no longer – 'Lovely lady, know for certain, once men used to bring me richer cups. But "horn" is the English word for what you took round just now. If you, for love of him I've just named, will offer me the horn full of wine that I saw you give to your lover just now, I will share this drink with you.' ...

She felt such grief at heart, she almost fainted. When she recovered, she stopped and reflected. She thought he might be a messenger from Horn. She did not dare to recognize that it was he himself. (199–200, p. 97)]

Still hovering between belief and scepticism as to whether this really is Horn (this passage is reminiscent of the Oxford *Folie Tristan*),[61] Rigmel brings out the drinking-horn, and he slips the ring into it – the one she had given him as a love-token. He drinks half and returns the horn to her. She recognizes the ring, and after further dark speeches that test Rigmel's loyalty, she realizes that it really is

Horn, and they hatch a plot to rescue her and defeat Wikele's plans. Rather than being the start of a relationship, this is instead the 'coming home' or repayment of a gift. Nevertheless, the elements of interruption, misrecognition and suspense are present here, and the episode acts not only as a conclusion but as a departure from an established narrative pattern that would frequently end a romance – the wedding of the heroine and feasting in the hall. Thus the return of one object or interest may also precipitate the interruption or initiation of another.

This scene revolves around the identity or interpretation both of the horn drinking vessel, and of Horn the hero. Horn and the horn need to come together in order to close the narrative and gift cycle. They do this partly by the play on the name 'horn' ('Mes "corn" apelent "horn"   li engleis latimier'), and also by Horn's placing the ring into the drinking horn, so that it metaphorically wears or carries the power of the love-token, and also evokes the sexual union of the two lovers in the symbols of horn and ring. Both the ring and the horn are precious and circular objects. They both could be taken to represent or reflect the narrative as a whole: circling back at this point, with a meaning that must be decoded, and exceeding its value as exchangeable commodity. A moment of exchange, as Sarah Kay has fruitfully argued in the context of *chansons de geste*, can take on the quality of *mise en abîme*, acknowledging its own fictionality and dwelling on the creative process that brought it into existence. Similarly, Donald Maddox has drawn attention to 'specular' moments in Old French narratives, especially those of Marie de France and Chrétien de Troyes – that is, moments that demand a heightened quality of reflection, recognition, or coming to terms with one's identity.[62] This scene in *The Romance of Horn* answers to both these ways of reading by multiplying the horn's meaning: it embodies the identity of the hero; it is a figure for desire; a test of truth – both of the heroine and the narrative; a symbol of the lordship that Horn comes to claim; and also, perhaps, a figure for the poem as meaningful artwork itself.[63] In addition, I would argue that the guise of pilgrim that Horn adopts at this point places him in a textual/ethical position close to Thomas the author in his outspoken moralism and interrogative power in the story. Horn is seen to be shaping and commenting on the narrative as well as participating in it. As Jonathan Parry comments, an attention to movements of the gift helps break down boundaries between person and thing: Horn is actor and acted upon; person and text; crafter and object; giver and gift. The resonances of his exchange with Rigmel here go beyond the demands of the plot and suggest more complex ways in which (re)telling the story acts to shape the tellers themselves.

At the end of *The Romance of Horn*, and at the moment when a final reckoning or conclusion might be looked for, Master Thomas once again raises the prospect of his own departure, but in the process also starts a new cycle of narrative obligations, by passing on to his own son Wilmot the responsibility for telling the story of Horn's son:

> Entritant de sorjorn cum iluc sorjornat,
> Le vaillant Hadermod de Rimel engendrat,
> Ki Asf[r]iche cunquist e qe pus [i] regnat
> E ki tuz ses parenz de paens [i] vengat;
> De pruesce e de sen trestuz les ultreat,
> Cum cil purrat mustrer ki la estorie savrat.
> Icest lais a mun fiz, Gilimot, ki·l dirrat,
> Ki la rime apré mei bien controverat –
> Controvures ert bon: e de mei [ce retendra]. (5225–33)

[In the time he stayed there, he fathered on Rigmel the valiant Hadermod, who conquered and then ruled Africa, and took revenge on the heathen for all his kin. In bravery and wisdom he surpassed them all, as he who knows the story can reveal. I leave this to my son Wilmot to tell, who after me will compose the poem well – he will be a good poet: he inherits that from me. (245, p. 120)]

The power of the gift to reduplicate and deepen its obligations is, then, prospective as well as retrospective in this romance. The poem's ending also reflects on how a 'gift' like poetic skill is transferable, and it draws into correspondence the heroic qualities of Aalof, Horn and Hadermod with those of the romance writer. The text too, then, becomes an expression of inherited value(s) that reaches out beyond its own immediate production.

Dominica Legge and, more recently, Judy Weiss, have suggested that *The Romance of Horn* may have been written for a Christmas feast in Dublin in 1171–2, when Henry II was visiting Richard FitzGilbert of Clare, known as Strongbow, who after a series of adventures was made tenant-in-chief of Leinster by the King.[64] In such a context, the web of obligations, exchanges and loyalties stretches out of the text and into the developing Angevin polity too. Horn's movement across Brittany, Britain and Ireland through exile is not an exact match for the post-Conquest settlement and expansion of Angevin power, but he can stand as a resonant figure for conquest, Christian heroism, and the forging of allegiance across the waters. The poem personalises this narrative so that, although Horn's trajectory is to recover a lost inheritance of land, the narrative is focused on how his personal authority achieves that amalgamation. This happens through physical prowess (even Christlike perfection); through continual reference to God's ordaining power in the narrative; and also to Horn's status as both object of exchange, teller of exchange stories, and actor in exchanges. As the drinking horn was passed around Strongbow's hall, its identity with Horn perhaps reminded the poem's listeners of the bonds that they were re-creating through the exchanges of body, words and goods that feudal relationships constantly demanded.

The Horn story was reworked several times in Insular contexts over the next few hundred years, moving from French to different English-lanugage versions, as shifts in audience expectations and linguistic situations took place.[65] The ways in which different adaptations or performances of the story negotiate moments of giving and exchange can help us to understand both the continuities of narrative and expectation, and the points of tension or development that these structures underwent. Before drawing together some of the ideas introduced in this chapter, I will discuss two of the English inflections of the Horn narrative – *King Horn* and *Horn Childe and Maiden Rimnild* – with a focus on how they manage particular acts of exchange.

'Icomen ut of the bote': the movement of exchange in *King Horn* and *Horn Childe and Maiden Rimnild*

King Horn is well known for its stripped-back style of narration, with protagonists being placed in a barely sketched environment.[66] Certainly its aesthetic is markedly different from the detailed descriptive texture of *The Romance of Horn*; instead there is relatively little evocation of the material world of its protagonists. Nevertheless, *King Horn*'s narrative is also driven forward by the energies of the gift given and received. The poem begins with a few lines about Horn's father (in this version called Murry), but the focus soon shifts to Horn, using superlatives drawn from natural imagery to highlight his God-given presence in the story:

> Fairer nis non thane he was:
> He was bright so the glas;
> He was whit so the flur;
> Rose red was his colur. (13–16)

While without much of the speculative or contextual material in *The Romance of Horn*, nor its interest in openly exploring the motivation of its protagonists, *King Horn* quickly builds a set of interlocking relationships of obligation or revenge that power the narrative. We find Horn's father slain by Saracens for being a Christian; Godhild, Horn's mother, praying to Christ for him; Christ credited with creating Horn; and the Saracens both holding back from killing him because of his beauty, and predicting that were he to grow up, he would repay their crimes against his family: 'Yef thu mote to live go ... Ye scholde slen us alle' (101, 104); 'if thu were alive, / With swerd other with knive, / We scholden alle deie, / And thi fader deth abeie' (111–14). Horn and his companions are then identified with the boat in which they travel. It is both a literal vehicle for their exile; a figure for the narrative itself; and in its mingling with Horn, it becomes an image for his role as a given or traded object too: 'Horn ich am ihote, / Icomen ut of the bote, / Fram the se side' (205–7).[67] Shortly before this, Horn addresses the boat as if a protagonist in the story: 'Schup bi the se flode, / Daies have thu gode' (143–4), asking it to act as an envoy by passing on a message of hope to his mother, and of predicted revenge to the pagans: 'And seie that hei schal fonde / The dent of myne honde' (155–6). The boat is to speak about Horn's involvement in the narrative, but also this passage of the poem facilitates Horn's role in telling his own story, and this interchange between person and thing, both circulating objects whose trajectories overlap, deepens *King Horn*'s texture at this important moment.[68]

King Horn does not have *The Romance of Horn*'s extended play with the lavish gifts that Rigmel (Rymenhild in *King Horn*) presses on Herland (Athelbrus). Instead, Athelbrus faces a moral dilemma about what Rymenhild wants to do with Horn, and so brings Horn's companion Athulfe as a substitute. The English romance still uses the scene as a way comically to evaluate Horn against other men. After Rymenhild 'gan wexe wild' (300) and lies him down on her bed, Athulfe admits to her that he is not the Horn she is getting excited about: 'Horn is fairer and riche, / Fairer bi one ribbe / Thane eni man that libbe' (318–20). Horn's value is still being weighed up and described in diverse metaphorical contexts, but rather than the extended description of Rigmel's gift-giving in *The Romance of Horn*, *King Horn* concentrates our attention on a moment of exchange between the lovers. Rymenhild gives Horn a ring with her name inscribed on it: 'Ther is upon the ringe / Igrave "Rymenhild the yonge"' (569–70). As with Horn's mingling of roles with his boat, the ring is a promise of Rymenhild's love, a prophecy of his victories in battle, and a text that narrates their romance, within the romance text of *King Horn* as a whole.[69] The embedding of these meaningful objects that circulate and interweave with the human protagonists is one way in which *King Horn* generates a sense of depth, notwithstanding its simple style. Like *The Romance of Horn*, the English text also establishes a web of connections between the protagonists as given or received, the story they perform or tell, and the romance that is heard or read.

The Horn narrative's pattern of discovered hero, repeated exile and the eventual reclaiming of lovers and land yielded numerous variations as the story itself travelled around and beyond Britain. The Auchinleck Manuscript (Edinburgh, National Library of Scotland, Advocates MS 19.2.1) is the only witness to another Middle English version, *Horn Childe and Maiden Rimnild*. Its editor Maldwyn Mills makes a case for its close relationship with *The Romance of Horn* or some version derived from it, though it makes a number of adjustments to the story, for example having Horn travel to Wales.[70] Matthew Holford has suggested that many of *Horn Childe*'s distinctive features are linked to its nostalgic political vision of England as dominant within Britain, looking back from a point in the early fourteenth century when the authority established by Edward I was being eroded under Edward II.[71] *Horn Childe* foregrounds the exchange of gifts, payments and loyalties more explicitly and pragmatically than *King Horn*, though these dynamics nevertheless contribute to an overall pattern of prestations that give shape and coherence to the story. For example, in the section where Rimnild has summoned Horn, and Arlaund (Herland in *The Romance of Horn*; Athelbrus in *King Horn*) instead brings Haþerof (Haderof *RH*; Athulfe *KH*), the reckoning of payments and value is more obvious. There is no elaborate gift-giving scene involving Arlaund; instead, this is displaced onto Haþerof, whom Rimnild believes to be Horn. After giving him fruit, spices and wines from a cup and horn, she produces gifts for him:

> Þan a seriaunt sche bad go,
> A gentil goshauk forto ta
> (Fair he was to fliȝt),
> Þerwiþ herten gloues to
> (Swiche was þe maner þo)
> & ȝaf Haþerof of her ȝif[t]:
> Sche wende bi Haþerof, Horn it were,
> Þat loued hunting noþing more,
> On him hir loue was liȝt.
> A les of grehoundes forþ þai brouȝt;
> & he forsoke & wald it nouȝt
> & seyd Haþerof he hiȝt. (337–48)

The abundance of material goods in this passage becomes analogous to the strength and value of Rimnild's feelings, but because she is mistaken about Haþerof's identity the effect is to emphasize their superfluity and, perhaps, undermine her role in the story as an equal participant in the love narrative. Whereas *The Romance of Horn* balances its finely detailed material descriptions with philosophical and ethical speculation or reflection, and *King Horn* leaves aside circumstantial description to focus on key moments of giving and receiving, in *Horn Childe* the value of the material world seems to be bound up with the textual weight of the poem, which informs and inducts its audience into the gift-laden world of the romance past ('Swiche was þe maner þo'). The scene with Haþerof neatly incorporates comic bathos when after the long build-up of objects Haþerof finally reveals his identity. The previous stanza echoes 'Horn' (327) with 'horn' (336) in rhyme position, which reminds the audience of the layers of reference in the hero's name.

Horn Childe and Maiden Rimnild continues to use gifts as a gauge for the status of relationships between the protagonists. When

Arlaund does bring Horn to Rimnild, she presents gifts to him with mini-ekphrases of horse, horn, robe and sword:

> 'Horn,' sche seyd, 'is þi name:
> An horn Y schal ȝiue þe ane,
> A michel & vnride;
> Al yuore is þe bon,
> Sett wiþ mani a riche ston,
> To bere bi þi side.' (385–90)

The gifts are closely bound up with Horn's progress to knighthood and therefore into a new identity as someone of the appropriate status to return her love. Here Rimnild's alignment of Horn and the gift of the horn rather unsubtly reinforces his position as a tradeable and moving object, though *Horn Childe* does not exploit the Horn/horn identity when Rimnild serves the disguised Horn at her wedding feast, preferring a wine cup as the vessel into which Horn drops the ring (lines 994–5).[72] The poem also uses gift exchange at the level of metaphor – Horn 'ȝaf þe maiden loue wound' (416) in implicit response to her fine gifts; and she in return makes a more literal promise of '[h]ir maidenhod to mede' (420), *mede* being a word, of course, whose meanings cross over between gift, reward and payment.[73] Moreover, expectations and economies of reward and exchange run through this part of the text. King Houlac's relationship with Horn and his companions links his giving of 'gold & fe' (469) to advice that they should marry. The false Wikard and Wikel then accuse Horn and Rimnild of treachery due to their sexual relationship, and the King believes the accusation because she had given Horn a fine horse: 'Forþi ȝaf sche him þe stede, / Lesing it is nouȝt' (494–5). Horn's rift with King Houlac is sealed when his gift of five harts, offered to placate the King, is refused, but Horn's bond with Rimnild is immediately reinforced when she gives him a ring with special powers and symbolism: 'Loke þou forsake it for no þing / It schal ben our tokening' (568–9). Thus *Horn Childe and Maiden Rimnild*, in its narrative-focused, more pragmatic mode, uses moments of exchange as the currency of human relationships and judging loyalties, as well as their forming a layer of messages in the text about value, longevity, faith, power, storytelling and desire.[74]

The three versions of the Horn legend that I have discussed in this chapter are all, I believe, energized by reading via the structures of exchange that they develop, and we can gain more access to those structures, more questions to ask of the texts, by paying attention to the notion of give and take studied by Mauss and Malinowski, and debated since then. It has been my argument that in *The Romance of Horn* and the other Horn texts here, the eponymous hero acts as a gift both within the story and to the story. Each moment of arrival incognito; or gift from king to budding knight; or exchange between lovers, gains power from the unequal elements of the exchange at the time it takes place, but is then embedded in a system of overall prestations that embodies romances' drive to present balanced accounts, even if their bottom line is reached via some extraordinary sacrifices or super-human acts. My further claim is that such energies of give and take give force to the act of story-telling itself, within these texts and of the texts. Not every medieval romance, or every story, will have as clear a relationship with acts of giving and receiving as *The Romance of Horn*, with its overlapping identification of protagonist and tradeable object. But Eliot's 'make believe of a beginning' is often generated in medieval romances by the kind of occluded origin given to Horn when he twice arrives as an exile at a new court.

Conclusion: creative misrecognition

This idea of the gift's occluded origin, or at least its point of departure, is one to which I should like to return now in closing this chapter. It resonates strongly, as we have seen, with the pattern of the hero's apparently unmotivated arrival in the narrative, and with the recovery of origins in retrospect that many medieval romances stage. Earlier I noted that the 'forgetting' of origins at the moment of discovery or giving helped give narrative energy to a romance story – helped it to initiate the workings of exchange and act as a gift. I would like to connect this to Bourdieu's larger sense that unknowing, or misrecognition, is important to exchange relationships of many kinds, allowing the flow of objects and obligations to continue without pausing at each moment to acknowledge and potentially derail their structural, symbolic or performative functions:

> To stop short at the 'objective' truth of the gift, i.e. the model … is to ignore the fact that the agents practise as irreversible a sequence of actions that the observer constitutes as reversible. … The temporal structure of gift exchange, which objectivism ignores, is what makes

possible the coexistence of two opposing truths, which defines the
full truth of the gift … [T]he operation of gift exchange presupposes
(individual and collective) misrecognition (*méconnaissance*) of the
reality of the objective 'mechanism' of the exchange.[75]

Bourdieu's acknowledgement of the power of gift as a form of
narrative as opposed to the totalizing vision of structuralist analysis
may also be used in our reading of stories, including those of Horn.
Similar acts of *méconaissance* permeate the structures of these texts,
and of an audience's engagement with them as narrative. We can
move between our knowing that a larger pattern of reciprocity
surrounds a text, and our forgetting of that pattern in order to take
part in the text's productive energy: in this sense I am positing a
dynamic where misrecognition is not (only) a lack of knowledge or
a wilful forgetting of the real, tougher, world, but (also) a more
deliberate and generative act. In a later reflection, Bourdieu returned
to the ambiguous characteristics of the gift in a way that addresses
the paradox posed by Derrida too – the relationship between gift
as unmotivated and gift as part of an exchange system. Bourdieu's
framing of this ambiguity in terms of knowledge, time and performance is, I believe, valuable for our own reading of narrative
structures and relationships:

> The major characteristic of the experience of the gift is, without a
> doubt, its ambiguity. On the one hand, it is experienced (or intended)
> as a refusal of self-interest and egoistic calculation, and an exaltation
> of generosity – a gratuitous, unrequited gift. On the other hand, it
> never entirely excludes awareness of the logic of exchange or even
> confession of the repressed impulses or, intermittently, the denunciation
> of another, denied, truth or generous exchange – its constraining and
> costly character.[76]

Bourdieu's 'ambiguity' and Godelier's 'enigma' are a powerful source
of energy for the continuing work of time and narrative in fiction,
including medieval romances. They involve the sort of willing
misrecognition that Bourdieu refers to when quoting Mauss, in what
he calls 'one of the most profound sentences that an anthropologist
has ever written: "Society always pays itself in the counterfeit coin
of its dream"'.[77] In a complex set of trajectories and relationships,
the act of giving (and, I argue, of telling) is both a moment to set
aside the structures demanding reciprocity or return, and a moment

when those very structures are most acutely activated and set in motion. In the next chapter, I shall pursue ideas of reciprocity, the itineraries of people and objects, and the role of keeping as well as giving, in some Middle English romances.

Notes

1 See e.g. Susan Crane, *Insular Romance: Politics, Faith, and Culture in Anglo-Norman and Middle English Literature* (Berkeley: University of California Press, 1986); Elizabeth Salter, *English and International: Studies in the Literature, Art and Patronage of Medieval England*, ed. Derek Pearsall and Nicolette Zeeman (Cambridge: Cambridge University Press, 1988), ch. 1; David Wallace (ed.), *The Cambridge History of Medieval English Literature* (Cambridge: Cambridge University Press, 1999), chs 1–6; Peter Damian-Grint, *The New Historians of the Twelfth-Century Renaissance: Inventing Vernacular Authority* (Woodbridge: Boydell Press, 1999); Jocelyn Wogan-Browne, *Saints' Lives and Women's Literary Culture, c.1150–1300: Virginity and its Authorizations* (Oxford: Oxford University Press, 2001); Laura Ashe, *Fiction and History in England, 1066–1200* (Cambridge: Cambridge University Press, 2007); Jocelyn Wogan-Browne et al. (eds), *Language and Culture in Medieval Britain: The French of England, c.1100–c.1500* (Woodbridge: Boydell & Brewer, 2009); M.T. Clanchy, *From Memory to Written Record: England, 1066–1307*, 3rd edn (Oxford: Wiley-Blackwell, 2012); Elaine Treharne, *Living through Conquest: The Politics of Early English, 1020–1220* (Oxford University Press, 2012); Orietta Da Rold et al. (eds), *The Production and Use of English Manuscripts, 1060 to 1220* (2010, rev. 2013), www.le.ac.uk/english/em1060to1220, accessed 20 February 2018; Laura Ashe, *Conquest and Transformation*, Oxford English Literary History 1: 1000–1350 (Oxford: Oxford University Press, 2017); and for regional identities and communities, Emily Dolmans, 'Regional Identities and Cultural Contact in the Literatures of Post-Conquest England' (doctoral dissertation, University of Oxford, 2017).
2 M. Dominica Legge, *Anglo-Norman Literature and its Background* (Oxford: Clarendon Press, 1963), pp. 98–100; Judith Weiss, 'Thomas and the Earl: literary and historical contexts for the *Romance of Horn*', in Rosalind Field (ed.), *Tradition and Transformation in Medieval Romance* (Cambridge: Brewer, 1999), pp. 1–14, at pp. 1–7.
3 Ian Short, 'Language and literature', in Christopher Harper-Bill and Elisabeth van Houts (eds), *A Companion to the Anglo-Norman World* (Woodbridge: Boydell Press, 2003), pp. 191–213, quoting p. 211. See

also Ruth Kennedy and Simon Meecham-Jones (eds), *Writers of the Reign of Henry II: Twelve Essays* (Basingstoke: Palgrave Macmillan, 2006), especially chapters by John Gillingham, 'The cultivation of history, legend, and courtesy at the court of Henry II', pp. 25–52; and Rosalind Field, 'Children of anarchy: Anglo-Norman romance in the twelfth century', pp. 249–62.

4 Thomas, *The Romance of Horn*, ed. Mildred K. Pope, 2 vols (vol. 2 rev. and completed by T.B.W. Reid), ANTS 9–10, 12–13 (Oxford: Blackwell, 1955, 1964), II.122–3, quoting 122; see also *The Birth of Romance: An Anthology*, trans. Judith Weiss (London: Dent (Everyman), 1992), pp. xiii–xiv. Many scholars would now call the language of the poem French of England: see Jocelyn Wogan-Browne, 'General introduction: what's in a name: the "French" of "England"', in Wogan-Browne et al. (eds), *Language and Culture*, pp. 1–13.

5 See Weiss, 'Thomas and the Earl', pp. 7–13.

6 *Romance of Horn*, ed. Pope, II.21–121 and 124 (quoting 124).

7 *Romance of Horn*, ed. Pope, I.ix–xv, includes brief descriptions of the three manuscripts with substantial amounts of text: along with the Cambridge manuscript, these are Oxford, Bodleian Library MS Douce 132; and London, British Library MS Harley 527, and she notes the two other fragments, described and edited in E.G.W. Braunholtz, 'Cambridge fragments of the Anglo-Norman "Roman de Horn"', *Modern Language Review* 16 (1921), 23–33. They are Cambridge University Library MSS Add. 4407 and 4470.

8 All quotations of *The Romance of Horn* are from Pope's edition; translations are from *The Birth of Romance*, trans. Weiss (here quoting laisses 1–2; p. 1). Pope's edition is also available (in a rather ponderous format) via the Anglo-Norman On-Line Hub, www.anglo-norman.net, accessed 20 February 2018.

9 The question of narrative voice, narrator, author and teller in romance is not straightforward. See especially A.C. Spearing's illuminating readings of romance and narrative voice: *Readings in Medieval Poetry* (Cambridge: Cambridge University Press, 1987), chs 2, 3; *Textual Subjectivity: The Encoding of Subjectivity in Medieval Narratives and Lyrics* (Oxford: Oxford University Press, 2005); and 'What is a narrator?', *Digital Philology* 4 (2015), 59–105. In *The Romance of Horn*, Thomas presents himself as author-persona at the start and end of the text, and the narrating voice co-opts the poem's audience into moral judgements and predictions about the story, but that does not necessarily imply a consistently 'authorial' narrator throughout the poem.

10 *Horn Childe and Maiden Rimnild: edited from the Auchinleck MS, National Library of Scotland, Advocates' MS 19.2.1*, ed. Maldwyn Mills (Heidelberg: Winter Universitätsverlag, 1988), pp. 59–61.

11 For detailed discussion of the role of the Saracens, see Morgan Dickson, 'Twelfth-Century Insular Narrative: The *Romance of Horn* and Related Texts' (doctoral dissertation, University of Cambridge, 1996), ch. 4.

12 See *AND*, s.v. *line* (1), with meanings ranging from 'string, cord; line, rope'; to 'line (of writing)'; to 'lineage, family'.

13 See in particular E. Jane Burns, *Courtly Love Undressed: Reading through Clothes in Medieval French Culture* (Philadelphia: University of Pennsylvania Press, 2002), and *Sea of Silk: A Textile Geography of Women's Work in Medieval French Literature* (Philadelphia: University of Pennsylvania Press, 2009). For romance's colonial and orientalist fantasies, see Geraldine Heng, *Empire of Magic: Medieval Romance and the Politics of Cultural Fantasy* (New York: Columbia University Press, 2003).

14 Personal communication, 2012. *AND* uses this line to illustrate the meaning 'boon, gift': s.v. *eur*, meaning 2.

15 See e.g. Brewer, *Symbolic Stories*, pp. 100–2, though recent work on romance sees more flexibility here.

16 This is imagined as in the South West of Britain, perhaps approximately modern-day Devon: see *Romance of Horn*, ed. Pope, II.4.

17 Crane, *Insular Romance*, pp. 24–7, quoting p. 25; for exile-and-return structures in French of England romances, see Liliana Worth, 'Exile-and-Return in Medieval Vernacular Texts of England and Spain, c.1170–1250' (doctoral dissertation, University of Oxford, 2015).

18 Crane, *Insular Romance*, p. 26.

19 Mauss, *Essai sur le don*, p. 71; *The Gift*, p. 61 (italicized in Mauss's text).

20 Mauss, *The Gift*, trans. Guyer, p. 70; *Essai sur le don*, pp. 82–4.

21 See from a medievalist's point of view Patrick Geary, 'Gift exchange and social science modelling: the limitations of a construct', in Algazi et al. (eds), *Negotiating the Gift*, pp. 129–40.

22 Notably, Raymond Firth, *Economics of the New Zealand Maori* (Wellington: Shearer, 1972; first published as *Primitive Economics of the New Zealand Maori* (London: Routledge, 1929)); and Claude Lévi-Strauss, 'Introduction à l'oeuvre de Marcel Mauss', in Marcel Mauss, *Sociologie et anthropologie*, 11th edn (Paris: Presses Universitaires de France, 2004), pp. 9–52.

23 Marshall Sahlins, *Stone Age Economics* (London: Routledge, 2017; first published 1972), pp. 134–67, quoting p. 144, 146.

24 Maurice Godelier, *The Enigma of the Gift*, trans. Nora Scott (Cambridge: Polity Press, 1999), pp. 8–32; quoting p. 12. Godelier cites Annette Weiner as an influence; I discuss her work further in Ch. 2. In *The Senses in Late Medieval England* (New Haven, CT Yale University Press, 2006), pp. 29–62, C.M. Woolgar discusses medieval understandings

of how physical and less tangible qualities might be passed into or through a thing from someone associated with it.

25 For a 'textual environment' as a flexible understanding of historical and social context, see Paul Strohm, 'The textual environment of Chaucer's "Lak of Stedfastness"', in his *Hochon's Arrow: The Social Imagination of Fourteenth-Century Texts* (Princeton, NJ: Princeton University Press, 1992), pp. 57–74. Much less detailed contextual information is known about *The Romance of Horn*, and so the textual environment would have to be drawn more loosely.

26 *AND*, s.v. *bon*.

27 My evocation of textual pleasure echoes Roland Barthes, *Le plaisir du texte* (Paris: Éditions du Seuil, 1973), and is influenced by the important discussion of romance and pleasure in McDonald, 'A polemical introduction', pp. 10–17.

28 Malinowski, *Argonauts*, pp. 177–91, quoting the subheadings on pp. 177, 189.

29 Jonathan Parry, '*The Gift*, the Indian gift and the "Indian gift"', *Man* new series 21 (1986), 453–73, at p. 454.

30 Hyde, *The Gift*, p. 15. This seems to be Hyde's distillation of Malinowski, *Argonauts*, pp. 81–104, esp. pp. 95–9: Malinowski's famous discussion of Kula exchange undertaken by the Trobriand islanders (necklaces circulating in one direction; armshells in another). Godelier has argued that Malinowski's understanding of Kula was skewed by his focusing on an idiosyncratic example of its operation (*Enigma of the Gift*, pp. 85–8). Parry ('*The Gift*') also discusses Firth's and Sahlins's scepticism about disinterested gifts, which is related to their critique of Mauss. Miyazaki, 'Gifts and exchange', includes a perceptive review of debates over gift versus commodity, exploring recent attempts to move beyond what he calls the 'problem–solution framework' of Mauss's analysis.

31 *Klaeber's Beowulf*, 4th edn, ed. R.D. Fulk et al. (Toronto: University of Toronto Press, 2008), lines 20–4. Even this balancing of obligations is a compression into a total system (gifts for loyalty) that plays out over many years, through numerous individual, uneven instances of give and take. On gift exchange in *Beowulf* see Robert E. Bjork, 'Speech as gift in *Beowulf*', *Speculum* 69 (1994), 993–1022; John M. Hill, 'Beowulf and the Danish succession: gift giving as the occasion for complex gesture', *Medievalia et Humanistica* new series 11 (1982), 177–97.

32 See Crane, *Insular Romance*, pp. 34–40, and Ashe, *Fiction and History*, pp. 154–5, for ideologies of land, region and nation at work in the text.

33 This opening of a space in which to start the story is comparable to the sense of wonder in romance narrative that Mikhail Bakhtin describes in 'adventure time': 'Forms of time and of the chronotope

in the novel', in his *The Dialogic Imagination*, ed. Michael Holquist; trans. Caryl Emerson and Michael Holquist (Austin: University of Texas Press, 1981), pp. 84–258, esp. pp. 86–92. However, *The Romance of Horn*, for all that Horn seems to spring into the narrative fully charged as a hero/gift, does contain shifts in maturity and perspective that Bakhtin thought absent in the Greek romances he discusses; see the variegation and development discussed by Rosalind Field, 'Courtly culture and emotional intelligence in the *Romance of Horn*', in Perkins (ed.), *Medieval Romance and Material Culture*, pp. 23–40.

34 Parry, '*The Gift*', p. 457.

35 Further to debates over the *hau* and kinds of exchange noted above, distinctions and relationships between gift and commodity are influentially discussed by Gregory, *Gifts and Commodities*, and brilliantly deployed to analyse the Middle English romance *Sir Amadace* in Putter, 'Gifts and commodities in *Sir Amadace*'.

36 On the characteristic rhetorical structures of gift-giving in *chansons de geste*, see Jean-Pierre Martin, 'Les offres de présents dans les chansons de geste: structures rhétoriques et conditions d'énonciation', *Romania* 107 (1986), 183–207.

37 E.g. lines 1653 (81, p. 38); 375–81 (18, p. 9); 392–4 (19, pp. 9–10). Horn's name links him with the decorated, sometimes inscribed drinking- and sounding-horns that were a familiar feature of elite culture; see Dickson, 'Twelfth-Century Insular Narrative', ch. 3; Morgan Dickson, 'The role of drinking horns in medieval England', *AVISTA Forum Journal* 21 (2011), 42–8; Avinoam Shalem, 'The second life of objects: ivory horns in medieval church treasuries', in Gudrun Bühl et al. (eds), *Spätantike und byzantinische Elfenbeinbildwerke im Diskurs* (Wiesbaden: Reichert Verlag, 2008), pp. 225–36; Avinoam Shalem and Maria Glaser, *Die Mittelalterlichen Olifante* (Berlin: Deutscher Verlag für Kunstwissenschaft, 2014), e.g. pp. 138–43; 159–62; 179–81. Examples of surviving horns from medieval England include the famous Savernake Horn: see below, pp. 73–7, and the Pusey Horn: London, Victoria and Albert Museum, no. 220-1938, described in Richard Marks and Paul Williamson (eds), *Gothic: Art for England, 1400–1547* (London: V&A Publications, 2003), p. 315.

38 *AND*, s.v. *trover*; *graver* (1); *graver* (2).

39 I use 'character' advisedly here, though the term is problematic for medieval romance, and risks our bringing assumptions drawn from what we think post-Romantic fiction is doing; see Spearing, *Textual Subjectivity*, and on 'character' as writing and as literary invention, J. Hillis Miller, 'Character', in his *Ariadne's Thread* (New Haven, CT: Yale University Press, 1992), pp. 28–143.

40 See Dickson, 'Twelfth-Century Insular Narrative', pp. 214–17: '[t]he
    fundamental problem with the wooing woman is that she is not her
    own to give' (p. 214). See also Judith Weiss, 'The wooing woman in
    Anglo-Norman romance', in Maldwyn Mills et al. (eds), *Romance in
    Medieval England* (Cambridge: Brewer, 1991), pp. 149–61 and 'The
    power and weakness of women in Anglo-Norman romance', in Carol
    M. Meale (ed.), *Women and Literature in Britain, 1150–1500*, 2nd
    edn (Cambridge: Cambridge University Press, 1996), pp. 7–23. Sarah
    Kay, *The 'Chansons de geste' in the Age of Romance: Political Fictions*
    (Oxford: Clarendon Press, 1995), pp. 43–8, powerfully reads women,
    especially Saracen princesses, in the *chansons de geste* as involved in
    structures of gift exchange, but also at times 'exercis[ing] an uncanny
    authority at the level of their *telling*' (p. 46). I discuss Kay's work
    further in Ch. 3.
41 For a survey of longstanding debates over feudalism and feudal
    relationships, see Richard Abels, 'The historiography of a construct:
    "feudalism" and the medieval historian', *History Compass* 7 (2009),
    1008–31, https://doi.org/10.1111/j.1478-0542.2009.00610.x, accessed
    20 February 2018.
42 Wikele's 'merie' is from *merir*, 'to merit, deserve; to reward; to pay
    back'; see *AND*, s.v. *merir*.
43 See e.g. *De amore*'s first dialogue, between a man and woman both of
    common (i.e. bourgeois) rank. Responding to the woman asking him
    for deeds worthy of the rewards he seeks, his rhetorical ploy imagines
    love as a gift set aside from equivalent repayment: 'your glory will be
    enhanced more if you grant me your love, or the prospect of love, out
    of kindness [*ex tua gratia*] alone than if you yield it to me as payment
    [*remunerationem*] for past deeds; for in the second case you would
    appear to be paying a debt, whereas in the first it is generosity [*largitas*]
    pure and simple' (Andreas Capellanus, *On Love*, ed./trans. P.G. Walsh
    (London: Duckworth, 1982), pp. 52–5). Don A. Monson remarks of the
    De amore: 'From the entire discussion an important conclusion emerges:
    the impossibility of separating love from the material and financial
    contingencies that surround it' (*Andreas Capellanus, Scholasticism, and
    the Courtly Tradition* (Washington, DC: Catholic University of America
    Press, 2005), p. 273). John of Salisbury's *Policraticus* V.15 provides an
    example from the mirror for princes genre: he warns against greed and
    advises only accepting gifts in moderation. See *Ioannis Saresberiensis
    episcopi Carnotensis Policratici; sive, De nugis curialium et vestigiis
    philosophorum, libri VIII*, ed. C.C.J. Webb, 2 vols (Oxford: Clarendon
    Press, 1909), I.575–8; John of Salisbury, *Policraticus*, trans. Cary J.
    Nederman (Cambridge: Cambridge University Press, 1990), pp. 95–8.

John looks back to Classical models in his scepticism about gift-giving culture, whereas *The Romance of Horn* embraces gift exchange but examines how motivation is also crucial to the proper functioning of such relationships.

44 Crane, *Insular Romance*; Dickson, 'Twelfth-Century Insular Narrative', pp. 36–8. Field, 'Courtly culture', perceptively draws out distinctions between the courtly environments of Suddene and Westir. For a broader approach to narrative units as 'memes' and how their varying deployment generates and deepens romance narrative, see Helen Cooper, *The English Romance in Time: Transforming Motifs from Geoffrey of Monmouth to the Death of Shakespeare* (Oxford: Oxford University Press, 2004).

45 The relationship between Gudreche and Gudmod as names in themselves links Horn/Gudmod with his new environment. The '-reche' element of Gudreche is possibly to be identified with the OE *reccan* (to extend, instruct, narrate, wield authority) or *reccan/rēcan* (to care for, be interested in); see *MED* s.v. *recchen* (v.(1)) and (v.(2)). See also Jane Bliss, *Naming and Namelessness in Medieval Romance* (Woodbridge: Brewer, 2008), pp. 88–94, who describes naming in *The Romance of Horn* as an act of 'identity gaming' (p. 94).

46 This episode resonates, of course, with the later moment when Rigmel and Horn drink from a horn, but is also suggestive of other texts in which wisdom and ethics are judged through a beautiful woman offering a vessel of wine. In Book 6 of Geoffrey of Monmouth's *Historia regum Brianniae*, for example, the British King Vortigern recklessly grants Kent to Hengest and Horsa in return for marrying Hengest's beautiful daughter, Ronwein (Rowena), after she offers him a golden cup of wine after dinner; see *The History of the Kings of Britain*, ed. Michael D. Reeve, trans. Neil Wright (Woodbridge: Boydell Press, 2007), pp. 128–31. Thanks to Jaclyn Rajsic for highlighting this episode to me.

47 Field, 'Courtly culture', pp. 29–37, quoting p. 31.

48 For example, *Chevrefoil*, lines 107–18, in Marie de France, *Lais*, ed. Alfred Ewert (London: Bristol Classical Press, 1995); *The Lais of Marie de France*, trans. Glyn S. Burgess and Keith Busby (London: Penguin, 1986). Echoes of or resistance to the Tristan legend seem to recur in *The Romance of Horn*.

49 See also Morgan Dickson, 'Female doubling and male identity in medieval romance', in Phillipa Hardman (ed.), *The Matter of Identity in Medieval Romance* (Cambridge: Brewer, 2002), pp. 59–72, at p. 68, who discusses the way in which the Westir episode enhances Horn's heroic value by testing him and viewing him as an object of desire in this new environment.

50 For the concept of *jouissance* as interruption, see Barthes, *Le plaisir du texte*. On the dangers of hasty repayment, see Hyde, *The Gift*, p. 15, following Malinowski, *Argonauts*, p. 96.

51 Pierre Bourdieu, *The Logic of Practice*, trans. Richard Nice (Cambridge: Polity Press, 1990), p. 105.

52 *King Horn*, in *Four Romances of England: King Horn, Havelok the Dane, Bevis of Hampton, Athelston*, ed. Ronald B. Herzman et al., TEAMS (Kalamazoo, MI: Medieval Institute Publications, 1997), http://d.lib.rochester.edu/teams/publication/salisbury-four-romances-of-england, accessed 1 February 2018, lines 1–4; *Sir Gawain and the Green Knight*, in *The Works of the Gawain Poet: 'Sir Gawain and the Green Knight', 'Pearl', 'Cleanness', 'Patience'*, ed. Ad Putter and Myra Stokes (London: Penguin, 2014), lines 30–1. Subsequent quotations will be from these editions.

53 Bourdieu, *Logic of Practice*, p. 103.

54 Derrida, *Given Time I*, p. 7.

55 Jacques Derrida, 'Women in the beehive: a seminar with Jacques Derrida', *differences* 16.3 (2005), 138–57, at p. 151.

56 Derrida notes the (linguistically contingent) employment of the concept of the circle in Malinowski and Mauss; *Given Time I*, pp. 24–5.

57 See Parry, 'The Gift', for the ways in which Mauss's later interpreters characterized his work as naïve; and also Jarvis, 'Gift in theory'; Miyazaki, 'Gifts and exchange'.

58 Derrida, *Given Time I*, pp. 30–1.

59 I use gender-neutral language here, since female or occasionally gender-changing protagonists also have the same capacity, though in the *Horn* narrative it is the hyper-masculinized Horn who carries most of these connotations. For romances in which female protagonists raise similar questions, see Nicholas Perkins, 'Ekphrasis and narrative in *Emaré* and *Sir Eglamour of Artois*', in Rhiannon Purdie and Michael Cichon (eds), *Medieval Romance, Medieval Contexts* (Cambridge: Brewer, 2011), pp. 47–60.

60 George Eliot, *Daniel Deronda*, ed. Graham Handley (Oxford: Oxford University Press, 2014), p. 3. Thanks to Peter McDonald for discussing this passage of Eliot with me.

61 See e.g. *The Birth of Romance*, trans. Weiss, p. 137. For the relationship of this episode to the *Folie Tristan* and *Gesta Herewardi*, and the ideas of identity and disguise they each explore, see Morgan Dickson, 'Verbal and visual disguise: society and identity in some twelfth-century texts', in Judith Weiss et al. (eds), *Medieval Insular Romance: Translation and Innovation* (Cambridge: Brewer, 2000), pp. 41–54.

62 Kay, *'Chansons de geste'*, pp. 201–7; Donald Maddox, 'Specular stories, family romance, and the fictions of courtly culture', *Exemplaria* 3 (1991), 299–326.

63 For the horn as a symbol of lordship, and connections between Horn and the horn, see Dickson, 'Twelfth-Century Insular Narrative', pp. 68–88.

64 Legge, *Anglo-Norman Literature*, pp. 98–100; Weiss, 'Thomas and the Earl', pp. 1–7. For FitzGilbert's career, see further Marie Therese Flanagan, Irish Society, *Anglo-Norman Settlers, Angevin Kingship: Interactions in Ireland in the Late Twelfth Century* (Oxford: Clarendon Press, 1989), pp. 112–36.

65 I do not have space here to comment on the relationship between French and English romances in the multilingual environment of Britain. For the context, see e.g. Wogan-Browne et al. (eds), *Language and Culture*; Jonathan Hsy, *Trading Tongues: Merchants, Multilingualism, and Medieval Literature* (Columbus: Ohio State University Press, 2013).

66 See e.g. Spearing, *Readings in Medieval Poetry*, pp. 24–43. For discussion of *King Horn* in the context of its surviving manuscripts, see *King Horn: An Edition based on Cambridge University Library MS Gg.4.27(2)*, ed. Rosamund Allen (New York: Garland, 1984), pp. 1–16; Susanna Fein (ed.), *Studies in the Harley Manuscript: The Scribes, Contents, and Social Contexts of British Library MS Harley 2253*, TEAMS (Kalamazoo, MI: Medieval Institute Publications, 2000); Kimberly K. Bell and Julie Nelson Couch (eds), *The Texts and Contexts of Oxford, Bodleian Library, MS Laud Miscs. 108: The Shaping of English Vernacular Narrative* (Leiden: Brill, 2011).

67 See also the return of this phrase, recharging the hero's entry into a new environment when he arrives in Ireland and takes a new name: '"Cutberd," he sede, "ich hote, / Icomen ut of the bote"' (773–4). Miyazaki ('Gifts and exchange', p. 253) discusses the overlapping identities of the decorated canoes involved in Kula exchange and the people who shape and travel on the canoes, citing Nancy Munn: 'a canoe, as the medium *within* which Gawans travel, and in which they first arrive on non-Gawan soil, is itself a resurfacing of the person' (see *The Fame of Gawa: A Symbolic Study of Value Transformation in a Massim (Papua New Guinea) Society* (Cambridge: Cambridge University Press, 1986), p. 147). This suggestive idea of the boat as a 'resurfacing of the person' might be applied to objects in a number of romances.

68 Repeated references to Horn as a harper and singer (e.g. 235–6; 244) also help to develop this relationship he has to telling the story as well as being its protagonist.

69 Horn later looks at the ring to remind him of Rymenhild and steel his
     courage against pagan enemies: 'He lokede on the ringe, / And thoghte
     on Rymenilde; / He slogh ther on haste / On hundred by the laste'
     (617–20); see also 881–2; 1495–6.
70 *Horn Childe*, ed. Mills. Quotations will be taken from this edition.
71 Matthew Holford, 'History and politics in *Horn Child and Maiden
     Rimnild*', *Review of English Studies* 57 (2006), 149–68.
72 See below, pp. 75–6.
73 *MED*, s.v. *mede* n.(4). *Horn Childe* line 102 is the first cited instance
     in *MED* of meaning 1(a): 'a gift; noble or royal endowments; a suitor's
     blandishments', though the word has a rich set of linked meanings
     stretching back to OE *med*. For a rewarding analysis of how the
     varying connotations of *mede* can be exploited, see James Simpson,
     'Piers Plowman': An Introduction, rev. edn (Exeter: University of Exeter
     Press, 2007), pp. 37–54.
74 For English romances as creating a narrative-focused aesthetic at odds
     with traditional critical modes of analysis, see two valuable essays by Ad
     Putter, 'The narrative logic of *Emaré*', in Ad Putter and Jane Gilbert (eds),
     The Spirit of Medieval English Popular Romance (Harlow: Longman,
     2000), pp. 157–80; and 'Story line and story shape in *Sir Percyvell of
     Gales* and Chrétien de Troyes' *Conte du Graal*', in McDonald (ed.),
     Pulp Fictions, pp. 171–96.
75 Pierre Bourdieu, *Outline of a Theory of Practice*, trans. Richard Nice
     (Cambridge: Cambridge University Press, 1977), pp. 5–6. See also
     Bourdieu, *The Logic of Practice*, ch. 6.
76 Pierre Bourdieu, 'Marginalia—some additional notes on the gift', in
     Schrift (ed.), *Logic of the Gift*, pp. 231–41, at p. 231.
77 Ibid.

2

'Kepe þou þat on & y þat oþer': giving and keeping in Middle English romances

Objects, events, and keeping-while-giving

In Chapter 1, I explored some ways in which we can read romance narrative, and in particular the Horn romances, through the lens of theories of the gift. I suggested that the romance protagonist could be analogous to a gift object, at times arriving unexpectedly, or only subsequently revealing the entanglements of fortune, family or the trajectory of exchange relationships that had set the action of the romance in play. Further, I read *The Romance of Horn* as a text in which recalling or recounting those engagements – retelling the story of lineage or revenge or love – also acts as a form of gift both within the text and out to the audience. I showed that this way of initiating narrative can fruitfully be understood alongside critical discussion of how a gift might be generated and how it can retain its claims to power while also depending on prior engagements and debts. Marcel Mauss's discussion of the relationship between systems of reciprocity and individual, apparently one-way, moments of giving; Jacques Derrida's meditation on the apparently impossible pure gift, and yet the paradoxical need to 'think gift'; and Pierre Bourdieu's understanding of the acts of misrecognition that allow the power of giving to be harnessed, can all help to read these moments of narrative beginning, and of creative mythmaking. I also discussed the debate over Mauss's description of the *hau*, which has its own circle to square, between spirit and payback, yield and surplus. Analogous acts of misrecognition or of 'allowing for' can help to align the presentation of *hau* as yield from a gift, with *hau* as spirit or quality. In this chapter, I will continue to hold these ideas in mind while reading a number of Middle English romances.

I shall focus on two kinds of dynamic. One relates to what can or should be given, and what should be kept back. It includes the decisions that protagonists make about engaging in exchange, and how those decisions then guide the narrative and ethical path of the text. It also involves anxieties about how value is created and dispensed in social and literary contexts. The other dynamic is how objects themselves are presented: as description or as narrative; thing and/or event. These two dynamics are connected both by moments of exchange in narrative, and by the relationship between stasis and action involved in each.

Annette Weiner's influential book *Inalienable Possessions* draws attention to things that are kept back from exchange, in a way that (she suggests) had been underplayed by Mauss and those following him. She argues that the early theorists of the gift, especially Malinowski, rooted their ideas of exchange in nineteenth-century theories of economy and the centrality of reciprocity, and so produced a 'simplified but pioneering classification of "gift" and "counter-gift", theorizing that reciprocity was the basis for social relations in "primitive" societies'. Weiner argues that this leaves out a more fundamental classification, which is between objects that may circulate, and those that do not: 'searching for the kinds of possessions that people try to keep out of circulation is far more theoretically meaningful than assuming that exchange simply involves the reciprocity of gift giving'. We could query the touch of polemic about Weiner's 'simply' in this sentence – Mauss, Malinowski and later writers rarely think of reciprocity as straightforward or in equilibrium, and Mauss describes a class of objects for the Kwakiutl and Tshimshian peoples that are '*sacra*, of which the family can divest itself only with great difficulty, and in some cases never'.[1] Nevertheless, Weiner's challenge is important, urging us to variegate our understanding of the gift away from sets of interlocking exchanges to a fuller appreciation of how things do and do not circulate in the act of developing social relations. Weiner further argues that exchange theories classically exclude or minimize the role of women in social relations: 'Exchange theories reveal strongly entrenched gender biases because the relevant subject matter remains what males exchange between one another'.[2] In the societies that Weiner focuses on, she highlights the ways in which the production, value and retention of cloth goods by women in families is central to those families' identities and sense of hierarchy:

> Intricate symbolic meanings semantically encode sexuality, biological reproduction, and nurturance so that such possessions, as they are exchanged between people, act as the material agents in the reproduction of social relations ... cloth possessions may also act as transcendent treasures, historical documents that authenticate and confirm for the living the legacies and powers associated with a group's or an individual's connections to ancestors and gods.[3]

Rather than focusing on movement and reciprocity as inevitable (and male-dominated) features of exchange, Weiner suggests that people's relationship to possessions importantly involves items that they seek to keep out of exchange; and that the continuing possession of such items accrues status and value to their keepers: 'The societies I discussed in the last chapter clarify how essential it is to the development of hierarchy that certain possessions authenticate a kin group's descendants and origins.'[4]

Weiner's focus on the variegated dynamics of possession, and how significant efforts are made to commit exchangeable items to transactions precisely to avoid putting inalienable items into circulation, also signals that the gift in narrative might not act as straightforwardly as the overt energies of movement and payback suggest. Hyde's emphasis on movement and consumption and Derrida's concern with the turning of the circle of exchange[5] can be supplemented by Weiner's understanding of the complexity and strategic play involved in Kula exchange paths:

> Instead of perceiving Kula transactions simply as gifts and counter-gifts, it is essential to visualize the maze of plays and strategies as *layers* of exchanges which one must constantly build up over time and then keep track of.[6]

Weiner describes how some Kula shells accrue not only value but a history that describes the rise and fall of reputations and of family honour: these shells have a kind of personality and set of narrative associations. The continuing play of Kula exchange is a risk to those engaged in it, but removing shells completely so that they are truly inalienable 'defeats the very processes that constitute authority and renown.'[7] At the end of her book, Weiner wishes to widen the applicability of her claims about the interaction of giving and keeping,

an interaction that for her constitutes the work of creating difference
and hierarchy in social relationships – what she terms the 'universal
paradox of keeping-while-giving':

> The creative human imagination has made things as diverse as myths,
> shrouds, crowns, cloaks, and bones into inalienable possessions—the
> coveted prizes around which wars are fought, leaders installed, and
> local groups assert their authority.[8]

Weiner's work challenges the assumption that exchange itself is at
the core of social relations, and that male–male transactions are the
core of exchange. In her examples, women are intimately involved
in the production, retention and distribution of cloth wealth, signifying
the importance of matrilineal connections, of the sister–brother
relationship, and of women's own spheres of influence, though she
sees their status as under threat from men including 'Hawaiian
priests, Inka rulers, Greek philosophers, Christian clergymen, and
Western capitalists'.[9] In a brief survey of the development of Western
European understandings of reciprocity as the basis of early anthropological assumptions, Weiner characterizes medieval reciprocity as
working between gift exchange and developing mercantile activity,
establishing a commitment to a 'norm of reciprocity', but that these
exchanges can only be understood in relation to the value or power
of inalienable property, land or rights, such as noble status or the
'cosmological authentication' provided by the Church.[10] Weiner's
fieldwork and the focus of her discussion is based on Oceania, and
so the history of Western exchange acts for her primarily as a way
of thinking about the formations of Western anthropological and
critical assumptions; there are thus dangers in mapping her descriptions of giving-while-keeping and the role of women in the production
of inalienable goods onto medieval romance stories. What I shall
do, however, is reflect on her work to develop our reading of exchange
and giving in romance, a genre that in its own exchange between
people acts as a 'material agent […] in the reproduction of social
relations', and in some cases as a document that ratifies or mytholo-
gizes the history of a person's or group's place vis-à-vis social
hierarchy, political power or religious belief. While romances often
do powerfully present exchange between high-status men as the
fundamental set of relationships that governs land, possessions and
identity – co-opting women as objects of exchange or as reinforcing

hierarchies – romances' openness to alternative possibilities and moments of decision can also allow for voices, powers and anxieties about giving and keeping to emerge, or to shadow more ideologically stabilizing modes of exchange.

For Weiner, the production of narratives alongside physical possessions ('myths, shrouds, crowns, cloaks, and bones') plays a part in this value creation, and narratives interweave with objects. Since her book was published, relationships between object, person(hood) and narrative have come to prominence in anthropological and archaeological debate, including interest in the changing use or meaning of possessions over time, whether they are exchanged or kept in families or institutions. Dan Hicks has summarized this dynamic as one where 'things are always events – more or less visible depending on the constant changes in the human and non-human world.'[11] Hicks's positioning of material culture studies sees objects and persons as having interacting narratives and creating contexts for one another: 'Life, both human and non-human, as it is encountered in Archaeology and Anthropology involves not relations between fixed entities, but life as the ongoing flow of permeabilities, and the emergence of worlds.' These permeable interactions – the ways in which objects stand for human relationships in romance texts, are given or kept as defining features of those relationships, and also how they raise the very question of what remains fixed and what moves or changes in time – help us understand the narrative power that romance stories exert on their audiences. In the rest of this chapter, I will draw on the set of questions outlined above to help read romance narratives and objects as they are exchanged, kept, valued and debated.

The Savernake Horn and *Horn Childe*

As an example of an object-as-event that helps us to navigate the relationship between people, things and time, I shall briefly consider a treasured object from medieval England: the Savernake Horn, one of the most important surviving examples of a medieval sounding horn.[12] The elephant tusk from which it is made was perhaps carved in the twelfth or thirteenth century in northern or western Europe, and would have had a carrying strap secured through a slit near the mouth of the horn and knotted at the mouthpiece end. In the fourteenth century, the horn gained new decoration and a baldric with heraldic designs. Richard Camber and John Cherry associate the baldric's repeated heraldic motifs with the Randolf Earls of Moray in the early fourteenth century, arguing that the baldric was most likely made for Thomas Randolf, the first Earl of Moray and regent of Scotland between the death of Robert the Bruce in 1329 and his own in 1332. The Earls of Moray possessed baronial forests in Annandale, and so Camber and Cherry argue that 'it is reasonable to assume that the baldric was made for a horn belonging to the Randolf Earls of Moray which they used in their forests.'[13] Also in the fourteenth century, two bands of enamelled silver (one silver gilt) were added to the horn near its mouth. They are stylistically associated with England. Their decorative compartments depict creatures of the forest, and the top mount has adjacent compartments showing a king, a bishop and a forester, who blows a horn. This little tableau is both a declaration about the prestige of the object (added or adapted perhaps a hundred years after its creation) and a narrative about its own origin. It seems to memorialize the granting of a forest or rights over forest lands. The Savernake Horn's early history is not clearly established, but it is possible that by the mid-fourteenth century it was in England. While the scene of king, bishop and forester does not seem to relate to Savernake Forest, the Horn at some point came into the possession of the Sturmy family, hereditary wardens of the forest (near Malborough in Southern England) from the late eleventh or twelfth century, until the wardenship passed to the Seymour family by marriage in the fifteenth century. The Seymours' possession of the horn and its important place in their family identity is indicated by a drawing of the horn in a Seymour genealogy dating from 1604, and in William Camden's description of the horn as part of the history of the Seymour Earls of Hertford at Wolfhall.[14] By Camden's time, the Horn represented the longevity and permanence of the Seymour/Sturmy connection with the forest, embodying and marking their own claims.

The Savernake Horn, then, has its own trajectory and accruing associations, from its origins as elephant tusk to being carved as a horn; seemingly possessed by the Earls of Moray whose arms appear on its baldric; adapted and added to with the fourteenth-century bands; and coming into the ownership of the Sturmys and then

Seymours.[15] Its own object life and the stories of ownership and inheritance into which it is bound then prompt further stories to be told. By the early seventeenth century this is an object claimed to be an inherited, stable possession embodying the worth of its owners, and in some ways licensing their own identity as a noble family in possession of inalienable rights and qualities. However, it has also previously been hunted, traded, crafted, granted and perhaps captured by numerous people over hundreds of years and from Africa or Asia to Europe. It is a material object, an event, a narrative and a possession whose exchange and ownership validates other stories about the people who own or use it. Likewise, these meanings cannot be contained in a single narrative or contextual frame: 'An artifact, or a performance such as an exchange, perceived as an image, is not reducible to the coding explanations that accompany it, or vice versa'.[16]

I suggest that these characteristics of the Savernake Horn are analogous to aspects of the romance tradition. It has long been a feature of romance reading to look for the interrelationship between, for example, family history, myth and claims of ownership or nobility in romance narrative.[17] Likewise, as Vance Smith has demonstrated, claims about value and property are deeply embedded in many Middle English texts, whose imaginative path often travels widely in exotic territory, but whose underlying structures and the interests of whose audiences are tied into the tasks of reckoning value; managing the household, or seeking reward.[18] This set of relations between what is stable and what travels; what is claimed as valuable and what is suppressed in the act of making value, is present in *Horn Childe*, which I briefly discussed in Chapter 1, and which survives uniquely in the Auchinleck Manuscript, a book copied at about the same time as the Savernake Horn was being altered to suit new owners and mark further exchanges.[19] The last section of the poem is lost, because a leaf is missing from the manuscript between what are now fols 323 and 324, almost certainly cut out because of the value of the picture that would have accompanied the start of the following text, the *Alphabetical Praise of Women*. The *Horn Childe* narrative reaches its climax just before the lost leaf. In this section of the poem, the debts, gifts and promises set in play in the poem are closed or paid back through the return of Horn, his revenge on the traitors Wikard and Wikel and his marriage to Rimnild, having bested her would-be husband Mogin in a wedding tournament. Arriving at the wedding feast of Rimnild and Mogin as a beggar, Horn is served wine by Rimnild from a cup, and drops into it the magic ring that she gave him earlier in the story: 'Þe ring of gold he kest þerinne: / "[þi] tokening, lo, it here"' (995–6). This ring was initially a gift, of course, but is also a 'tokening' of the stability and inalienability of the lovers from one another despite the many journeys that Horn undertakes. As the action moves towards its denouement, Horn frames his actions as repayment, for example for the blow that Wikard struck him ('His buffeyt schal be bouȝt' (1047)), and Rimnild also phrases Horn's revenge in the same way: 'Horn schal him his dettes quite, / Toniȝt it schal be bouȝt' (1067–8). After Horn has triumphed and married Rimnild, Houlac confirms his settlement to Horn: 'Half mi lond ichil þe ȝiue / Wiþ mi douȝter while Y liue / & al after mi day' (1114–6). The romance breaks off when Horn is seeking another return, by re-taking his father's lands. Horn's punning identity with a horn as symbol of land tenure, social exchange, or virile masculinity, is only partially obscured by the change in this version from drinking horn to cup as the meaningful object by which, in receiving the ring, the lovers are reunited.

Horn acts both as an object whose exchange fosters productive or agonistic relationships, and as a person whose own exchanges guide his place in those relationships. In Hicks's vocabulary, Horn creates his own contexts for action; his relationships with other people, and with entities such as inheritance and integrity, are also shot through with his status as romance hero, object of admiration and embodiment of certain political, literary and gendered values. The romance is a speculative account of how these kinds of exchange and relation can operate in the superlative environment of romance, but *Horn Childe* can itself be read as a valued object and event, whose trajectory from French to English adaptation is marked by the investments and paybacks of its audience and adaptor(s). Texts and variants too have their object life or itinerary, whose returns usually produce further movement and creative revision. Equally, a large collection such as the Auchinleck Manuscript provides a reader with a range of responses to objects that are entered into or kept back from exchange, and the relationships between persons and objects that mark the eventful histories of romance narrative. Amongst its eighteen romances I shall discuss three more that approach these dynamics in differing ways. *Amis and Amiloun* centres on given objects that then seal a brotherly bond; *Tristrem* examines what happens when such a bond is fractured, amidst flows of objects and exchanges that constitute Tristrem's own biography; *Orfeo* explores the fear of losing something inalienable, and the acts both generous and calculating that help to restore Orfeo's ability to exchange and to rule.

Amis and Amiloun

Amis and Amiloun appears relatively early in the Auchinleck Manuscript (fols ?48r (now a stub, hence the uncertainty) to ?61va (also a stub)) as part of booklet 2, after the *Speculum Gy de Warewyke* and before a *Life of St Mary Magdalene*.[20] Like *Horn Childe*, it derives from a French romance,[21] and it also uses drinking vessels to symbolize the connection between its two main protagonists. These are the friends Amis and Amiloun, whose relation of love and blood-brotherly bond places many of the other exchanges and relationships in doubt, or describes them in light of how they test or reinforce the connection between the two central figures. Susan Crane argues, both in relation to *Amis and Amiloun* and the earlier French *Amis et Amilun*, that while 'this process honors Christian principles by finding a place for them in a secular tale, that place is finally defined and delimited by the capacity of Christian principles to support the tale's secular ideal of brotherhood'.[22]

We could, then, read *Amis and Amiloun*'s narrative through the central transaction between the two friends, and its consequences for the flow of debts and obligations that their careers entail. The moment of their commitment to one another is suffused with the rhetorical and syntactical balancing of their reciprocal commitment:

> On a day þe childer war & wiȝt
> Treweþes togider þai gun pliȝt:
>   While þai miȝt liue & stond
> Þat boþe bi day & bi niȝt,
> In wele & wo, in wrong & riȝt,
>   Þat þai schuld frely fond
> To hold togider at eueri nede,
> In word, in werk, in wille, in dede,
>   Where þat þai were in lond,
> Fro þat day forward neuer mo

> Failen oþer for wele no wo;
> Þerto þai held vp her hond.[23]

In this stanza, the importance of their agreement is signalled by the alliterating and rhythmic pairings that echo their own linked qualities: 'war & wiȝt'; 'liue & stond'; 'bi day & bi niȝt'; 'wele & wo, in wrong & riȝt'; 'In word, in werk, in wille, in dede'; 'for wele no wo'. This exchange underscores Amis and Amiloun's unbreakable bond. It provides a system of overall prestations within which the later services and gifts between the two, and through or from others, can operate. It also sets up a series of questions about which obligations or gifts may be offered or more widely circulated, and which must not.

Their relationship is also manifested through the identical gold cups that Amiloun produces, giving one to Amis:

> Kepe þou þat on & y þat oþer;
> For Godes loue, heuen-king,
> Lete neuer þis coupe fro þe
> Bot loke heron & þenk on me;
> It tokneþ our parting. (268–72)

Unlike gifts whose power relies on the gap of time between giving and reciprocation, or the imbalance of exchange, here the identical cups attempt to fix the relationship as a context within which other acts take place: 'Lete neuer þis coupe fro þe'. The cups are both 'tokens' of their friendship in the sense of symbols of it, but they also become more physical 'tokens' or proofs of identity later in the narrative.[24] In that sense, the cups are objects with their own narrative trajectory and event-hood, acting as resonant things at key moments in the text when the bond between the two seems in danger of being broken. For example, later in the story Amiloun has been ejected from his home by his wife, disgusted by his now-leprous body. Amiloun and his faithful companion Owain/Amourant are reduced to begging, food is scarce, and people have stopped giving them alms. Nevertheless, Amiloun declares that he will never sell his gold cup, even though they have to sell their asses to buy food:

> Ouer al þat lond þurth Godes wille
> Þat hunger wex so gret & g[r]ille
> As wide as þai gun go;
> Almest for hunger þai gan to spille,

Of brede þai no hadde nouȝt half her fille,
Ful careful were þai þo.
Þan seyd þe kniȝt opon a day
'Ous bihoueþ selle our asse oway
For we no haue gode no mo,
Saue mi riche coupe of gold,
Ac certes þat schal neuer be sold,
Þei hunger schuld me slo.' (1749–60)

Plenty of poetic resources are used to describe the feast and famine cycle of the rural economy. Amiloun and Amourant are given food by the locals when the town is doing well, but cannot sustain this generosity in hard times. Amourant is then given two asses by Amiloun's estranged wife in a bid to remove them from the neighbourhood: a gesture more of contempt than generosity. The economic cycle has a larger context of 'Godes wille', inviting moral and biblical readings of Amiloun and Amourant's sufferings. As Vance Smith demonstrates, Middle English texts of this period are often acutely tuned to the fine distinctions between charity and waste and to the movements of desire or lack that shape people's actions in the practical and imaginative spheres.[25] Here, the exceptional nature of the gold cup allows for different realities or narrative trajectories to be accommodated in the text. *Amis and Amiloun* is alert to the suffering not only of aristocratic protagonists but of the marginal poor in a 'chepeing-toun' (1764). On the other hand, Amiloun's cup is beyond economic calculation, and represents a yield or promise of his friendship with Amis. The cup itself completes a journey away from and then back to its companion. In such an environment, the cup invokes other biblical analogies too, for instance with the counter-intuitive logic of the parable of the merchant's lost pearl.[26]

A reader of the Auchinleck Manuscript could view this passage in apposition to the previous text, the *Speculum Gy de Warewyke*. This poem takes Guy's turn away from secular knighthood as a grounding point for ethical and spiritual advice, delivered by a cleric named Alcuin, to give 'gret profyt' to Guy's soul.[27] The end of the text has been damaged due to the loss of the leaf that also contained the start of *Amis and Amiloun*, but just before this point, it retells the story of the prophet Elijah and the widow of Zarephath (I Kings 17:7–16). God has told the prophet to ask the widow for food, and while she can provide water for him, she tells him that she only has a small amount of flour and some oil. She is gathering sticks to make a fire, to provide a meal for her and her son, 'that we may eat it – and die'. The prophet tells her to go home and make bread, and to give some to him. Miraculously, there is enough for the woman, her family and Elijah:

> 'Ne dred þe noht, womman, in þi þouht
> Þi mele ne shal wante noht,
> And þin oyle shal waxen sikerli;
> Þi lome shal noht ben empti.'
> Gret plente hadde þe widewe þo,
> While she liuede euere mo.
> Now þu miht knowe in þi mod,
> Þat in almesse dede is double god. (999–1006)

The lesson of this exemplum is explicitly drawn towards the giving of alms to the poor, as 'double god': a gift that has both spiritual and, the text implies, practical, yield to the giver.[28] In *Amis and Amiloun*, no such miraculous yield from the townsfolk occurs, and Amiloun's and Amourant's asses still have to be sold. Nevertheless, Amiloun's refusal to sell the cup paradoxically disrupts expected economic outcomes in a similar way to the exemplum of Elijah and the widow, focusing the narrative on longer-scale benefit and on the cup as marker of the stored energy in his distance from Amis and from his former life: stretched like an elastic band whose tension seeks return. It also aligns claims of aristocratic distinction with the Christian imagery and inflections of the story.[29] Those claims to distinction and hierarchy are the kind of claims that, as we have seen, Weiner argues are central to efforts at keeping-while-giving, so that valued objects are held back as a self-fulfilling token of status.

Later, the cups again provide a vessel for the energies of what has been given and retained, as markers of identity and homecoming. Amiloun and Amourant have arrived at Amis's castle, where he is now a rich and powerful duke. They gather with others to beg for alms at the gate. One of Amis's knights sees the ravaged Amiloun with the beautiful Amourant. In another instance of the refusal of immediate gain, Amourant declines the knight's offer to come and serve the Duke:

> Þe gode man asked him anon,
> ȝif he wald fro þat lazer gon
> & trewelich to him take;

> & he seyd he schuld, bi seyn Jon,
> Serue þat riche douke in þat won
>   & richeman he wald him make.
> & he answerd wiþ mild mode
> & swore bi him þat dyed on rode
>   Whiles he miȝt walk & wake,
> For to winne al þis warldes gode
> His hende lord þat bi him stode
>   Schuld he neuer forsake. (1881–92)

Once more, devotional language and Christian grace ('bi him þat dyed on rode') accompanies the refusal of immediate exchange here. Amourant's reply prompts the onward impetus of the text towards retelling and revelation, as the knight goes back to Amis and describes the anomalous scenario of the handsome young man caring for the leper. The conversation between knight and duke also plays with the different possibilities for action in the economic and ethical sphere: what sort of a person, or object, or event, is Amourant? How does this story (that of the knight, and that of the poem) reconcile the competing pressures of duty and gain? From within the romance, Amis speculates on the different kind of narratives and economies from which Amourant's seemingly mad loyalty to Amiloun might stem:

> Þan seyd þe douke 'þei his lord be lorn,
> Par auentour þe gode man haþ biforn
>   Holpen him at his nede,
> Oþer þe child is of his blod yborn,
> Oþer he haþ him oþes sworn
>   His liif wiþ him to lede.
> Wheþer he be fremd or of his blod
> Þe child' he seyd 'is trewe & gode,
>   Also God me spede.
> ȝif ichim speke er he wende,
> For þat he is so trewe & kende
>   Y schal quite him his mede.' (1941–52)

Amis's list includes the echo of his own relationship with Amiloun, who both has sworn oaths with Amis, and has '[h]olpen him at his nede', making Amourant a shadow figure of Amis's gratitude in the story, as the name Amourant hints. In this way, Amis's declaration that he will 'quite him his mede' applies proleptically both to Amourant's and Amiloun's loyalty.

The gold cups belonging to the two friends are still to have a decisive role in the narrative's repayments. As in the horn/cup and ring in the Horn romances, or delayed recognition tokens in other romances, the fact that Amiloun, a leper, has the matching cup to Amis's provokes a crisis. The token of the friendship, the gift that must not then be further circulated, nearly destroys the friendship itself when Amis attacks Amiloun, thinking that he has stolen the cup that is in his possession. In a stanza missing from the Auchinleck copy (and supplied in Foster's edition from Oxford, Bodleian MS Douce 326) Amourant upbraids Amis and reminds him of the debt that he owes, in language tellingly echoing Amis's earlier promise to 'quite' Amourant 'his mede':

> And ys thi brother, sir Amylioun,
> Þat whilom was a noble baroun
>   Bothe to ryde and go,
> And now with sorwe ys dreue adoun;
> Nowe God þat suffred passioun
>   Breng him oute of his wo!
> For the of blysse he ys bare,
> And thou yeldyst him all with care
>   And brekest his bones a two;
> Þat he halp the at thi nede,
> Well euell aquitest thou his mede,
>   Alas, whi farest thou so? (2113–24)

Delayed (or mis-)recognition is of course the stock-in-trade of romance narrative, but I suggested in Chapter 1 that it is also one of the characteristics of the narrative of gifts. Here, the 'quitting' of a cycle of exchange or debt is dramatized through the misrecognition of Amiloun. His marked and diseased body is set in apposition to the cup – the latter representing the permanent value of the bond between Amis and Amiloun, the former the costs of repaying that bond. Amourant's appeal to 'God þat suffred passioun' is an important marker here of the allusions to salvific sacrifice (to redemption in its etymological sense of 'buying back') that are interwoven through *Amis and Amiloun*.

Amis's decision to sacrifice his children to bathe Amiloun's leprous body in their blood (prompted by the advice of an angel in a dream) likewise shifts the generic and ethical parameters of the text towards hagiography and passion narrative, aligning the gift/bond of the protagonists with that power. Romance's gifted narratives allow for speculation to surface about alternative story paths, whether that is gifts (not) retained and returned, or promises (not) kept. It is likely that one reason for the popularity of the Amis and Amiloun story was not only its extremes of action, devotion, debt and repayment; not only the frisson of mingling courtly with religious desire and language; but also the opportunity for its audiences to debate or challenge the paths taken, the ways in which the story almost literally doubles and confuses its protagonists, allowing for other storylines to shadow the narrative, and for sceptical commentary to be provoked from within the story itself. A striking example of this is in Amis's exchange with Belisaunt, the daughter of the duke in whose service he has been raised. Like Rimnild in *Horn Childe*, Belisaunt is a 'wooing woman' who has fallen in love with the desirable Amis: 'Wher þat sche seiȝe him ride or go / Hir þouȝt hir hert brac atvo' (423–4). Amis lamenting his parting from Amiloun, and Belisaunt lovesick, they meet in a garden: an environment charged with narrative potential, especially since the Duke and most of his courtiers are meanwhile 'dere-hunting' (445). Belisaunt asks Amis to

> Pliȝt me þi trewþe þou schalt be trewe
> & chaunge me for no newe
> Þat in þis world is born,
> & y pliȝt þe mi treuþe also,
> Til God & deþ dele ous ato
> Y schal neuer be forsworn. (531–6)

As in the Horn stories, Amis reminds her of her higher status (and exchange value). As a duke's daughter, he tells her that it is 'michel vnriȝt / Þi loue to lain opon a kniȝt / Þat naþ noiþer lond no fe. (546–8). Belisaunt's response, however, breaks out of this dynamic of reckoning values to assert her own claims and mock the preachy quality of Amis's response:

> sir kniȝt, þou nast no croun;
> For God þat bouȝt þe dere,
> Wheþer artow prest oþer persoun
> Oþer þou art monk oþer canoun
> Þat prechest me þus here?
> Þou no schust haue ben no kniȝt

> To gon among maidens briȝt;
> Þou schust haue ben a frere.
> He þat lerd þe þus to preche,
> Þe deuel of helle ichim biteche,
> Mi broþer þei he were. (562–72)

Ironically using the pious phrase of salvific economics 'For God þat bouȝt þe dere', Belisaunt also disrupts the generic and gendered expectations of this scene. She then pressurizes him into having sex with her by threatening to cry rape if he refuses. While Amis manages to delay their union by a week, he does exchange vows: 'He graunted hir hir wil þo, / & pliȝt hem trewþes boþe to, / & seþþen kist þo tvai' (615–17). Of course, this exchange is a variant on the well-worn romance theme of a young couple exchanging vows or more, notwithstanding the context of family and rank. In *Amis and Amiloun*, there is a special charge to this embedded truth-plighting in relation to Amis's oath to Amiloun. Subsequently, Amis's enemy the steward is able to exploit one of these (the illicit relationship with Belisaunt) in order to repay his bitterness about the other (his attempt – rebutted by Amis – to form an alliance with Amis after Amiloun has departed). One exchange of body, word and object is, then, influenced or provoked by another. *Amis and Amiloun* acutely tracks the crises of *trawthe* as they are weighed up or commented on by the protagonists as if they are stepping aside from the boundaries of the text and its system of overall obligations. This applies equally to the reactions of Amiloun's wife to his becoming a leper, and to the reflection on loss and gain in Amis's later decision to kill his children in order to cure Amiloun with their blood. Gift-exchange; reckoning of value; the cups as tokens travelling through the narrative; the work of time on the gift relationship or on the recognition of that relationship; and the forces of God's gift of salvation and sacrificial economy – all these work to complicate and enrich the individual decisions and moments of exchange in the story. To put it simply, the text foregrounds decisions about how things are valued, and how or whether they can be exchanged. The bond between Amis and Amiloun becomes a prime instance of keeping-while-giving around which the other relationships circulate, and the romance's extremes of fortune create an additional narrative pleasure in the unlikely returns of the last part of the story. What the audience takes for keeps, as it were, is a powerful sense of *trawthe* as an inalienable quality whose keeping justifies all kinds of other actions, even if they are costly and apparently harmful (though the text might also provoke debate in its audience about what exactly constitutes the *trawthe* being kept if it entails so much destruction).[30] Amis's and Amiloun's gold cups remind us of this untarnished quality that gives distinction to the protagonists and allows the text to stake its claims to sacred language and values despite its ethically dubious plot, sitting as it does amidst exempla and hagiography in this part of the Auchinleck Manuscript.

Tristrem

Other Auchinleck romances may be read with attention to the object lives embedded within them, and to the layers of giving and keeping that power their plots. In *Degaré*, the eponymous hero's identity is bound up with the objects he has been left with as a baby. Degaré is the product of a rape by a fairy knight, and his mother leaves the baby at a hermitage, along with some gold, a letter, and some gloves that will only fit her. He later marries his mother before realizing her identity, and she passes to him a damaged sword left by his father. The sword marks the anxiety and shame in his inheritance from his father, but also the narrative path by which he makes the family unit improbably whole again. *Floris and Blancheflour* revolves around Floris's attempts to regain Blancheflour from a harem in Bablyon, after she has been sold to merchants by her parents in exchange for money and a cup decorated with scenes from the Trojan War. The near-identity of the couple attracts a reading in which fears about the muddying of aristocratic, Christian or aesthetic value by the forces of commodifying – in the spheres of status, belief or culture – are played out in a psychological narrative of loss and restoration.[31] While Guy of Warwick's career famously turns on his rejection of worldly value for a means to ally his knightly qualities with the lasting treasure of religious vocation, his son Reinbroun himself becomes a traded good in his eponymous romance, carried off by merchants towards Russia, before being diverted to Africa and presented to a king as a gift. While any of these might repay further scrutiny, I am here going to discuss *Tristrem*, which appears in booklet 9 of the Auchinleck Manuscript along with *Orfeo*.

In *Tristrem*, a number of object lives and trajectories are woven into a text that has been described as 'the best example of a Middle English romance as a "life"'.[32] Like the cups which help to fix Amis and Amiloun's relationship, the accidental drinking of a love potion binds Tristrem and Ysonde so that their path is always measured by their identity or distance. Meanwhile, the other transactions are also moments of narrative transition or crisis: they interact with the central relationship between Tristrem and Ysonde, but they work at numerous levels, with varying routes in and out of the text. *Tristrem*'s reputation has suffered by comparison with the great Tristan texts of the twelfth and thirteenth centuries, including the fragmentary *Tristan* of Thomas, of which the Middle English version is an adaptation. Alan Lupack reads *Tristrem* as a parody, because of its colloquial or less heroic descriptions of fighting, but also because of *Tristrem*'s interest in the details of payments, money, gifts and bribes. For example, in the scene where Tristrem plays chess against merchants, Lupack suggests that Tristrem is shown as 'a chess hustler' who cleverly lets his opponents win at first to dupe them. Likewise, the 'practical, almost mercenary, interest in specific amounts of money' here and elsewhere seems to Lupack to undercut the romance of the text.[33] I would not describe the effect of these as parodic, but they do help open this long narrative to a wide set of responses, from practical and adventurous, to ethical, to tragic, and they keep the text alive to a variety of forms of exchange, not only an aspiration to aristocratic forms of noble giving.

Early in the story, Tristrem's mother Blanchflour gives Rohand (friend of Tristrem's father Roland) responsibility for Tristrem's upbringing, passing him a ring, which is proleptic of remembrance and mourning:

> A ring of riche hewe
> Than hadde that levedi fre;
> Sche toke it Rouhand trewe.
> Hir sone sche bad it be:
> 'Mi brother wele it knewe;
> Mi fader gaf it me.
> King Markes may rewe
> The ring than he it se
> And moun.
> As Rouland loved the,
> Thou kepe it to his sone.' (221–31)

The ring later proves Tristrem's identity, after he has been abducted by the chess-playing merchants, and later (in a romance reflex of the Jonah story) been set off from their boat, landing with his chess winnings, the ring and some bread. While many of the payments and gifts in *Tristrem* contribute to immediate narrative impetus (for example, Rohand paying the porter to gain access to Mark's court, accompanied with the saying 'He was ful wise, Y say / That first gave gift in land' (626–7); or Tristrem paying ten shillings to pilgrims he meets to take him to the king), others act at a longer timescale. Thus, in fighting the Irish giant Mourant, a piece of Tristrem's sword lodges in the former's brain. This is the way that Isonde later realizes that Tristrem is the killer of Mourant, who is also her uncle. Later, Isonde recognizes a ring that she previously gave Tristrem 'to tokening' (2602) when it is on the finger of Ganhardin, brother of Isonde of the White Hands. The ring has already had its effect of drawing Tristrem's thoughts back to the first Isonde, even when he is with Isonde of the White Hands (for example, line 2685).

The cup from which the lovers drink their love potion is likewise a resonant object, whose description overlaps with the moment that fixes the madness of their desire:

> The coupe was richeli wrought:
> Of gold it was, the pin.
> In al the warld nas nought
> Swiche drink as ther was in.
> Brengwain was wrong bithought.
> To that drink sche gan win
> And swete Ysonde it bitaught.
> Sche bad Tristrem bigin,
> To say.
> Her love might no man tuin
> Til her ending day. (1662–72)

This stanza appears naive in its simple statements, but it operates as a very efficient form of narrative compaction. It serves as a micro-ekphrasis of the cup, including the detail that its 'pin' was gold. Lupack glosses 'pin' by reference to the *MED* definition, s.v. *pin* 6(b): 'a pin inserted in a drinking vessel marking equal portions of the contents'.[34] The cup is, then, set up to provide equal draughts of the potion and ensure the lovers' mutual dependency, though of course it is meant for Ysonde and Mark. The very proximity and brevity of their descriptions mingles the richness of the cup, power of the drink, and *swete*-ness of Ysonde. Likewise, the movement between thought, gift and word ('wrong bithought'; 'bitaught'; 'bad') is so close as to mingle cause and effect, almost as though the drinking of the potion has *caused* the wrong thinking that brought it about, and irrevocably shifted the grammar of the story from singular ('Sche') to plural ('Her'). A listener's own imaginative engagement might include a reminiscence of Eve's giving Adam the apple to eat in the garden of Eden (the potion as a death draught of knowledge, sin and desire), and the exchanges of a marriage ceremony. In these kinds of exchanges, *Tristrem* (and other romances) achieves a layered sense of how story co-opts objects, intentions and actions, in ways that are not always logical but which have their own balance and power. Moments of giving and receiving are especially open to that power. At this moment too, the exchange is then stabilized into an inalienable connection between the two of them, so that giving becomes keeping: 'Her love might no man tuin / Til her ending day'.

Much later in the romance, Tristrem has images of his own romance story carved in the hall that Beliagog (a giant he has defeated) undertakes to create. The Middle English poem moves quickly through this episode compared to the meditation on loss and representation in other versions.[35] Nevertheless, *Tristrem* still allows an audience to reflect on how objects interchange with people: sending messages, yielding emotion, and developing ideas about the self and relations with others in a work of art (both the images and the poem):

> At his des in the halle
> Swete Ysonde was wrought;
> Hodain and Pencru, to calle;
> The drink hou Brengwain brought;
> Mark yclad in palle;
> And Meriadok ful of thought;
> (So liifliche weren thai alle
> Ymages semed it nought
> To abide);
> And Tristrem, hou he faught
> With Beliagog unride. (2839–49)

In a previous essay, I argued that the trope of ekphrasis helped romance narratives to prompt reflection, intertextual reference and meditation on the work of storytelling itself, as protagonists merged with or were portrayed in relation to resonant objects.[36] In this case, the power of representation is enough to make Ganhardin fall in love with Brengwain on seeing her picture.

> Ganhardin schamed sore;
> His heved ran on blod.
> Ysonde he seighe thore
> And Brengwain fair and gode.
> Brengwain the coupe bore.
> Him rewe, that frely fode,
> He swore bi Godes ore.
> In her hond fast it stode
> Al stille.
> 'Tristrem, we ar wode
> To speken ogain thi wille.
>
> 'Nis it bot hertbreke,
> That swithe wele finde we,
> And foly ous to speke
> Ani worde ogaines the.
> Mi wille yif Y might gete,
> That levedi wold Y se.
> Mine hert hye hath ysteke,
> Brengwain bright and fre,
> That frende.
> Blithe no may ich be
> Til Y se that hende.' (2982–3003)

Ganhardin is left reeling from the violent power of representation, the physical and emotional force of Tristrem's retelling of his story in physical form, with the cup as central to this power to re-enact. Seeing Brengwain with the cup seems to have a similar effect on Ganhardin as actually drinking the potion did on Tristrem. The image is also an object that causes physical and narrative effects. As with the power of the gift/hero's arrival that we encountered in Chapter 1, here this sudden revelation sets the story in motion again, enabling the flows of desires, gifts and returns to reach their ends. In talking to Ganhardin about the breakdown of his relationship with Ysonde of the White Hands, Tristrem says:

> 'Of hir kepe Y namare;
> A gift Y geve the.

> To a levedi wil Y fare
> Is fairer than swiche thre
> To frain.'
> Ganhardin longeth to se
> That levedi, naught to lain. (2920–6)

This 'gift Y geve the' operates as an idiomatic dismissal of the second Ysonde, returning her as property to her brother. However, Tristrem immediately enables Ganhardin to take part in the value of the first Ysonde. The unexpected gift he receives is being stricken with desire when reading/seeing the romance of Tristrem, in which he is now a participant. If Ganhardin's response is a model for the audience of *Tristrem* to follow, then the effects of this story-as-gift are striking and disturbing.

Fourteenth-century audiences of romances such as *Tristrem* or *Amis and Amiloun* were familiar with the ways in which personal gifts told stories, or had stories inscribed on them: not only from imagining their power in a romance text, but from their own material practices. Clothing and objects, including personal gifts, were integral to the selfhood and relationships of medieval people.[37] Likewise, heraldic motifs and associated stories turned the people displaying them into a form of living storytelling, tracing origins and inalienable claims, but also updating or adapting those stories through marriage, inheritance or patronage.[38] Less public forms of storytelling through objects were also familiarly used. One example is a gold ring made in England or France c.1400, found in Norwich and now in the Victoria and Albert Museum.[39] Its bezel is set with two stones, a sapphire and a garnet. Around the inside of the ring has been carved 'Due tout mon coer' (with all my heart). Like many other personal rings probably given as gifts, this object both represents a love story, and constitutes part of that story too. It is narrative and symbol; an object in motion that is also an event. It is likely that the two stones represent the giver and receiver of the ring, either through some symbolic or associative connection, or for more personal reasons. In addition, behind the gems at the back of the bezel, there is a little panel that can be slid away to reveal a cavity. In this could be placed a lock of hair or some other memento. The ring may thus literalize the romantic metaphors that also appear on posy rings, such as that a part of the lover, though absent, remains with their beloved.[40] This object illustrates the complex interdependence that things and people have in the ways that they mutually constitute identity and relations.[41] While, then, the stories of Amis and Amiloun and of Tristrem and Ysonde are in some sense fantasies whose dramatic or miraculous exchanges and gifts are far removed from an early audience of the Auchinleck Manuscript, in other ways their lessons about giving, yielding, and relational knowledge via exchanged objects resonate with how a fourteenth-century audience for romance might understand their own lives. Though *Tristrem* is more loosely organized – drawing in a variety of exchanges, bonds and objects that intersect with his biography – it might make us remember that *Amis and Amiloun* also operates across a spectrum of giving, trading and keeping, from the absolutism of the gold cups to the bartering and alms-giving of the town. Before leaving the Auchinleck Manuscript, I shall explore how these lessons in giving, keeping and exchanging are examined in the text copied immediately after *Tristrem* in booklet 9 of the manuscript: *Orfeo*.

Orfeo

Orfeo has long attracted critical attention, amongst other reasons for its complex attention to the relationship between human social duties and ties, and the challenge to those assumptions represented by the otherworld. The poem's suggestive richness has encouraged a wide range of interpretations, from psychological to theological, while in another of the poem's three manuscript versions (Oxford, Bodleian MS Ashmole 61) the poem is titled 'Kyng Orfew', emphasizing its theme of governance at the level of court, household and/or self.[42] The narrative centres on acts of giving, taking and valuing, and the fear of loss; and on the drive towards recovery or reciprocation that those acts provoke. It follows a fundamental form of romance telling, from integration to disintegration to reintegration,[43] with the accrued knowledge with which that breaking and remaking marks its protagonists: as in the best *da capo* arias, return is never just the same again. A reading of *Orfeo* focusing on these losses, debts and recoveries could observe how absolute and relative values are noticed and managed. At the start of the story, Orfeo is defined by positives and absolutes: a king, descended from (euhemeristic) gods, dwelling in a noble city (25–50). His queen Heurodis is immediately figured through her superlative value. She is 'a quen of priis'; 'Þe fairest leuedi for þe nones / Þat miȝt gon on bodi & bones' (51; 53–4). Heurodis's 'priis' signals her status as an inalienable treasure in Orfeo's world. She is not merely more beautiful than other women, but her beauty is inexpressible: 'no man may telle hir fairnise' (56). After she sleeps under an 'ympe-tre' (70) and has a horrifying vision, a sense of time and loss are invoked through her physical change, narrated through Orfeo's words:

> 'O lef liif, what is te
> Þat euer ȝete hast ben so stille
> & now gredest wonder schille?
> Þi bodi, þat was so white ycore,
> Wiþ þine nailes is al totore.
> Allas, þi rode þat was so red
> Is al wan, as þou were ded,
> & also þine fingres smale
> Beþ al blodi & al pale.
> Allas, þi louesom eyȝen to
> Lokeþ so man doþ on his fo.' (102–12)

Notions of past and present, comparisons and the fear of future loss enter into the poem at this point, having been 'stille' before. The fear that human value is transient, that status cannot finally resist loss (or death, or sin), is realized when Heurodis is taken the following day, despite Orfeo's knights attempting to protect her inalienable status. Orfeo's inability to keep Heurodis out of circulation provokes his own exile, with only his harp and 'sclauin' (cloak, or pilgrim's mantle) as the continuing identifiers of his potential for exchange:

> He þat hadde had castels & tours,
> Riuer, forest, friþ wiþ flours,
> Now, þei it comenci to snewe & frese,
> Þis king mot make his bed in mese.
> He þat had yhad kniȝtes of priis
> Bifor him kneland, & leuedis,
> Now seþ he noþing þat him likeþ,
> Bot wilde wormes bi him strikeþ.
> He þat had yhad plente
> Of mete & drink, of ich deynte,
> Now may he al day digge & wrote
> Er he finde his fille of rote. (245–56)

Like Nebuchadnezzar's transformation into a beast before returning to God through humility, Orfeo remakes his potential for give and take first through losing the markers of conventional value. His recovery starts from the gift of song and joy:

> His harp whereon was al his gle
> He hidde in an holwe tre;
> & when þe weder was clere & briȝt
> He toke his harp to him wel riȝt
> & harped at his owhen wille.
> Into alle þe wode þe soun gan schille
> Þat alle þe wilde bestes þat þer beþ
> For ioie abouten him þai teþ;
> & alle þe foules þat þer were
> Come & sete on ich a brere
> To here his harping afine,
> So miche melody was þerin. (267–78)

Orfeo's recovery from his loss, his being able to enter reciprocal relationships, is bound up in exercising his 'owhen wille', his 'gle'. As with the initiation of narrative in *The Romance of Horn* which seems to stem from Horn's God-given quality, in *Orfeo* this sense of joy is the way in which the story derives its energy once more, turning the previously threatening wilderness into Orfeo's (and *Orfeo*'s?) audience of 'bestes' and 'foules' taking joy in his gift.[44]

Just as the removal of Heurodis to the Fairy kingdom was an act transgressing usual boundaries of reckoning, so Orfeo recovers her by an exchange that cannot easily be accounted for. In imaginative terms too, the motif of the rash promise is a marker that we are in a narrative world outside the normative frameworks of equivalence. Orfeo has arrived at the Fairy King's court in disguise as a minstrel, and a rather unprepossessing one at that. He performs for the king, who then offers him a reward. The text tellingly interweaves two sets of expectations about this: first, that Orfeo's song is so beautiful that it escapes equivalence (there is therefore a logic to Orfeo audaciously reclaiming one of the taken in return). The other is that minstrels are familiar members of a medieval gig economy, whose performances are commodities, paid for piece by piece with scarcely a gesture to the notion of song as gift. (When Orfeo arrives at the castle gate, he characterizes his value as providing his 'gle' at the king's 'swete wille' (383, 384), rather than out of his own creative desire, as happened in the forest.) There is comedy in the Fairy King's surprise at being outwitted by the minstrel, and in his comparison of Orfeo as 'lene, rowe, & blac' (459) and Heurodis as 'louesum, wiþouten lac' (460). Had the Fairy King been familiar with the romance of *Tristrem*, he would have known that minstrels cannot be trusted or allowed to walk off with queens. King Mark makes this schoolboy error with a similar rash promise to an Irish lord who harps for him, and who claims Ysonde as a prize. Tristrem gives Mark a ticking off: 'Gifstow glewemen þi Quen? / Hastow no nother thing?' (1851–2), and then turns the tables on Ysonde's abductor by playing his rote for the queen and escaping with her. The trope of the rash promise to a minstrel, then, allows for a number of different associations to be activated: with song as gift; with song as service and commodity; with the trickster figure outwitting the king; with the value of a promise as gift; with how to reckon the equivalence between persons (the dishevelled Orfeo; the beautiful Heurodis); and with the power of romance narrative that can itself raise the dead, or at least reclaim them from the fairy otherworld. In the final scene, Orfeo's being misrecognized is also crucial to allowing him to test his steward and return as a gift back to his own court, using the power of song again to signal joy and a suspension of reckoning. Whereas the outward movement of the text has echoes in the biblical parable of the merchant seeking a lost pearl and giving up all that he has to find it, here the shadow of the narrative is the return of the prodigal son. These narrative shadows give further depth to the story pattern of the romance, along with its Classical roots and folktale treatment. At different points in the story Orfeo can then take on different relationships with the value that is inscribed into Heurodis; into the court culture that he leaves and then rejoins; and into his harp. It is notable that Heurodis is given very little scope to effect her own exchanges; in some reading traditions of the myth she is explicitly treated as an aspect of Orfeo's psyche or a figure for his sin.

Orfeo reminds us that the movements of property in romance narrative are not simple, and romances' treatment of value or of exchange is not fully readable through one kind of lens. As Weiner argues, the line between what should and should not be given, what relates to exchange and what relates to retention with a group or family, is a recurring tension in social structures; it is also central to many of these narratives.[45] It would be hazardous to characterize the Auchinleck romances as a whole for a coherent response to these concerns about the relationship between value, exchange and story. Even the texts that I have discussed in this chapter have varying priorities and approaches. Something that I would like to emphasize, though, is their response to gift as story, and their notion of gift objects as carrying or representing symbolic power, emotional value and narrative process. In these romances, objects act both as events and stories. As objects themselves, the romances are also events that can be exchanged and valued. Further, we might see the Auchinleck Manuscript as a lively economy of debate and reflection on exchange, personhood, objects, on what to give and what to keep. The manuscript itself forms a system of interlinked prestations that both contains the multiple pathways of exchange within its narratives, and allows for cross-currents of exchange between texts.[46] These exchanges are not necessarily simultaneous or immediately cross-directional: that is, they are not a binary exchange of the kind that Weiner warns us against being satisfied with in analyses of such systems; instead, their potential is complex and layered. Thus the story of Elijah and the widow in the *Speculum Gy de Warewyke* gives additional purchase to the description of alms-giving in *Amis and Amiloun*. The yield of the richly wrought gold cups in *Amis and Amiloun*, exchanged between two men inextricably bound by loyalty pressurizes our reading of the rich cup in *Tristrem*, which secures a bond between a woman and man whose futures are already mortgaged to other loyalties. Tristrem's response to loss in seeking another Ysonde and bringing his past to life through ekphrastic depiction enriches a reading of Orfeo's reaction to Heurodis's abduction, followed by the tantalizing encounters he has with her in the train of the Fairy King and asleep in the sculpture garden of death at the King's palace. An impatient reader might want to call these themes and leave it at that; after all, in a manuscript with eighteen romances, we are bound to find some parallels and thematic strands. I partly accept that critique: we might certainly describe these as shared motifs or themes. However, I should like to make a case for the more active model of prestation that encountering a manuscript compilation suggests: the surplus that each text provides can be a gift to reading a new narrative; a form of energy that stimulates our response to story, and allows for their meditations on loss, possession and value to gain more power. The social life of these texts is thus enriched by thinking of their having economic interactions, as one narrative or idea lends value to another. It also allows more fully for what readers bring to the manuscript to be factored into the relationship between texts and their performance, and in the case of the Auchinleck Manuscript, between texts and their illustrations. Thus, while I am sceptical about totalizing claims of the kind sometimes attributed to Mauss, I think that models of interaction derived from his work – especially the movement of value between persons and things within larger systems of meaning – can be a helpful guide for the rich set of dealings that poets, bookmakers and audiences might have with books such as the Auchinleck Manuscript.

In the final section of this chapter, I will discuss *Sir Gawain and the Green Knight*, another fourteenth-century romance whose verbal, physical and ethical exchanges encapsulate the dynamics of giving, keeping, telling and reflecting that we have seen at work in the Auchinleck romances. I will argue that the ambivalence of giving and keeping, and of Gawain as both protagonist and given object, are held in tension in the poem, encouraging its readers to look for a balancing of gift and return, but at the same time complicating that search by reflecting on its own narration as a form of giving.

Sir Gawain and the Green Knight: 'The forme to the fynisement   foldes ful selden'

Many of the motifs and structures of exchange that we encountered in the Auchinleck romances are also found in *Sir Gawain and the Green Knight*, a romance bound together by exchange, bargain, and return. As Stephanie Trigg argues in a perceptive essay, *Sir Gawain and the Green Knight* is 'a poem which not only sets the exchange of objects, promises, and secrets at the center of its plot, but also underlines the uncertainty of value and the impossibility of symmetrical exchange in those negotiations.'[47] In a classic essay, Jill Mann had already demonstrated the centrality that ideas of price and value have in the poem, and she linked these to the audience she envisaged the poem having, spanning aristocratic and mercantile interests.[48] In the same year as the publication of Trigg's essay, Britton

J. Harwood focused on the concept of the noble gift, and on the relationship between chivalry, Christianity, the Law and reciprocity in the poem. Harwood argues that the Christian values represented in the Pentangle are undermined by the way in which the outward signs of faith have become habitual for Gawain: 'Christianity does not sustain Gawain in his anxiety'. With a single tap on the neck, the Green Knight repays Gawain both for the beheading and for his failure to restore the girdle: 'The tap that interconnects two gift exchanges thus disturbs the basis of reciprocity itself'.[49] Harwood figures Gawain's final encounter with the Green Knight as one involving both challenge and forgiveness: 'The Green Knight challenges the Arthurian court so that, when Gawain fails to make a return, the aggression manifest in the original challenge can be disclosed as latently love: Gawain receives "the grace ... of his live" (2480)'. This experience of forgiveness, in Harwood's reading, is, potentially the beginning of hope for Gawain.

More recently, Walter Wadiak has argued that the gift of/as violence is a central organizing feature of this poem and of others based on the story: 'These romances organize themselves around a specific gesture of violence: the glancing "tappe" (2357) that the Green Knight bestows upon Gawain at the end'.[50] Wadiak's powerful reading foregrounds the problematic claims of chivalric ideology as vitally important to the poem's meaning, at work at least as strongly as the operation of Christian ethics: '[v]iolence informs the structure of the poem at a fundamental level, however much it (or we) might fantasize about the sublime return of a gift that has been effectively purged of aggression, transformed into a sign of God's love.'[51] I accept the importance both of violence (or the threat of violence) and of excess that Wadiak builds into his reading, but I am more ambivalent about the nature of the poem's relationship to chivalric ideology, seeing that relationship as itself structured around ambiguity and surplus, and more consciously sceptical about how codes of knightly virtue are ever wholly compatible either with Christian ethics or the facts on the ground. In what follows, I shall return to the ways in which the poem manifests those uncertainties, imbalances and surpluses that Trigg, Harwood and Wadiak all perceive as important to its narrative economy. There are of course other discussions that gain traction from the nature of exchange in the poem.[52] Rather than tackling all of those questions, here I focus on links between the powerful symbolic objects in the text (especially the pentangle and girdle); Gawain as the carrier of objects and as a given object himself; and the dilemmas of giving and keeping. I suggest that the *Gawain*-poet's ekphrastic mode of description focuses the energy of the poem on what is stored and released by objects as events, marking the ambiguity and potential undecidabilty of both the gift and the story.

The detailed description of Gawain's arming fuses him with the value and material heft of his clothing and equipment.[53] He is clasped, bound and enclosed by them:

> Dubbed in a dublet   of a dere tarse,
> And sithen a crafty capados,   closed alofte,
> That with a bryght blaunner   was bounden withinne;
> Then set thay the sabatouns   upon the segge fotes;
> His legges lapped in stele   with luflyche greves. (571–5)

The verbs referring to Gawain continue to underscore his entanglement with the worth of the signifying layers by which he is enveloped: 'piched' (576); 'knaged' (577); 'closed' (578); 'Umbe-weved' (581); 'hasped' (590). Gawain is being gift-wrapped for delivery to the edge of the circle of civilized values, and his reception is uncertain. Is he a kind of potlatch object, to be destroyed as a statement of the court's determination to stand by its word and show that even valuable objects are expendable? This seems to be a likely outcome, one already prepared for by his fellow courtiers: 'That thou, lede, schal be lost,   that art of life noble! / To fynde his fere upon folde, in fayth, is not ethe' (675–6). They grumble about the loss of Gawain on the grounds that the exchange is not on equal terms and that trading blows with an 'alvisch man' (681) is unfair. On the other hand, Gawain-as-gift might also, by opening himself to the Other, allow that Other to reciprocate and become part of a larger sociable network.[54] The Green Knight's representation as both aggressive and fashionably elegant, and his game of gifts/blows as both playful and deadly serious, keeps those prospects in tension for much of the poem.

Gawain is, then, both a *participant* in exchange with the Green Knight, according to the 'forwardes' (378) proposed and accepted the previous New Year, and the *object* in a larger exchange. The poet's description of the pentangle with its five sets of five interlinked virtues completes this interpenetration of idea, thing, person and gift. Gawain has already slung the shield round his neck ('aboute the halse castes' (621)) by the time we are given a description of 'why the pentangel apendes   to that prince noble' (623).[55] The value of Gawain, the pentangle, the act of description and the stylistic intricacy deployed in that description are all synthesized at this moment, the narrating voice insisting that it is 'in tente you to telle,   thogh tary hit me schulde' (624). As in George Eliot's celebrated chapter seventeen of *Adam Bede*, 'In which the story pauses a little', here the pause for a formal *descriptio* is also a prompt to the listener or reader to take notice of the value and meaning of objects and signs; to notice how verbal artifice makes things happen, producing both events and ethical stances in narrative. Here, though, we are not (yet) given an explicit narratorial meditation on how 'needful' it is for fiction to represent human dullness or frailty.[56] Instead, the pentangle's interlocking stability and absolute virtues are a sign of aspiration and ideal (literally backed by the image of the Virgin Mary), but one that will encounter the reality of human imperfection. In that sense the *Gawain*-poet has affinities with Eliot's claimed focus on the 'rare, precious quality of truthfulness' in Dutch genre painting, despite the poem's romance connections with the mysterious and superlative.[57] With Gawain an object in motion, and an event whose narrative trajectory reaches even beyond the pages of MS Cotton Nero A.x into the story's audiences and reimaginings, the apparently closed loops of the 'endeles knotte' (630) are already under pressure. This ekphrasis, then, which mingles person and object, is a powerful, dangerous combination, which inevitably has to shift when he/it must act in the world. One of the striking characteristics of the *Gawain*-Poet's craft is that he enables his audience to look through the apparently closed protective layer of chivalric idealism to see the 'ugly, stupid, inconsistent' actions even of those who carry the most aspirational values into the world.[58] In pressing the question of how Gawain relates to or is identifiable with resonant objects such as the pentangle, and later, the green girdle, the poet also asks questions about the nature of exchange itself, its motivations, its acts of misrecognition and its ambivalence.

The *Gawain*-Poet's understanding of how the material world carries value but also proffers change or uncertainty has already been demonstrated in a telling passage on the turning of the seasons.

This set-piece description is one of the ways in which an alliterative poet can display their virtuosity. The term 'set piece', however, underplays the movement and power with which the seasons are described:

> After the sesoun of somer   with the soft wyndes,
> When Zeferus syfles himself   on sedes and erbes,
> Welawynne is the wort   that waxes thereoute,
> When the donkande dew   dropes of the leves,
> To bide a blysful blusch   of the bryght sunne.
> Bot then hyes Hervest   and hardenes him sone,
> Warnes him for the wynter   to waxe ful ripe.
> He drives with droght   the dust for to rise,
> Fro the face of the folde   to flye ful highe.
> Wroth wynd of the welkyn   wrasteles with the sunne,
> The leves lausen fro the lynde   and lyghten on the grounde,
> And all grayes the gresse   that grene was ere;
> Then all rypes and rotes   that ros upon firste,
> And thus yernes the yere   in yisterdayes mony,
> And wynter wyndes agayn,   as the world askes
>   No fage,
>   Til Meghelmasse mone
>   Was comen with wynter wage.
>   Then thenkes Gawan ful sone
>   Of his anious vyage. (516–35)

Here and in the preceding section describing autumn and winter, the poet sets verbs of contest and contrary motion against those of onward momentum: 'syfles'; 'waxes'; 'dropes'; 'hyes'; 'hardenes'; 'drives'; 'rise'; 'flye'; 'wrasteles'; 'lausen […] and lyghten'; 'all rypes and rotes   that ros'; 'yernes'; 'wyndes agayn'; 'comen'. The Michaelmas moon comes with (and in some sense becomes) the 'wage' of winter: the promise or harbinger of winter, with *wage* meaning both a pledge or surety, and in other contexts a payment or reward.[59] The passage describes arcs of time and reciprocity that are exemplary of human relationships (and of the game/contest undertaken by Gawain), but are also capable of unfolding to make human agreements and reciprocal acts a microcosm of these larger structures themselves. The poet's meditation on enfolded structures of time, reciprocity and human relationships is, I believe, analogous to anthropologists' attempts to come to terms with how gift relations both represent and constitute social structures in their complex interaction. In addition, the poet is here not only describing a separated, imaginary idea of the natural seasons as an antidote from 'real' exchange, but a system of yield and return which is the basis of the late-medieval economy too. The vocabulary of richness, swelling, struggle, value, and exchange that suffuses the description is also integral to perceptions of economy and of ecology in this period. The narrating voice's comment that 'A yere yernes ful yerne   and yeldes never like: / The forme to the fynisment   foldes ful selden' (498–9) expresses this relationship of circularity and momentum in a brilliantly compressed form: what a year 'yeldes' grows out of and at the same time is distinguishable from the act of tracing its progress ('yernes ful yerne') both verbally and thematically. Equally, the image of a start and finish that 'foldes ful selden' (very rarely matches up) is one both of return on investment, and of the energy of continuing debts and promises. It is an image enacted when, in returning to Arthur's court, Gawain brings back a yield (and burden) of knowledge that is proffered as a gift and challenge to the court and to the poem's audience.

In literal terms, of course, what Gawain returns to the court are the girdle given to him by Bertilak's wife, and the scar on his neck. Both are a surplus or yield of the exchanges entered into during the narrative.[60] Gawain explains his decision to keep the girdle by acknowledging and then setting aside its beauty and cost, but then replacing those with its value as a sign:

> 'Bot your girdel,' quoth Gawan,   'God yow foryelde!
> That wil I welde with good wille,   not for the wynne golde,
> Ne the saynt, ne the silk,   ne the syde pendauntes,
> For wele ne for worschip,   ne for the wlonk werkes,
> Bot in syngne of my surfet   I schal see hit ofte.' (2429–33)

Here 'surfet' – the transgression of not revealing and exchanging the girdle in his game of winnings with Bertilak – becomes a supplement to his identity and arms, excessive and yet now inextricable. It is also supplementary in the sense that it is a sign, an object, that represents Gawain's experience and emotion, but is also destined to stand in for that experience and survive beyond it. The 'surfet' corresponds with the yield of gift exchange, making a return unequal to the original outlay and binding the receiver into a set of obligations and potentially further expenditure, its difference thus becoming also a form of surplus. In this case, the repeated sight of the girdle will prompt Gawain to acts of remorse and readjustment of the value he places on his worth. In a phrase similar to the rising and falling, swelling and retreating of the seasons, Gawain predicts that 'when pryde schal me prik [stimulate, excite]   for prowes or armes, / The loke to this luf-lace   schal lethe [lower, bring down] my herte' (2437–8). This little psychological narrative is also a story of ecology and economics, enabling Gawain to manage cyclical imbalances in his valuation of his self-worth, and aligning the gift of the girdle with a form of productive penitential stimulus too.

The ambiguity and multiplicity of the girdle's value and meaning has long been a feature of readings of the poem. Bertilak's wife raises the whole question of reciprocal exchange directly by offering Gawain a costly ring as, pointedly, a gift without need for reciprocation:

> 'Nay, hende of high honoures,'
> Quoth that lufsum under lyne,
> 'Thagh I nade oght of youres,
> Yet schulde ye have of myne.' (1813–6)

The ring's value is 'ful huge' (1820), and of course the description of its pure gold setting and gleaming stone evokes the gifts of rings between lovers in romances such as the Horn narratives and *Tristrem*. The beautifully graded give-and-take of the verbal exchanges here establish that Gawain's resistance to the gift(s) is not absolute, but conditioned by time; he seeks to lessen the impact of his refusal by temporal modifiers: 'I wil no giftes, for goode,   my gay, *at this tyme*' (1822); 'he nay that he nolde […] Nauther gold ne garysoun   ere *God him grace sende* / To acheve to the chaunce   that he had chosen there' (1836–8; my emphases). These concessions soften (before he has even made it) his statement that he will 'hit never / To graunt' (1840–1) the offer of the girdle, and potentially link the later acceptance of the gift to the 'grace' from God of completing his adventure. Gawain, then, along with the poem's audience, can align the hidden 'costes' of the girdle with a gift from God rather than from the Lady, justifying for the time being the incompatible understandings, relationships and duties to which this gives rise, and which are encapsulated in the phrase 'the sleghte were noble' (1858) [the trick would be a noble/excellent one].

These reflections on gifts and their surplus of meaning are central to the text's own processes of exchange and forward momentum, where the absence of an exact match between 'forme' and 'fynisement' drives further action. They appear in the playful exchange of 'yeres-yiftes' amongst Arthur's courtiers in their festive games, who '[d]ebated busily aboute tho giftes' (67, 68). They are evident in the Green Knight's claim that the pride and renown of the Round Table could be '[o]verwalt with a word of on wyes speche' (314), which spurs on his offer of the beheading game. They are self-consciously debated in the reckoning of winnings that Bertilak promotes, and in the ekphrastic comparison of the women in the text: Guinevere, the old woman in the castle, and Bertilak's wife, with Mary as an incomparable point of comparison. They are still powerfully present in the conversation that Gawain has with the Green Knight at the Green Chapel, where Gawain's body serves as the account book of gains and losses from the narrative. Whereas in *Amis and Amiloun* miraculous intervention brings Amis's children back to life, whose sacrificial blood has served to heal the 'surfet' of the protagonists' actions, and in *Tristrem* a thigh wound representing his sin or lack helps bring about the deaths of the lovers, here Gawain's wound and his decision to wear the green girdle are neither argued away nor precipitate his death, but become features of his self, his heraldic blazon, and of the narrative:

> The hurt was hole that he had hent in his nekke,
> And the blykkande belt he bere thereaboute
> Abelef as a bauderyk bounden by his side,
> Loken under his lyft arme, the lace, with a knotte,
> In tokening he was tan in tech of a faute. (2484–8)

As we saw in the figure of 'surfet' in Gawain's speech accepting the girdle, this final movement of the poem is one of return and of surplus. This consists not only in the physical superfluity of the blood rushing to Gawain's face in shame when he recounts what happened ('The blod in his face con melle / When he hit schulde schewe for schame' (2503–4)).[61] Gawain's homecoming is also a form of return gift to the court ('gayn hit hem thoghte' (2491))[62] in the form of his newly marked body with its 'nirt in the nek' (2498), and in the retelling of the story of his adventures and exchanges ('all the costes of care that he hade' (2495)), turning

Gawain into a Gawain-poet and the poem's audience into the Arthurian courtiers. The court's much-debated response to Gawain's 'token of untrauthe' (2509) is also based on a form of supplementary exchange, especially in the laughter that counters Gawain's shame, and their addition to their arms of a green band worn as 'a bauderyk … A bende abelef him aboute   of a bryght grene' (2516–17). That sense of payback with interest is present in the poet's recalling of another badge of shame that has been turned to gain: the crown of thorns ('Now that bere the crowne of thorne, / He bryng us to His blisse' (2529–30)), as a supplement to the return to Trojan history that the poem's final lines otherwise bring us. It also extends out from the poem to the debate amongst its audience about whether Gawain's shame or the court's laughter are the more appropriate responses to his story – a debate that has continued ever since. *Sir Gawain and the Green Knight* thus enacts the idea that 'The forme to the fynisment   foldes ful selden' (499), marking the final moments of the text as a series of returns with interest on our investment in the narrative.

Walter Wadiak argues that the poem explores the possibility of an absolute gift – one made without the hope for return – but must also turn away from that possibility: 'If *Sir Gawain* seems engrossed with the possibility of such a gift—a gift that would erase chivalry by enacting it to its limits—it is in part because such a gift is what the poem most fears'.[63] Wadiak discusses the 'persistence' of chivalry through its alignment of violence and the gift: a chivalry that needs violence to underpin the social structures that at the same time license hierarchy, generosity and sacrifice – as long as that sacrifice confirms the status of the chivalric elite. In this reading, Arthur's court cannot face the violent truth about chivalry, and they conceal the marker of this (Gawain's wound) with their adoption of the girdle. This is a coherent but also rather determined approach to a text that I see as opening a number of at times competing notions of gift, exchange and objects. Fears about chivalry's hegemony are undoubtedly expressed in the poem as well as through the defiant motto of the Order of the Garter appended to the text: 'Hony soyt qui mal pence'. Fears about another potential threat to chivalric ideology – women's power – are also voiced both through Gawain's antifeminist rant in lines 2409–28 and, depending on how we read it, by a rhyme in the voice of a sorrowful lover added to the manuscript on fol. 125r/129r: 'Mi minde is mikul on on þat wil me noȝt amende / Sum time was trew as ston & fro schame couþe hir defende'. However, I would not say that 'the poem' most fears a threat to chivalry through imagining an absolute gift. In my view, the representation of giving, and the reflection on chivalric ideology in the poem are more fractured and multiple than this. Reading through Weiner, Hicks, and the other romances we have encountered in this chapter, I think that *Sir Gawain and the Green Knight* exposes both the opportunities and costs of giving-while-keeping, and the permeability between object and giver in relationships of exchange. At Hautdesert, Gawain seeks to keep the qualities of *trawthe* described in the pentangle, and at a crucial moment, to preserve his life by receiving and concealing the girdle. What he gives are the freighted compliments and intricate language of the exchanges between him and Bertilak's wife, and the kisses gained or accepted via those exchanges. Of course, this conception of giving and keeping in the poem is not exactly the same as the larger systems of Kula exchange that Weiner discusses, and which constitute a wide and public set of exchanges and hierarchies. Those larger systems are more comparable to the circulation of high-value gifts, land and people in late-medieval society; nevertheless, the world of Hautdesert is a microcosm of those moments of giving and keeping. What Weiner's work helps us to see is that exchange is happening or being withheld at numerous levels of the narrative and the relationships within it: a 'maze of plays and strategies as *layers* of exchanges'.[64] Obligations to give and receive are powerful but are variegated by drives to preserve and store, or to set objects or values aside from exchange. Likewise, an understanding of an object as event(s) in time helps us to see Gawain himself as an object/text moving through the narrative but also travelling through *Sir Gawain and the Green Knight* into other texts and contexts. The poem allows for a rich understanding of the ways that individuals can take part in exchange and value objects, but are also themselves bound up in systems of exchange that are larger than them, or which they can only partly comprehend.

Earlier I suggested that we might read the Auchinleck Manuscript as a system of prestations, in which texts had layered relationships of give and take between them, and out to readers and listeners. I do not have space to explore in detail how this proposition might work for MS Cotton Nero A.x, but in closing this discussion I should like briefly to suggest that *Sir Gawain and the Green Knight*'s concern with giving and keeping might itself be part of a larger pattern of thinking in the manuscript. In *Pearl*, the possibility of reckoning value between the human and divine spheres is at the heart of the debate between the dreamer-persona and the pearl maiden, with the workings of time and/as value being integral to their verbal exchanges. In *Cleanness*, one of the central biblical exempla details the sinful misuse of precious vessels from Jerusalem's temple at Belshazzar's feast, vessels that had been captured but then honoured and reserved as inalienable by his father Nebuchadnezzar. In *Patience*, Jonah must come to terms with God's ability to make and unmake the world through acts of creativity, exchange and destruction – in particular that of the gourd that Jonah has grown and delights in as a (mistaken) sign of his power and longevity: something that he believes he can keep out of circulation, but that in fact must be given up, like all human goods, through time and God's will. These concerns with value, property, matter, exchange and time are seeded throughout the poems that make up MS Cotton Nero A.x, making a larger context for the debate about exchanges of property and of the body that take place in *Sir Gawain and the Green Knight*.

Throughout this chapter, I have argued that the objects of medieval English romance provoke layered reflections on exchange, time, and how to represent human relationships. Annette Weiner's revision of established theories of reciprocity helps us to broaden our approach to these objects and narratives, so that we not only understand them as part of reciprocal processes, but as stories of keeping, reserving or passing on, as well as giving, exchanging, or trading. Protagonists in these stories take part in relationships of exchange, resist those relationships, and themselves become valued or exchanged, sometimes playing different roles simultaneously at different levels of interaction. In the romances discussed above, choices to withdraw from circulation (Amis and Amiloun's gold cups); to stabilize a relationship through the giving-then-keeping of an object (Horn's ring); or to regulate different obligations through giving and not giving (Gawain's and Lady Bertilak's kisses, and the girdle; the reluctant exchanges of *Orfeo*) are scrutinized both as part of an ethical work demanded of their audiences, and as a form of telling itself. The object's movement or stasis is traced with the narrative of its exchange, its value and its trajectory out from the text's own confines. In the next chapter, I will discuss two poems of Chaucer in which these questions – especially of how people might respond to their own status as exchangeable objects – come to the fore.

Notes

1 Mauss, *The Gift*, p. 132; *Essai sur le don*, p. 161. This comes in a section titled 'The force of things', *The Gift*, pp. 130–8.
2 Weiner, *Inalienable Possessions*, paragraph quotes pp. 2, x, 12.
3 Ibid., p. 3. This observation is particularly resonant for me when I think about my paternal grandmother Florence Perkins, a seamstress by training, whose surviving work in lace, cross-stitch and tapestry is redolent of the social relations in which she participated.
4 Ibid., p. 131.
5 Hyde, *The Gift*, ch. 1; Derrida, *Given Time I*, pp. 6–33.
6 For Kula exchange, see e.g. Malinowski, *Argonauts*, pp. 81–104; Hyde, *The Gift*, pp. 8–9; Godelier, *Enigma of the Gift*, pp. 78–95; also Derrida, *Given Time I*, p. 7. This quotation is Weiner, *Inalienable Possessions*, p. 141.
7 Weiner, *Inalienable Possessions*, p. 146.
8 Ibid., 154.
9 Ibid., p. 153. For cloth production and its cultural resonance, see Annette B. Weiner and Jane Schneider (eds), *Cloth and Human Experience* (Washington, DC: Smithsonian Books, 1991); and for medieval culture, Monica Wright, *Weaving Narrative: Clothing in Twelfth-Century French Romance* (University Park, PA: Penn State University Press, 2009); Burns, *Sea of Silk*; E. Jane Burns (ed.), *Medieval Fabrications: Dress, Textiles, Clothwork and Other Cultural Imaginings* (New York: Palgrave Macmillan, 2004). I have argued that the ekphrastic description of the embroidered cloth worn by the eponymous protagonist of *Emaré* creates a symbiotic relationship between object and person, representing and re-enacting the intertextual romance tradition: Perkins, 'Ekphrasis and narrative'.
10 Weiner, *Inalienable Possessions*, p. 29; and see pp. 28–36. On the Church, gifts and property, see above, Introduction note 16; Bernhard Jussen, 'Religious discourses of the gift in the Middle Ages: semantic evidences (second to twelfth centuries)', in Ananya Jahanara Kabir

and Deanne Williams (eds), *Postcolonial Approaches to the European Middle Ages: Translating Cultures* (Cambridge: Cambridge University Press, 2005), pp. 173–92. Silber, 'Gift-giving in the great traditions' draws on Weiner's work to discuss medieval religious donations and inalienability.

11 Dan Hicks, 'The material-cultural turn: event and effect', in Hicks and Beaudry (eds), *Handbook of Material Culture Studies*, pp. 25–98, at p. 84. See also Chris Gosden and Yvonne Marshall, 'The cultural biography of objects', *World Archaeology* 31 (1999), 169–78. 'Biographies' is modified by the more flexible 'itineraries' in Hans Peter Hahn and Hadas Weiss, 'Introduction: biographies, travels and itineraries of things', and David Fontijn, 'Epilogue: cultural biographies and itineraries of things: second thoughts', both in Hahn and Weiss (eds), *Mobility, Meaning and Transformations of Things* (Oxford: Oxbow, 2013), pp. 1–18; 183–95. For medieval contexts and discussion, see Roberta Gilchrist, 'The materiality of medieval heirlooms: from biographical to sacred objects', in Hahn and Weiss (eds), *Mobility, Meaning and Transformations of Things*, pp. 170–82, and *Medieval Life: Archaeology and the Life Course* (Woodbridge: Boydell, 2012). I briefly discuss some of these developments in Perkins, 'Materiality of medieval romance'. For the questions of agency interleaved with the notion of object biography, see Janet Hoskins, 'Agency, biography and objects', in Christopher Tilley et al. (eds), *Handbook of Material Culture* (London: SAGE Publications, 2006), pp. 74–84.

12 London, British Museum 1975, 0401.1. For description and discussion, see Richard Camber and John Cherry, 'The Savernake Horn', in Richard Camber (ed.), *Collectors and Collections: The British Museum Yearbook 2* (London: British Museum Publications, 1977), pp. 201–11, to which this paragraph is indebted.

13 Ibid., p. 208.

14 Ibid.; the reference to the Horn ('Cornum … magnum … et argento ornatum') is in the 1607 Latin edition of William Camden, *Britannia …* (London: [Eliot's Court Press], 1607), p. 185, http://gateway.proquest.com/openurl?ctx_ver=Z39.88-2003&res_id=xri:eebo&rft_id=xri:eebo:citation:99857309, accessed 8 August 2019.

15 The Savernake Estate's website still stresses the Forest's longevity and inalienability: 'Since it was put into the care of one of the victorious knights who fought at the Battle of Hastings in 1066, Savernake Forest has passed down from father to son (or daughter, on 4 occasions) in an unbroken line for 31 generations, never once being bought or sold in a thousand years, and today it is the only Forest in Britain still in private hands.' As Weiner discusses, however, inalienability has its costs,

and possessions are very rarely completely removed from the tides of exchange or the fall of fortunes. The Savernake Horn was acquired by the British Museum in 1975. The now-dilapidated Palladian mansion on the edge of the Forest, Tottenham House, was sold by the Estate's trustees against the wishes of the head of the family, the Earl of Cardigan, in 2015: savernakeestate.co.uk, accessed 23 June 2018. At the time of writing, the current owners plan to restore it for use as a (240-room) private family home.

16 Marilyn Strathern, 'Artifacts of history: events and the interpretation of images', in her *Learning to See in Melanesia* (Chicago, IL: Hau Books/Society for Ethnographic Theory, 2013), https://haubooks.org/learning-to-see-in-melanesia, accessed 20 February 2019, pp. 157–78, quoting p. 168.

17 See e.g. Matthew Giancarlo, 'Speculative genealogies', in Paul Strohm (ed.), *Middle English* (Oxford: Oxford University Press, 2007), pp. 352–68.

18 See esp. Smith, *Arts of Possession.*

19 See above, pp. 54–7.

20 For the booklet structure, context and facsimiles of the manuscript, see *The Auchinleck Manuscript,* ed. David Burnley and Alison Wiggins, https://auchinleck.nls.uk/editorial/project.html, accessed 10 May 2018; *The Auchinleck Manuscript: National Library of Scotland, Advocates' MS. 19.2.1,* intr. Derek Pearsall and I.C. Cunningham (London: Scolar Press, 1977); Timothy A. Shonk, 'A study of the Auchinleck Manuscript: bookmen and bookmaking in the early fourteenth century', *Speculum* 60 (1985), 71–91; Fein (ed.), *The Auchinleck Manuscript.*

21 See *Amis and Amiloun: Zugleich mit der altfranzösischen Quellen,* ed. Eugen Kölbing (Heilbronn: Henninger, 1884), and *Amys e Amillyoun,* ed. Hideka Fukui, ANTS Plain Texts Series 7 (London: ANTS, 1990). The French romance is translated in *The Birth of Romance,* trans. Weiss.

22 Crane, *Insular Romance,* p. 118.

23 Lines 93–104. Quotations of *Amis and Amiloun* are from *The Auchinleck Manuscript,* ed. Burnley and Wiggins, but I have indented the *b*-rhyme lines in its tail-rhyme for ease of reading.

24 See *MED,* s.v. *token* (n.), meanings 1 and 4.

25 Smith, *Arts of Possession,* chs. 3, 5; see also Stephanie Trigg, 'The rhetoric of excess in *Winner and Waster*', *Yearbook of Langland Studies* 3 (1989), 91–108.

26 Matthew 13:45–6.

27 *Speculum Gy de Warwyk,* in *The Auchinleck Manuscript,* ed. Burnley and Wiggins, line 60.

28 On alms and/as gifts in the wake of Mauss, see especially Parry, 'The Gift'.

29 For the Christian framework and imagery of the narrative, see also Crane, *Insular Romance*, pp. 117–28; and Jill Mann, 'Messianic chivalry in *Amis and Amiloun*', *New Medieval Literatures* 10 (2008), 137–59.

30 See my discussion of *The Franklin's Tale* below, Ch. 4.

31 On *Degaré* and *Floris and Blancheflour* see e.g. James Simpson, 'Violence, narrative and proper name: *Sir Degare*, 'The Tale of Sir Gareth of Orkney', and the *Folie Tristan d'Oxford*', in Putter and Gilbert (eds), *Popular Romance*, pp. 122–41; Christopher Cannon, *The Grounds of English Literature* (Oxford: Oxford University Press, 2004), pp. 188–92; Wadiak, *Savage Economy*, pp. 19–29.

32 Phillipa Hardman, 'The true romance of *Tristrem and Ysonde*', in Corinne Saunders (ed.), *Cultural Encounters in the Romance of Medieval England* (Cambridge: Brewer, 2005), pp. 85–100, at p. 87, citing Maldwyn Mills.

33 '*Lancelot of the Laik*' *and* '*Sir Tristrem*', ed. Alan Lupack, TEAMS (Kalamazoo, MI: Medieval Institute Publications, 1994), http://d.lib .rochester.edu/teams/text/lupack-lancelot-of-the-laik-and-sir-tristrem-sir-tristrem-introduction, accessed 8 June 2018. Quotations from *Tristrem* are taken from this edition. Hardman, 'True romance', defends the skill and structure of the poem, and see also Dana M. Symons, 'Does Tristan think, or doesn't he?: The pleasures of the Middle English *Sir Tristrem*', *Arthuriana* 11 (2001), 3–22, which focuses on its foregrounding of narrative pleasure and action, rather than interiority or critical distance.

34 Gloss to line 1663.

35 The text of Thomas's *Tristan* is fragmentary, but versions influenced by it provide a fuller picture. See *Les fragments du Roman de Tristan: poème du XIIe siècle*, ed. Bartina H. Wind, 2nd edn (Geneva: Droz, 1960); Gottfried von Strassburg, *Tristan; with the Tristan of Thomas*, trans. A.T. Hatto (Harmondsworth, Penguin: 1960); and see also Jutta Eming et al. (eds), *Visuality and Materiality in the Story of Tristan and Isolde* (Notre Dame, IN: University of Notre Dame Press, 2012).

36 Perkins, 'Ekphrasis and narrative'.

37 See Eleanor Standley, *Trinkets and Charms: The Use, Meaning and Significance of Dress Accessories, AD 1300–1700* (Oxford: Institute of Archaeology, 2013).

38 See Susan Crane, *The Performance of Self: Ritual, Clothing and Identity during the Hundred Years War* (Philadelphia: University of Pennsylvania Press, 2002).

39 London, Victoria and Albert Museum, M. 189-1962, http://collections. vam.ac.uk/item/O377723/ring-unknown/, accessed 10 February 2019. Listed in Joan Evans, *English Posies and Posy Rings* (London: Oxford

University Press, 1931), p. 12. See Marian Campbell, *Medieval Jewellery in Europe, 1100–1500* (London: V&A Publications, 2009) pp. 72–5. I am very grateful to the V&A's curators for discussing this ring with me in advance of its loan to the Bodleian Library for the exhibition 'The Romance of the Middle Ages' in 2012.

40 Other examples recorded in Joan Evans, *English Posies*, include 'sauns de partter' (p. 13); 'mon cor aves' (p. 11, from Fressingfield, Suffolk; numerous rings have this or a variant); 'je cous tien t(enez) moy' (p. 10, BM 233).

41 For discussion in modern contexts, see Daniel Miller, *Stuff* (Cambridge: Polity Press, 2010).

42 For the manuscripts and a parallel text edition, see *Sir Orfeo*, ed. A.J. Bliss, 2nd edn (Oxford: Clarendon Press, 1966). I quote from his Auchinleck text, though note Bliss's radical reconstruction of the opening, lost in the MS; cf. *The Auchinleck Manuscript*, ed. Burnley and Wiggins. A summary of different critical approaches is given, with references, in the Introduction to *Orfeo* in *The Middle English Breton Lays*, ed. Anne Laskaya and Eve Salisbury, TEAMS (Kalamazoo, MI: Medieval Institute Publications, 1995), https://d.lib.rochester.edu/teams/publication/laskaya-and-salisbury-middle-english-breton-lays; supplemented by the equivalent in *Codex Ashmole 61: A Compilation of Popular Middle English Verse*, ed. George Shuffelton, TEAMS (Kalamazoo, MI: Medieval Institute Publications, 2008), https://d.lib.rochester.edu/teams/publication/shuffelton-codex-ashmole-61, accessed 12 August 2019.

43 See James Simpson, 'Derek Brewer's romance', in Charlotte Brewer and Barry Windeatt (eds), *Traditions and Innovations in the Study of Medieval English Literature: The Influence of Derek Brewer* (Cambridge: Brewer, 2013), pp. 154–72, at pp. 168–9.

44 For a cognate reading of the power of poetry and creativity in the poem, see Seth Lerer, 'Artifice and artistry in *Sir Orfeo*', *Speculum* 60 (1985), 92–109; see also Roy Michael Liuzza, '*Sir Orfeo*: Sources, traditions, and the poetics of performance', *Journal of Medieval and Renaissance Studies* 21 (1991), 269–84.

45 Weiner, *Inalienable Possessions*, e.g. p. 150: 'The inherent tension in keeping-while-giving follows from two fundamental contradictions: one, the challenge to give is at the same time a challenge to the ability to keep, and two, the challenge to surrender the documentation of difference between exchange participants is, at the same time, a challenge to the guardianship of autonomy.'

46 Arthur Bahr, *Fragments and Assemblages: Forming Compilations of Medieval London* (Chicago, IL: University of Chicago Press, 2013), ch. 2, reads booklet 2 of the Auchinleck MS as an assemblage, a concept

that bears some comparison to the idea here of a manuscript as a system of prestations. I discuss books and/as assemblages further in Ch. 5 below.

47 Stephanie Trigg, 'The romance of exchange: *Sir Gawain and the Green Knight*', *Viator* 22 (1991), 251–66, at p. 252.

48 Mann, 'Price and value'.

49 Britton J. Harwood, '*Gawain* and the gift', *PMLA* 106 (1991), 483–99, quoting 490, 491.

50 Wadiak, *Savage Economy*, p. 89.

51 Ibid., p. 96.

52 For example, Felicity Riddy, 'Giving and receiving: exchange in the *Roman van Walewein* and *Sir Gawain and the Green Knight*', *Tijdschrift voor Nederlandse Taal- en Letterkunde* 112 (1996), 18–29, who compares the English poem with the Dutch *Roman van Walewein* in the context of the relationships between urban and courtly cultures. R.A. Shoaf, *The Poem as Green Girdle: Commercium in 'Sir Gawain and the Green Knight'* (Gainesville: University Presses of Florida, 1984) explores commercial language, sin, forgiveness and regeneration, and the generation of signs in the poem.

53 On the importance of seeing and description, see Sarah Stanbury, *Seeing the 'Gawain'-Poet: Description and the Act of Perception* (Philadelphia: University of Pennsylvania Press, 1991; and on the dangers of looking, and the visual traditions in which the poet operates, see Hsin-Yu Hu, 'Delineating the *Gawain*-Poet: Myth, Desire and Visuality' (doctoral dissertation, University of Oxford, 2015).

54 For an analogous understanding of Gawain as the 'exemplary Young Man' in numerous romances, 'facing the marvellous or unknown, and rendering it manageable for the rest of his society' see Thomas Hahn, 'Gawain and popular chivalric romance in Britain', in Roberta L. Krueger (ed.), *The Cambridge Companion to Medieval Romance* (Cambridge: Cambridge University Press, 2000), pp. 218–34, at p. 223. My reading, however, seeks to retain something of the *un*manageable and *un*resolved in Gawain's opening of the circle of exchange. For the larger context of fantasies of power or absorption, see Patricia Clare Ingham, *Sovereign Fantasies: Arthurian Romance and the Making of Britain* (Philadelphia: University of Pennsylvania Press, 2001).

55 The verb 'apendes' here means 'be appropriate to' or 'pertain to', cf. *MED* s.v. *ap(p)enden*, 2(a), though also has a close physical cousin in its derivation from Latin *(a)pendere* (to hang something onto something), via French *apendre*.

56 George Eliot, *Adam Bede*, ed. Carol A. Martin (Oxford: Clarendon Press, 2001), p. 165.

57 Ibid., p. 166. J. Hillis Miller, *The Ethics of Reading: Kant, de Man, Eliot, Trollope, James, and Benjamin* (New York: Columbia University Press, 1987), pp. 61–80, discusses this passage of *Adam Bede* as a powerful speech act; the *Gawain*-Poet's description also carries perlocutionary force. In *An Introduction to the 'Gawain'-Poet* (London: Longman, 1996), pp. 45–68, Ad Putter discusses the *Gawain*-Poet's skill at mingling the realistic and fantastic.

58 Eliot, *Adam Bede*, p. 166.

59 See *MED*, s.v. *wage* (n.).

60 Vance Smith points out the poet's clear familiarity with the daily reckonings of the late-medieval household, and the problems of reckoning different kinds of exchange and gift: *Arts of Possession*, p. 11. On the text's visual poetics as contributing to shifting patterns of meaning and value, see Stanbury, *Seeing the 'Gawain'-Poet*, pp. 107–11.

61 On shame in the poem, see e.g. J.A. Burrow, 'Honour and shame in *Sir Gawain and the Green Knight*', in his *Essays on Medieval Literature* (Oxford: Clarendon Press, 1984), pp. 117–31; Stephanie Trigg, '"Shamed be...": historicizing shame in medieval and early modern courtly ritual', *Exemplaria* 19 (2007), 67–89.

62 See *MED* s.v. *gein* (adj.), meaning 2(b), 'beneficial, profitable, helpful; excellent, pleasing, agreeable'.

63 Wadiak, *Savage Economy*, p. 103.

64 Weiner, *Inalienable Possessions*, p. 141 (original emphasis).

3

The traffic in people: Chaucer's *Knight's Tale* and *Troilus and Criseyde*

Chapter 2 discussed how some English romances pay attention to what can be exchanged and what should be kept. These romances embed complex messages about love, service or obligation in the objects that are exchanged, and in how people relate to, or are bound up with, those objects, operating a network of relationships that at times rely on economic structures, and at other times apparently resist or refuse those structures. As I noted, people may be both participants in exchange, and themselves be exchanged between groups, or to satisfy the demands of others. However, even in stories whose end provides a formal or conservative closure (marriage; reconquest; reunion), there are openings in the narrative where possibilities of other relationships or exchanges are posited or imagined. Gift exchange is a particularly acute instance of this kind of moment of potential, where those other possibilities may be thought of, and romance as a genre is especially accommodating to imagining alternative paths, even when the generically normative path is the one usually chosen in time.

This chapter encounters two poems by Geoffrey Chaucer which reflect on these questions and relationships. They are both romance treatments of Classical narratives, both drawing on Boccaccio for their major narrative sources, and both focused on human relations in a time of war: *The Knight's Tale*, and *Troilus and Criseyde*.[1] Both have received extensive commentary in the context of gendered relations and the status of women in exchange. In this chapter I will connect those ideas to Chaucer's interest in people as both exchange-able and exchanging, in many contexts and alongside their gendered roles. My aim is not to deny the importance of gender in these narratives, but to put them in touch with ways in which

Chaucer imagines human (and elsewhere, non-human) protagonists in relations of exchange and power that also cross and complicate gendered and other divides.

'Captured by enemies'

I shall approach *The Knight's Tale* via a document recording Chaucer's own experience as an object of exchange. Chaucer was listed as a *valletus* and then esquire in King Edward III's household from 1367.[2] Before that, however, at least from April 1357 to October 1360, he was attached to the household of Elizabeth de Burgh, Countess of Ulster, and her husband Lionel, Earl of Ulster and second surviving son of the King.[3] Chaucer went to war in France as part of the English campaign of 1359–60, probably in the company led by Prince Lionel. The commander-in-chief of the division was probably Edward the Black Prince himself.[4] There is little evidence about Chaucer's activities on campaign. We do know, however, that he was captured by the enemy, and the King made a payment towards his ransom in March 1360. This is listed in the accounts of William de Farley, Keeper of the Wardrobe of the King's household, under a series of 'Dona' [grants, or gifts]: 'Galfrido Chaucer capto per inimicos in partibus Francie in subsidium redempcionis sue de consimili dono regis die et anno supradictis xvi li' [For Geoffrey Chaucer captured by enemies in French territories, to pay for his ransom, likewise by grant of the King on the aforesaid day and year [i.e. 1 March] 16 pounds].[5] The account for 1360 includes payments for journeys undertaken on the King's service, for a dead horse, and to repair a bridge damaged by Edward's army on its route, as well as to ransom those captured in battle. Other captives ransomed by the King during 1360 included John de York (the King's carter) and his seven fellows – £12 for the lot – Richard Dulle, an archer (40 shillings), and Richard Stury, an esquire of the King and a valuable prize at £50. Stury and Chaucer were later both involved in negotiations in France in 1377 over peace and a proposed marriage of Richard II to Princess Marie, the daughter of the King of France.[6]

The taking of prisoners and their later ransoming was an integral part of late-medieval warfare, creating connections, obligations and communication both across the battle lines and between those fighting and their comrades, other ranks and their wider families and groups of supporters. As Rémy Ambühl suggests in his study of 'ransom culture' in the Hundred Years War, the practice of ransoming had an impact on all ranks, and was intimately embedded in war: 'ransom culture embraced the whole social spectrum' and 'the process of ransoming could run smoothly and quickly enough to allow a succession of returns to service and further captures'.[7] Those on campaign could, then, either gain control over captured combatants, or could themselves become subject to ransoming and reliant on their family resources, contacts, comrades or lord(s) to secure their freedom. Chaucer's capture happened during a campaign to consolidate English victories in France, victories that had culminated in the Battle of Poitiers in 1356. At Poitiers, indeed, the greatest prize of all had been taken by the English: King John of France, along with numerous members of the French nobility.[8] In his *Chroniques*, Jean Froissart described the situation in the aftermath of the battle:

> [The English] found that their prisoners were twice as numerous as themselves, so they conferred together and decided to ransom most of them on the spot. The captured knights and squires found the English and Gascons very accommodating and many of them bought their liberty there and then, or were freed simply on their promise to surrender themselves at Bordeaux by Christmas or to deliver the payment there.
> The English took up their quarters for the night on the edge of the battlefield. Some disarmed, but not all, and they disarmed their prisoners. They made them as comfortable as they could, each attending to his own, for the prisoners captured in battle were theirs personally, to be freed and ransomed as they chose.[9]

This curious mixture of bloody conflict and respectful hospitality in many ways encapsulates the ambiguities of late-medieval chivalry.[10] The relationship between captive and captor is complex: from being roughly equivalent in rank, one has apparently turned into a piece of property, and yet his promise to return and pay his ransom is respected by his 'owner'. This two-way relationship exemplifies the economics of late-medieval war, in which individuals accrued debts and obligations as well as the potential for advancement or valuable spoils. However, it does not mean that commodity calculation is the only set of rules by which these relationships are governed. Since the word of the captured knight was sometimes enough to secure liberty in order to raise funds for the ransom, there was a recognition that the relationship is one of obligation as well as commodity valuation, an acknowledgement of the continuing status of the captured as well as their monetary value. Ambühl discusses the theory that practices of ransoming were linked to development of rules around tournaments, and that these have a give-and-take relationship with the practice of warfare – each setting expectations or adjusting action in the other sphere.[11] Staged, practice or fictional representations of battle, prisoner-taking and relationships of ransoming, then, both comment on and are part of a wider cultural experience of war and its reversals.

The Knight's Tale

Such relationships of honour, debt and reversal of fortune are of course the substance of Chaucer's *Knight's Tale*. The tale introduces us to its two major male protagonists, Palamon and Arcite, at the moment when they are taken prisoner after a bloody battle at Thebes:

> And so bifel that in the taas they founde,
> Thurgh-girt with many a grevous blody wounde,
> Two yonge knyghtes liggynge by and by,
> Bothe in oon armes, wroght ful richely,
> Of whiche two Arcita highte that oon,
> And that oother knyght highte Palamon.
> Nat fully quyke, ne fully dede they were,
> But by hir cote-armures and by hir gere
> The heraudes knewe hem best in special
> As they that weren of the blood roial
> Of Thebes, and of sustren two yborn.
> Out of the taas the pilours han hem torn,
> And han hem caried softe unto the tente
> Of Theseus; and he ful soone hem sente
> To Atthenes, to dwellen in prisoun
> Perpetually – he nolde no ransoun.
> And whan this worthy duc hath thus ydon,
> He took his hoost, and hoom he rit anon
> With laurer crowned as a conquerour;
> And ther he lyveth in joye and in honour

> Terme of his lyf; what nedeth wordes mo?
> And in a tour, in angwissh and in wo,
> This Palamon and his felawe Arcite
> For everemoore; ther may no gold hem quite.[12]

The economic consequences of the battle are thoroughly embedded in this passage. For example, scavengers or 'pilours' strip the bodies of dead combatants and here identify Palamon and Arcite as potentially valuable property.[13] The heralds are the next line of evaluation, using the cousins' heraldic symbols to identify their status. Ransom is specifically ruled out in their case, suggesting that it would have been a normal procedure, and Theseus's particularly draconian decision not to ransom the cousins is re-emphasized at the end of this passage: 'ther may no gold hem quite'.[14] Palamon and Arcite, then, are both recognized as objects of value, but whose affiliation with Thebes has brought the usual process of exchange to a halt. As with the Theban widows' complaint to Theseus that the tyrant Creon had not allowed their menfolk's bodies to be buried, here Theseus turns Arcite and Palamon into a form of negatively charged inalienable property.

Of course, the phrase 'what nedeth wordes mo?' invites more words. We hear later that both Palamon and Arcite do get out of prison, but by then a new object of interest has come into focus in the narrative:

> This passeth yeer by yeer and day by day,
> Till it fil ones, in a morwe of May,
> That Emelye, that fairer was to sene
> Than is the lylie upon his stalke grene,
> And fressher than the May with floures newe – ...
> She was arisen and al redy dight,
> For May wole have no slogardie anyght. (I.1033–7; 1041–2)

If we first saw Palamon and Arcite through the richness and exchange value of their arms, here we see Emily through the glinting worth of her femininity: 'fairer', 'fressher' and later 'shene' (I.1035; 1037; 1068); these act as an alternative form of heraldry by which she may be assessed. And she immediately becomes the focus of Palamon and Arcite's attention. This is love, but expressed as competition and possession. Emily, though, already 'belongs' to Theseus. He has won her, along with his own wife, Hyppolita, when he conquered the Amazon women-warriors:

> He conquered al the regne of Femenye,
> That whilom was ycleped Scithia,
> And weddede the queene Ypolita,
> And broghte hire hoom with hym in his contree
> With muchel glorie and greet solempnytee,
> And eek hir yonge suster Emelye. (I.866–71)

Emily, then, is a spoil of war, somewhat analogous to Palamon and Arcite. We do not know if she was an Amazon combatant, though the description of her as 'yonge' and later as an apparent ideal of fresh femininity militates against that possibility. As generations of readers of *The Knight's Tale* have noticed, she is mentioned here literally as a subclause to the winning of Hippolyta. When Theseus later discovers Arcite and Palamon fighting in a grove, he does accede to the pleas of the women to spare their lives, but he also promises to give Emily to the one who wins a tournament.

> [Whichever of you can] with his hundred, as I spak of now,
> Sleen his contrarie, or out of lystes dryve,
> Thanne shal I yeve Emelya to wyve
> To whom that Fortune yeveth so fair a grace. (I.1858–61)

These moments of (potential) exchange seem to position Emily as an object passed between powerful men. Theseus's patriarchal authority is clearly being exercised here, but it is notable that the agency of giving and the category of the gift shifts even within a pair of lines. Theseus is to 'yeve' Emily as a wife, but this is a dependent action upon Fortune's giving the grace of victory to one of the men. At this point, then, Emily is categorized partly as a young woman, and partly as the gift ('grace') itself of victory. Theseus has the power to give, but that power is tied to the gift of Fortune. Such mobile description accords with the language of exchange, payment and reward in Theseus's speech up to this point, for example the familiar image of lovers being part of the God of Love's paid retinue ('Thus hath hir lord, the god of love, ypayed / Hir wages and hir fees for hir servyse!' (I.1802–3)), and Theseus's statement that he can forgive the crimes of Palamon and Arcite partly because of his own experience of being in service to or captured by love:

> I woot it by myself ful yore agon,
> For in my tyme a servant was I oon.
> And therefore, syn I knowe of loves peyne
> And woot hou soore it kan a man distreyne,
> As he that hath ben caught ofte in his laas,
> I yow foryeve al hoolly this trespaas,
> At requeste of the queene, that kneleth heere,
> And eek of Emelye, my suster deere. (I.1813–20)

In Theseus's speech, Emily's position shifts or multiplies. She is equivalent to him in the sense of not having the least obligation to the lovers for their feelings: 'she for whom they han this jolitee / Kan hem therfore as muche thank as me' (I.1807–8).[15] She is his 'suster deere' whose entreaties have helped him spare the two men's lives: at this point, her inclusion with another 'eek' following acknowledgement of the Queen's influence is poised between value and relation. Emily is also the prize or gift of victory in Palamon and Arcite's later contest, set to establish a new relationship between Theseus and one of the lovers.

Emily's transformations and exchanges (spoil of war; victim of fortune; prisoner; suppliant; contestant; prize for victory) help power the narrative movement of *The Knight's Tale*, and we shall return to the multiple roles that Emily and other of its protagonists play. But it is as a woman exchanged between men that Emily's role has most often been scrutinized, amongst other such women in Chaucer's work. In *Chaucer's Sexual Poetics*, for example, Carolyn Dinshaw analyses *The Man of Law's Tale* via the exchange of women and exclusion or marginalization of their desire. Talking of the Sultaness and Donagild in that tale, she argues that they are excluded or demonized because they are women with independent desires: 'These desires do not originate in the desires of others, as they must in [a] society which is founded on the exchange of women. Emily in *The Knight's Tale* provides perhaps the clearest example in Chaucer of the feminine desire that conveniently adapts itself to the desires of those who trade her.'[16] Earlier, Dinshaw cites the 'traffic' in women between groups of men as an important structuring feature of the social systems in Chaucer's narratives, discussing there *Troilus and*

Criseyde in particular. Dinshaw's 'traffic' refers to an influential essay by Gayle Rubin, who cites and critiques Claude Lévi-Strauss, who himself is responding to Mauss's work on the gift.[17] Rather than re-run the history of this important set of debates, I shall focus briefly on an element of Lévi-Strauss's discussion of agency and voice, and Rubin's analysis of it. Lévi-Strauss attempted to describe an underlying structure for marriage as part of a larger system of exchange:

> The total relationship of exchange which constitutes marriage is not established between a man and a woman, but between two groups of men, and the woman figures only as one of the objects in the exchange, not as one of the partners ... this remains true even when the girl's feelings are taken into consideration, as, moreover, is usually the case. In acquiescing to the proposed union, she precipitates or allows the exchange to take place, she cannot alter its nature.[18]

This statement could of course be tested and compared with numerous medieval romances which purport to be 'about' the relationship between a man and a woman, but where male–male rivalry or transaction is central. In discussion of Lévi-Strauss, Rubin raises more detailed questions about the role of women in this so-called 'total relationship': are women exchanged for another woman always? Are they exchanged for bridewealth? Does a marriage form part of a chain of obligations or is it 'cancelled' out in the transaction itself? Rubin reformulates Lévi-Strauss's argument as: 'Kinship and marriage are always parts of total social systems, and are always tied into economic and political arrangements.'[19] This broader definition rings true for medieval marriage at many ranks of society, in which the marrying couple took their place amidst interests and pressures at (inter)national, regional or local levels, and it also to an extent loosens the gender binary of groups of men trading women as in Lévi-Strauss's formulation.[20]

Rubin also queries the connection that Lévi-Strauss imagines – his concluding metaphor – between social or political systems and language. Here I quote Rubin, who discusses and then quotes Lévi-Strauss:

> For instance, Lévi-Strauss sees women as being like words, which are misused when they are not 'communicated' and exchanged. On the last pages of a very long book, he observes that this creates something of a

contradiction in women, since women are at the same time 'speakers' and 'spoken'. His only comment on this contradiction is this:

> But woman could never become just a sign and nothing more, since even in a man's world she is still a person, and since insofar as she is defined as a sign she must be recognized as a generator of signs. In the matrimonial dialogue of men, woman is never purely what is spoken about; for if women in general represent a certain category of signs, destined to a certain kind of communication, each woman preserves a particular value arising from her talent, before and after marriage, for taking her part in a duet. In contrast to words, which have wholly become signs, woman has remained at once a sign and a value. *This explains why the relations between the sexes have preserved that affective richness, ardour and mystery which doubtless originally permeated the entire universe of human communications.* (Lévi-Strauss 1969: 496 [original emphasis])

This is an extraordinary statement. Why is he not, at this point, denouncing what kinship systems do to women, instead of presenting one of the greatest rip-offs of all time as the root of romance?[21]

I do not have space fully to explore the layers of argument and assumption in Lévi-Strauss and Rubin here, but there are a few questions that I should like to register as a way back into Chaucer's representation of gender, voice and exchange. First, can Rubin's objection that Lévi-Strauss presents 'one of the greatest rip-offs of all time' (that is, the suppression of women in the name of romantic mystery) as 'the root of romance' be equally applied to romance as a literary genre? Is romance *generically* part of that rip-off? and how would that relate to its narrative systems of exchange and gift? Lévi-Strauss's resort to mystery is one of those moments where structuralism reaches a limit of explanatory power and imagination, still being rusted into habits of thought about gender and society. His imagining of women as words in communication is embedded in a set of structuralist propositions about the generation of symbolic exchange, and Rubin takes aim at the problems both of logic and imagery that emerge in his characterization of women as both sign and value: spoken between men and yet capable of 'taking her part in a duet'. The resulting 'ardour' and 'mystery' constitutes a male, heterosexual and Western/Northern perspective on the mystery and exoticism of women (especially women of colour) – the kind of unknowable, quixotic figure familiar from male-voiced lyric and narrative poetry from the twelfth century onwards. Rubin's critique challenges Lévi-Strauss's clumsy figurations, suggesting that, like other key male thinkers that she discusses, he constructs an explanation for gendered inequality around assumptions about difference.[22] I think that this is where the 'leakiness' of the literary text can be used as a way of moving around the problem of treating social systems as prior and reified structures, into which people fit or to which they react.

Up to now, that is, the romances that I have discussed have on the whole celebrated or reinforced narrative goals of heterosexual marriage and the securing of land and dynasty. Many of them can indeed be read as attempts to justify the suppression of women in the name of romance. However, they have not always done so straightforwardly or without imagining other kinds of choices and outcomes. Rather like the double time of gifted narrative that we encountered in Chapter 1, where the listener encounters moments of giving 'as if' unreciprocated while also appreciating the overall system of prestation to which a narrative pays attention, the fictional text may represent social structures as performance and narrative or ethical choice, alongside or in the face of already-formed systems. This does not by any means invalidate a feminist or other critique of medieval texts' representation of gender. However, it does allow us to read these texts as both creating and representing ideas remade in performance (rather than describing fixed structures) and as including the possibility of alternative thinking, however constrained that possibility is. One might argue to the contrary that this idea of choice or performance is chimerical, tricking the audience into acceptance of its own subjection, or reinforcement of its own prejudice.[23] However, I would argue that the possibility of alternative outcomes, and the visible construction that goes into protagonists performing their assigned role in society, allow for enough chinks to see refracted possibilities glint through. In this reading, I am influenced by Nicola McDonald's proposition that romances allow for imagining extremes, the opposite of the eventual denouement; and the recent reflections of Derek Attridge on the mobile relationship between social conventions, the text and the audience(s) in the work of literature.[24] It is in this space for imaginative speculation, for play in the system, that I also see some of romance's most powerful work happening. Returning to Lévi-Strauss's metaphor of voice: who speaks and who is spoken for is precisely a matter for negotiation and variety in romance, and agency is not something that is a binary, or a zero-sum game. Readings of romance can emerge precisely where a flow of agency or relations meet and interact.

In an incisive essay on women and the gift in French romances and *chansons de geste*, Sarah Kay discusses a number of theoretical approaches to gender, desire and gift that illuminate these narratives and questions. Kay sees in the gift a way of looking beyond zero-sum calculations of power, agency or value, and instead as 'a topic which provides a means of analyzing the position of medieval women while at the same time challenging the received fabric of representation: the gift, that is, provides a tool both for recovering "experience" and for redefining our relationship to it'.[25] Kay rightly sees the development of debate around the gift as enabling new perspectives on agency and narrative in courtly literature – perspectives that are layered one on another, rather than necessarily singular. She gives as an example Beroul's *Tristan*, in which Iseut is not only an object of exchange, but also shows her awareness of her own role in 'perpetuating the alliance' between households that her marriage to Mark represents. Iseut, Kay argues, is shown 'not just an item of *goods* but a *person*, and thus capable of giving in her turn'.[26] This reading of Beroul's Iseut is cognate with the awareness of narrative roles and choices that I believe female protagonists show in the Auchinleck romances discussed in Chapter 2, especially Belisaunt in *Amis and Amiloun*, Ysonde in *Tristrem* and Rimnild in *Horn Childe*. It is shown even more playfully and ambiguously by Bertilak's wife in *Sir Gawain and the Green Knight*, in a complex enmeshing of agency and power involving Morgan le Faye and Bertilak too, not to mention the influence of the Virgin Mary and God laced through the story. Sarah Kay's reading is informed by the work of Marilyn Strathern, whose 1988 book *The Gender of the Gift* is a rich exploration of gift, personhood, gender and agency, based on her fieldwork in Melanesia and also addressing more general questions in feminist theory and anthropological language. Her ideas offer a number of avenues for our reading of Chaucer's work.

Strathern's nuanced writing resists categorization and summary.[27] It is also a critique of Western habits of assuming that concepts like society, individual and gender may be mapped onto other cultures, or that these terms of reference are stable. For that very reason, it would be hazardous to read Chaucer's representation of pagan antiquity directly through Strathern's analysis of relationships in the Highlands region of Papua New Guinea. Instead, I shall outline some key challenges in Strathern's work that I think could inform our reading of Chaucer's own imaginative Anthropology. One example is the observation that acts of Melanesian exchange can be gendered, rather than thinking of inherently gendered persons taking part in exchanges:

> Often gifts subsume persons themselves, especially under patrilineal regimes where women move in marriage from one set of men to another, although this is not the only context in which objects, as they pass from donor to recipient, appear to be categorized as male or female. However, one cannot read such gender ascriptions off in advance, not even when women appear to be the very items which are gifted. It does not follow that 'women' only carry with them a 'female' identity. The basis for classification does not inhere in the objects themselves but in how they are transacted and to what ends. The action is the gendered activity.[28]

Strathern also explores the idea that persons who are exchanged have interests in those exchanges and can also be agents. That is, there is not a clear boundary or binary between exchanger (person) and exchanged (thing). In dialogue with Chris Gregory's work on gift and commodity, she argues:

> 'Gift economy', as a shorthand reference to systems of production and consumption where consumptive production predominates, implies, in Gregory's terminology, that things and people assume the social form of persons. They thus circulate as gifts, for the circulation creates relationships of a specific type, namely a qualitative relationship between the parties to the exchange. This makes them reciprocally dependent upon one another.[29]

Strathern questions where the boundaries of personhood are drawn, talking of partible or 'dividual' persons as opposed to the 'individual' as the entity from which agency and identity flow.[30] In Melanesia, she argues, persons are regarded as being constituted by their relationships, and when a person acts, this is the moment when in fact they are most expressing their being bound into those relationships, rather than their acts being largely an expression of self will and independence from others:

> Women being the 'objects' of exchange relationships are not deprived of such autonomy. Moreover, Hagen men's transformation of themselves into prestige-bearing name-carriers is not ultimately about fulfilling themselves as subjects. Ceremonial exchange works to make them objects in the regard of others. And men are also construed as aspects of women's social identities. In other words, it would be an error to see certain people as always the objects of others' transactions and equally an error to assume their natural, 'free' form is as subjects or agents. One might put it that people do not exist in a permanent state of either subjectivity or objectivity. The agent is a conduit.[31]

Strathern prompts her readers to scrutinize many of their assumptions about gender, power and agency, and while anthropological scholarship has absorbed and now to an extent moved on from the apposition of dividual/individual to describe human selves in (even) more fluid ways, her work is fundamental to that discussion and I shall further explore ideas of dividuality and multiplicity later in the chapter.[32]

Medieval discussions of the self and persons frequently did make gender a key marker of difference and status, but this was a contested field, as *The Canterbury Tales* itself shows. Strathern also draws a contrast between Melanesian concepts of person and relation, and the assumptions of Western society. Those assumptions form a necessary counterweight to her analysis of Melanesian ways of thinking, but are inevitably broadly drawn. Western medieval texts contain plenty of debate themselves about the extent to which persons possess or individually experience identity and agency.[33] Although, then, there are dis-alignments between Strathern's observations and Chaucer's fourteenth-century context, I believe that her observations have resonance for the way that medieval narratives imagine men and women, providing a vocabulary for exploring personhood and agency through or along with constraint, rather than agency as necessarily opposed to constraint. This resonates with my discussion of Auchinleck romances in Chapter 2, where both men and women are constructed as persons through the relationships in which they participate. Last, her work stresses that gift exchange creates relations, and further, that the knowledge carried by or represented by objects in exchange is also relational:

> As I would grasp that perspective, relations only appear as a conse-
> quence of other relations, forms out of other forms. Consuming
> knowledge about one form means making another form appear. This
> requires human effort. People tie the reason for knowing things to
> particular sequences of causes and their effects, for knowledge only
> makes sense if it is consumed by the right person at the right place
> and time. Otherwise it is mere surface phenomena, disembodied
> (unconsumed) things. Information does not exist in itself.[34]

In Melanesian society, she argues, information is bound into the person using it, and its working out in time and through relations. Once again, Strathern's intricately drawn commentary is partly framed to mark differences between contemporary Melanesian and Western understandings. However, the way that her book opens up the question of relations, persons and gender is productive for many fields of thinking, as a way of complicating gendered difference, the experience of knowledge, and assumed structures of power. For reading Chaucer, they likewise provide questions and opportunities.

Returning now to Emily in *The Knight's Tale*, she may be read using some of Strathern's challenges to contemporary Western modes of thinking about self, exchange and gender. Indeed, Emily could be seen as a partible person in the tale. Her identity is constituted by flows and relations, initially as Hyppolita's sister. The next time she is described, it is through the gaze of the narrative voice, overlap-ping with that of Palamon and Arcite. She is here the (fantasized) embodiment of natural beauty and innocence to them, but her actions are also in relation to an obligation: she has come to do homage to May, in language echoing the opening of the whole *Canterbury Tales*: 'The sesoun priketh every gentil herte, / And maketh it out of his slep to sterte, / And seith, "Arys, and do thyn observaunce"' (I.1043–5). We have already seen how Theseus later refers to her in at least three ways in his speech setting up the contest between Palamon and Arcite: as equivalent to him in her lack of obligation; as his dear sister, persuading him to clemency along with Hyppolita; and as the prize for the contest's victor and an embodiment of Fortune itself. Each of these roles is bound up in her relations to others. Each gives her rather different fields of action and agency, real or imagined. In each of them she might be regarded as an 'object', but saying that she is a (female) object traded between men in the tale would present an attenuated version of her roles, her relations and the cross-currents that both source and constrain her agency.

Perhaps the most obvious point at which Emily's agency is presented is when she prays to Diana in her temple. This scene both opens the listener to Emily's participation in the narrative as a protagonist who has voice and will, and it constrains that will, directing it back into a transactional outcome for the story as a whole. Emily's prime request is for the exchanging and trading to stop: 'wel wostow that I / Desire to ben a mayden al my lyf, / Ne nevere wol I be no love ne wyf' (I.2304–6). She also, though, acknowledges the high chance that she cannot herself close the cycle of transaction and thereby stop the narrative: 'Or if my destynee be shapen so / That I shal nedes have oon of hem two, / As sende me hym that moost desireth me' (I.2323–5). Emily's selfhood is woven through with prior debts and relations to others, as Hippolyta's sister, effectively Theseus's ward, as devotee of Diana, and as a romance protagonist who, however much she would prefer to be in a religious narrative of the preservation of chastity and transaction with the next world (something more like the *Life of Christina of Markyate* but with the chaste female Diana as object of devotion), has to align her desires with those of her rank, gender and the romance genre. Although I would stress more than she does that Emily's fortune is to be absorbed into a male-focused resolution whose premise she wants to reject, my reading has common ground with Jill Mann, who sees Emily's 'submission to marriage and child-bearing' (prospectively in this temple scene) as 'a submission to "aventure"; it parallels and re-enacts the knight's readiness to "take his aventure" (I.1186), making male and female experience a mirror for each other'.[35]

By 'showing the working' of alternative desire and accommodating others' interests as part of the make-up of her personhood, then, the narrative allows for those desires to be registered even as they are set aside by more powerful transactions and relations, and so we can see Emily not as totally defined by her gendered position, or by a prospective outcome. In this way I would supplement Dinshaw's comment (quoted above) that Emily's desire 'conveniently adapts itself to the desires of those who trade her'. Her alternative desire is clearly stated, markedly unromantic, and continues to provide a counter-current to the 'approved' narrative of male competition and reward in the tale, despite her later adaptation. In that sense, I see her position as closer to Palamon and Arcite (as suppliants to the gods, having to adapt their desires to other powers and fortunes) than is often allowed for. I also see some of the female desire constrained in the tale re-emerging in a different form in Alison's delight in sexual pleasure and choice in *The Miller's Tale*: still problematic, constrained by social rules and conflicted, still potentially stoking heterosexual male readers' fantasy, but resisting a standard idea of being traded, wedded and then curated as a piece of valuable property or used for her sexual and reproductive capacity.

Palamon's and Arcite's prayers at the temples of Venus and Mars respectively could be read as instances of their male desires and voices being heard by the gods and each accommodated in the story's outcome. However, Palamon and Arcite are themselves bound into relational constraints from the moment that they appear as barely living bodies found in the aftermath of battle. The fact that then they are recognized together by their coats of arms emphasizes the way in which it is wider systems of familial and political connections that go to create their personhood too. Their imprisonment, sight of Emily and lament at the workings of Fortune again tie them into the give and take of forces that they as individuals cannot comprehend or control. Their very identity is blurred by their parallel lives and responses, suggesting Palamon and Arcite as aspects of personhood and psychology, but not as clearly individuated agents.[36] All three young protagonists of *The Knight's Tale* are, then, constituted imaginatively as persons through the relations that flow through their acts and the responses of others to them, and these relations are especially apparent at moments of transaction, as with Palamon and Arcite being prisoners of war; or Emily accompanying her sister the defeated enemy and war bride. Although their rhetoric at times stakes claims to singular desire or agency, the larger contexts of their action are constantly being suggested to make their multiple roles, their partible status, apparent. From this point of view, I would suggest that they are characterized by what we could call multidentity, rather than individual or core identity, and it is a multidentity that can later be repeated with difference in the patterns of other Canterbury tales.[37]

The elaborate construction of the lists and stadium, with vivid ekphrastic descriptions of the three temples at which Palamon, Emily and Arcite pray, might tend to emphasize fixity, suggesting social structure or destiny as settled. However, the very effort of construction, the artifice of the temples and the artistic work that goes to make the painted narratives portraying, for example, Diana's power to save, transform or destroy, itself reminds us of the huge effort that societies make to monumentalize the narratives they live by. Robert Epstein has powerfully read the ekphrastic description of the stadium and its designs as symbolic violence in the sense that Bourdieu describes it: a form of domination that sublimates the distinction between what Bourdieu terms 'sense relations and power relations', and works through the very communication in which it is disguised.[38] The image-filled constructions are, then, a way of Theseus 'demonstrating his control' over the polity by making 'a model of the universe'. In Epstein's reading, the theatre of the lists and the temples 'celebrate temporal power' and link this to divine authority.[39] This is a strong reading of the dynamics of ekphrasis at play in *The Knight's Tale*, but my own instinct is to allow for the doubt or lack of knowledge underlying this effort to be more visible in our reading. For all Theseus's (or other monarchs') attempts to display power and link it to natural structures, I think that Theseus's buildings, and *The Knight's Tale* itself, become dramatic forms of expenditure to represent human creativity in the face of loss. In *The Knight's Tale*, Chaucer represents the Classical past not as a culture wholly confident and in control of its relations with past, present and future, or with the gods, but as a culture whose passing is written into the physical world it inhabits. The narrative outcome of the tale is resolved by Saturn's mediating between Mars and Venus: a mediation itself stemming from their family bonds and narrative entanglements. From the perspective of the pagan humans, this outcome must be accepted as part of the inscrutable chain of causes beyond understanding – a set of exchanges and relations into which human relations are placed, but whose beginnings and ends are not visible or controllable:

> Allas, the pitee that was ther,
> Cracchynge of chekes, rentynge eek of heer.
> 'Why woldestow be deed,' thise wommen crye,

'And haddest gold ynough, and Emelye?'
No man myghte gladen Theseus,
Savynge his olde fader Egeus,
That knew this worldes transmutacioun,
As he hadde seyn it chaunge bothe up and doun,
Joye after wo, and wo after gladnesse,
And shewed hem ensamples and liknesse. (I.2833–42)

Looking back from this vantage point, the elaborately constructed arena, ritualistic fighting and solemn marriage envisaged at the end of the tale could all be seen as a way of humans evading or masking what they perceive as the inscrutability, or worse, randomness, of divine providence.

The effort of expenditure and sacrifice of resources on the contest between Palamon and Arcite (financial, artistic and human) attempts to shore up and contain in socially defined or approved structures the fear of loss that stalks the text, but it cannot of itself guarantee those structures of belief or social relations. In that sense, Theseus's commissioning of the stadium accords with activities that Georges Bataille defines as unproductive expenditure:

> Human activity is not entirely reducible to processes of production and conservation, and consumption must be divided into two distinct parts. The first, reducible part is represented by the use of the minimum necessary for the conservation of life and the continuation of individuals' productive activity in a given society; it is therefore a question simply of the fundamental condition of productive activity. The second part is represented by so-called unproductive expenditures: luxury, mourning, war, cults, the construction of sumptuary monuments, games, spectacles, arts, perverse sexual activity (i.e., deflected from genital finality) – all these represent activities which, at least in primitive circumstances, have no end beyond themselves. Now it is necessary to reserve the use of the word *expenditure* for the designation of these unproductive forms, and not for the designation of all the modes of consumption that serve as a means to the end of production. Even though it is always possible to set the various forms of expenditure in opposition to each other, they constitute a group characterized by the fact that in each case the accent is placed on a *loss* that must be as great as possible in order for that activity to take on its true meaning.[40]

Bataille goes on to give jewellery, sacrifice, competitive games and artistic works as examples of such non-productive expenditure, that gain their meaning, satisfaction and power through loss. Bataille's remarks are part of an attempt to relate Mauss's descriptions of potlatch with Bataille's own belief in the inescapability of excess in the twentieth-century economy. Mauss's interpretation of potlatch has come under heavy scrutiny, and Bataille's version of it is itself partial.[41] Nevertheless, Bataille's perception that expenditure without immediate economic return is crucial to cultural and political acts of definition helps us to see *The Knight's Tale* as itself a monument to loss, whose expenditure generates meaning, and prompts a different kind of return. That return initially comes from the responses of the pilgrims, that 'it was a noble storie / And worthy for to drawen to memorie' (I.3111–12), with an emphasis on the higher ranked listeners ('And namely the gentils everichon' (I.3113)). It also comes from the series of responses and counter-responses that start with the Miller and which develop into the exchange economy of *The Canterbury Tales* as a collection, in which notions of excess, or of debt, power further storytelling and repayment.[42]

Returning to the dynamics of agency and gender in *The Knight's Tale* itself, Theseus, as Egeus had earlier, places human actions in a context of constantly circulating forces of life and death: 'speces of thynges and progressiouns / Shullen enduren by successiouns, / And nat eterne, withouten any lye' (I.3013–15). His reference to the 'Firste Moevere' (I.2987) hints for a medieval audience at an idea of a divine, providential force, but without his being able to grasp at its theological implications, living as he does before Christ. Human relations are envisaged as the continually exchanging flow of fortune, emotion and transformation. The pagan setting aids Chaucer's anthropological fiction, in which figures from another culture voice their explanation of their lived experience and their understanding of social relationships.[43] In turn they illuminate aspects of his own culture, including doubt and fear about human value, which are less easy to acknowledge directly. Chaucer's aim is not to develop the same sort of self-reflective description for which Strathern might strive. His engagement with pagan history is nevertheless complex and ambivalent, and his work is energized by questions about other cultures and beliefs that we might now regard as anthropological ones. In exploring those, he makes an effort to consider how such relations might be organized and how persons bound by and through those relations might also imagine them. Thus at moments when they seem most to speak for themselves, they are expressing their relational status, as when Palamon declares himself a lover and thus bound to Emily's imagined power to give or withhold: 'but I have hir mercy and hir grace ... I nam but deed' (I.1120, 1122). The tale explores such claims to self-definition, but at the same time acknowledges that individuality is something that is always defined in relation to others, and that protagonists' pathways to self-definition or self-awareness are also conduits for others' agency. This is especially the case when the terms of reference under which *The Knight's Tale* explores the conditions of humanity are those of movement, exchange and transposition.

In emphasizing this aspect of the text, I also want to put pressure on how far gender defines the protagonists' experience. Hyppolita has been conquered at the start of the story along with 'al the regne of Femenye' (I.866). Likewise Emily is brought back by Theseus as adjunct property to his victory, and he is able to hand her to the winner of a contest between two young men. And it is Emily's prayer to remain a virgin that is rejected by the gods. It would be ignoring the context both of the Classical setting of the narrative and of Chaucer's own environment to deny the particular constraints on women both fictionally and in his contemporary audience. But Chaucer's restless narrative imagination allows us to see both that all humans, like gifts and stories, are part of an extended set of relational bonds and obligations that begin before birth and stretch beyond death; and that the disproportionate constraints on some categories of persons are created not only in relation to their gender but also to politics, rank and fortune. The protagonists' multidentities are not limited to the powers or constraints governed by gender, and at times, it is in the interaction between gender and other qualities or constraints that the narrative gains force. Strathern's analysis of Melanesian gendered exchange has been influential beyond its field in reminding readers of the stories that gender relies on, its constantly constructed elements, people's ability to map qualities associated with one gender onto otherly-gendered bodies, and its cultural and relational meanings. *The Knight's Tale*, in the face of its status as epic-romance, suggests that these gendered constructions are part of the relational and exchange-oriented narrative from which romances gain part of their power, and allow for further debate, retelling and adjustment in the text's repayments, retellings and later quittings.[44]

Troilus and Criseyde

Another major poem that Chaucer worked on in the 1380s, with its own series of exchanges with *The Knight's Tale*, as well as with source and intertextual material in Boccaccio, Boethius and elsewhere, is *Troilus and Criseyde*. Like the Knight, the narrating voice of the poem is figured as taking part in an exchange with his audience. But that voice speaks from the position of servant, compiler and reporter, opening up a plethora of relationships and possible exchanges between the text(s) and its audience(s). The narrative movement of the story is also conceived as a continual series of movements and exchanges:

> The thynges fellen, as they don of werre,
> Bitwixen hem of Troie and Grekes ofte;
> For som day boughten they of Troie it derre,
> And eft the Grekes founden nothing softe
> The folk of Troie; and thus Fortune on lofte
> And under eft gan hem to whielen bothe
> Aftir hir course, ay whil that thei were wrothe. (I.134–40)

This is a beautifully sly passage, in which the greatest epic story in the Western tradition is summarized in a single stanza with the studied uninvolvement of a Frenchman describing a cricket match. It also diverts the audience's gaze from war as the prime subject of the poem, although that will keep soaking back into the structure, action and language of *Troilus and Criseyde* at many levels. Additionally, this stanza's very syntax is bound up in the give and take of the conflict, with its patterning of 'Troie ... Grekes ... Troie ... Grekes ... Troie', the metaphor of 'buying it dear', and the image of Fortune's wheel, whose destabilizing yet inescapable action works its way through the enjambments of the final three lines of the stanza. Though the figure of Fortune does not make many overt appearances in *Troilus and Criseyde*, there is a looming sense throughout the poem of the cycles of pain and joy that are her prerogative.[45] This includes the opening stanza of the poem, whose verbal patterning is echoed in the one quoted above:

> The double sorwe of Troilus to tellen,
> That was the kyng Priamus sone of Troye,
> In lovynge, how his aventures fellen
> Fro wo to wele, and after out of joie,
> My purpos is, er that I parte fro ye.
> Thesiphone, thow help me for t'endite
> Thise woful vers, that wepen as I write. (I.1–7)

Calkas and Criseyde, the Greeks and Trojans, *wo* and *wele*, and the working of *aventure(s)* move in cycles from the very start of the poem, while the siege itself was provoked when Paris snatched away Helen. This illegal trafficking in women precipitates the whole hostile set of exchanges of violence, revenge and destruction. An inverse gift relationship of revenge is thus powerfully embedded in the poem's workings. When Troilus scorns all lovers as 'veray fooles, nyce and blynde' (I.202), the God of Love 'gan loken rowe / Right for despit, and shop for to ben wroken' (I.206–7). Troilus's glance is then imagined to be like an arrow, piercing a crowded temple and striking home in Criseyde (I.271–3).

Within the first movements of the poem, then, layers of debt, repayment, exchange and revenge are being laid down, at different levels of distance, detail and chronology. Criseyde's appearance in the temple includes a pointed description of the power of her glance and appearance too, embedding her 'look' in him in return for his piercing 'eye':

> To Troilus right wonder wel with alle
> Gan for to like hire mevynge and hire chere,
> Which somdel deignous was, for she let falle
> Hire look a lite aside in swich manere,
> Ascaunces, 'What, may I nat stonden here?'
> And after that hir lokynge gan she lighte,
> That nevere thoughte hym seen so good a syghte.
>
> And of hire look in him ther gan to quyken
> So gret desire and such affeccioun,
> That in his herte botme gan to stiken
> Of hir his fixe and depe impressioun. (I.288–98)

Here we can see both the effect of a gift for Troilus – the sudden and apparently unmotivated arrival of Criseyde and love in his experience, like a romance foundling whose parentage is as yet unrevealed to the other protagonists – and the operations of the God of Love for the poem's audience, acting from despite and anger. The double workings of this action (gift and revenge; unmotivated and motivated) help to construct the set of narrative ironies integral to the poem, placing knowledge about process or agency at the centre of the protagonists' and the audience's experience.

Here I shall focus on some points in the narrative where that set of ironies or questions is at work, and where gift and exchange are especially prominent as its vehicles. Following my discussion of *The Knight's Tale* alongside Marilyn Strathern's work on gender and gift, I shall argue that Chaucer once again focuses on agency not as something that only works alongside power (agency as another word for having power in society or the narrative), but on agency working through and with constraint, and that gender can only be imprecisely mapped onto that investigation. It is no surprise to say that Criseyde's agency is limited because she is a woman, a widow, the daughter of a traitor, and reliant on patronage, and that the whole structure of Trojan politics is set to repeatedly claim women's lives and actions as collateral damage to epic conflict. This is a persuasive and powerful reading of the story. It also has certain limits, and I see Chaucer at his most acutely probing of agency and exchange at the moments when it is most constrained. I also believe that his exploration of these questions is tied to but not bound by gender, and that Criseyde is the figure whose agential process is most intimately seen as a test case for the audience themselves to absorb, both within and outside the fictional ambit of the text.

In an article using gift theory to read the characterization of the main protagonists, Jeff Massey has described Troilus as a participant in a gift economy, whose love is defined by absolutes and a lack of calculation – traits which, for Massey, help to feminize him – whereas Criseyde is more aligned with commodity exchange and the calculation of benefit: 'Criseyde acts as a masculinized woman operating within a commodity economy.'[46] For Massey, Pandarus becomes a translator between these poles, turning the language and expectations of one into those of another to bring them together. Massey's analysis relies heavily on a reading of Derrida's problematics of the motivated gift, but this carries its own problems, which I discussed in Chapter 1. It is plausible to see Troilus experiencing love as a sudden gift, and as we saw above, the temple scene in Book I seems to confirm the contrast between his understanding of events as sudden and unmotivated, and the audience's knowledge of the process that has set this circle in motion. However, I do not think this necessarily removes him from calculation in a 'feminized' moment of the gift, nor do I read Criseyde's position as a commodified and therefore masculinized one in the way that Massey does.

Rather than viewing Pandarus's literal role as go-between as also representing a linguistic or theoretical position between the two lovers, I read Pandarus as a figure whose reckoning of benefit and short-term fixing sits closer to commodity exchange, and the lovers as constituted through a number of forces related to exchange, power and gender, which are not fixed or on a binary scale. Criseyde initially expresses shock at the bald way in which Pandarus approaches matters in Book II:

> 'Now em,' quod she, 'what wolde ye devise?
> What is youre reed I sholde don of this?'
> 'That is wel seyd,' quod he. 'Certein, best is
> That ye hym love ayeyn for his lovynge,
> As love for love is skilful guerdonynge.
>
> 'Thenk ek how elde wasteth every houre
> In ech of yow a partie of beautee;
> And therefore er that age the devoure,
> Go love; for old, ther wol no wight of the.
> Lat this proverbe a loore unto yow be:
> To late ywar, quod Beaute, when it paste;
> And Elde daunteth Daunger at the laste.' (II.388–99)

Love for love is reasonable repayment, Pandarus argues, before describing age as a remorseless process eating away at her value. He has already raised – in the very act of denying it – the troubling suggestion that he is a kind of pimp ('baude' (II.353)) by bringing Criseyde together with Troilus. Pandarus's analysis of Criseyde's value – as a consumer good whose 'use by' date is fast approaching – shocks her; how can he present the exchange so starkly, without any mention of inalienable or intangible qualities like her virtue or reputation?:

> 'What, is this al the joye and al the feste?
> Is this youre reed? Is this my blisful cas?
> Is this the verray mede of youre byheeste?
> Is al this paynted proces seyd – allas! –
> Right for this fyn? O lady myn, Pallas!
> Thow in this dredful cas for me purveye,
> For so astoned am I that I deye.' (II.421–7)

The vocabulary of commodification ('mede'; 'proces'; 'fyn') is taken up by Criseyde, but to throw it back bitterly at Pandarus. Her call to Pallas compresses many of the emotions of Emily's prayer to that other virgin goddess Diana, making this stanza a *Knight's Tale* episode in miniature. On this evidence, Criseyde's position is not a masculinized commodifier in the story. Neither is she 'simply' a misogynist stereotype of the fickle woman: gender interacts with other expectations to help shape her and Troilus's status(es) and identities.[47] There are ways in which the episode would be inconceivable if its genders were reversed – it is, after all, presented as a female-marked dilemma. This might militate against my claim that Chaucer allows women's decisions and agency to be available models for those processes across and between genders – that is, to see gender as part of a set of relational constraints or actions; and that Chaucer's work resists the notion that gendered narratives are always already set to act out particular structures, however likely those structures are to be remade in each telling. Pandarus's claim that he too will die if she does not yield is a common male manipulative trope; Criseyde's similar feeling, expressed at the end of the stanzas quoted above, passes with much less comment or notice, partly because it is not tied into traditions of male-voiced love complaint. But as in Strathern's description of Hagen people as dividual, and agential when acting through the obligations and constraints on them, *Troilus and Criseyde* allows such multiple and sometimes conflicting qualities to inform the complex operation of the poem. Criseyde's constrained choices, and her movement towards loving Troilus, should not be diminished as acts of will or agency simply because they operate under constraint, nor thought of as 'masculine' when they involve pragmatic calculation. While the poem accommodates contradictory impulses, the operation of layered personhood through acts of giving and receiving makes a difference to how we read it. I shall discuss some of these passages now, and later I shall connect the relations I have described in them to the work of narrating and reading the text, which is shared between protagonists, tellers and audiences.

Shortly after the scene in Book II where Criseyde pushes back against Pandarus's framing of love as a matter of fair repayment before the value of Criseyde's body declines, Chaucer portrays the process of Criseyde's thinking and emotional movement in a famous sequence scarcely precedented in Western literature. Criseyde happens to see Troilus ride past her window, an object of desire and admiration; she debates in her mind the pros and cons of loving him; she listens to a song about love; and she hears a nightingale sing as she goes to sleep, later to dream of an eagle exchanging her heart for his, but without pain or fear. The journey that we as audience take with her is partly prompted by her unguarded comment to herself 'Who yaf me drynke?' (II.651). The phrase evokes a love-potion, perhaps the one in the Tristan story,[48] and a gift that is both life-changing and potentially fatal. One way of reading it is 'externally', from our position outside the narrative, aware of the intertextual web supporting the poem, and ready to mark this as part of a set of predetermined narrative moments leading to the sort of tragic love story typified by the Tristan and Iseut legend. The overall shape of this narrative is already available to us, not only from the well-known history of Troy, but from the opening stanzas of the poem. Despite this, though, the poem's exploration of Criseyde's processes of thinking and feeling – an experiment in speculation on personhood and emotion – shift our perspective and alter the momentum of the plot. The mysterious, intoxicating gift that Criseyde imagines has the effect both of suggesting her connection to the romance tradition of love as gift, love as potion; but also prompting a series of other perspectives on her willingness to love Troilus. These include the narrating voice's concern that the envious in the audience will 'jangle thus: / "This was a sodeyn love"' (II.666–7), and the denial of this imagined critique: 'For I sey nought that she so sodeynly / Yaf hym hir love, but that she gan enclyne / To like him first' (II.673–5). Here, the image of love as being given a potion, and of love itself as a gift, are placed before the reader, but also added to a much larger set of constraints and questions, with the rhetorics, generic connections and implications for personhood that they imply. In numerous medieval romances, the moment of loving between protagonists is both a 'sodeyn love' and a love overtly set alongside practical, familial and financial structures. This does not of itself turn love from a gift into a commodity, but in *Troilus and Criseyde* Chaucer is strikingly keen to show his audience not only the details of those intervening obligations and relations to which Troilus and Criseyde are bound, but also the indefinable moments of decision or of emotional traction that bring love into a narrative like this.[49] In my reading of this passage, the effect of such narrative dilation and overdetermination is to suspend simple relationships between cause and effect, receiving and giving. They create a sense that these various external and internal images, actions, experiences, are working together through Criseyde, prompting us not to deny her agency, but to think of it as interacting with the flow of relations, obligations and experiences that literally on the page make up her self.

The imaginative centre of this idea of love as reciprocal giving is in Book III: 'It semed hire he wiste what she thoughte / Withouten word, so that it was no nede / To bidde hym ought to doon, or ought forbeede' (III.465–7). Soon after this description of love as barrier-free exchange comes the build-up to Criseyde's visiting Pandarus's house, and the series of circumstances and actions that bring the lovers to bed together. Once again, the scene is over-determined by various contributing forces, including Pandarus's subterfuge and Troilus's complicity. These scenes are core to the understanding of Criseyde's position in the narrative as a person exercising agency and/or as someone trapped by gendered constraints and male power. Both Chaucer's interest in continuing exchange under all narrative circumstances, and Strathern's lessons on avoiding assumptions about agency, power and gender, can help us to navigate these passages of the poem, seeing that Troilus and Criseyde present a confluence of emotions, obligations and relations, and that neither can be characterized as consistently wielding or lacking power across this passage of the poem. Troilus is part of a plan to pressurize Criseyde, but he is also a desperate lover, and an experiment in romance rhetoric that pushes towards comedy. Criseyde is cornered by the men's plan and confused about which response to give to

Troilus, but yet powerfully demonstrates desire and selfhood at these moments: a partible selfhood whose conflict and constraint is exactly its recognizable quality.

Something of the complexity of agency and constraint built up in *Troilus and Criseyde* emerges in two acts of giving that Criseyde seeks to take part in during this passage of the poem. She listens to Pandarus claim that Troilus is at death's door because of a rumour that she loves Horaste, and reaches for an object that would in many romance narratives provide the perfect token of steadfast love:

> Quod tho Criseyde, 'Wol ye don o thyng
> And ye therwith shal stynte al his disese?
> Have heere, and bereth hym this blewe ryng,
> For ther is nothyng myghte hym bettre plese,
> Save I myself, ne more hys herte apese;
> And sey my deere herte that his sorwe
> Is causeles; that shal be sene to-morwe.'
>
> 'A ryng?' quod he, 'Ye haselwodes shaken!
> Ye, nece myn, that ryng moste han a stoon
> That myghte dede men alyve maken;
> And swich a ryng trowe I that ye have non.
> Discrecioun out of youre hed is gon;
> That fele I now,' quod he, 'and that is routhe.
> O tyme ilost, wel maistow corsen slouthe!' (III.883–96)

This exchange represents the cross-currents both of gender and genre at work in the poem. Criseyde's attempt to calm Troilus's fears through the gift of a ring echoes some other romances that I have discussed (*Horn Childe*; *Tristrem*). It fits the template of true lovers linked by a personal gift despite physical absence or proper caution. Pandarus's reply treats the idea like a hackneyed trope from an Auchinleck-style romance.[50] Instead, his characteristically urgent rhetoric – 'sped up and goal-centered' as Paul Strohm acutely characterizes it – literally has no time for substitutes for the physical exchange he is trying to expedite.[51]

Shortly afterwards, in the scenes leading up to Troilus and Criseyde going to bed, the layering of agency and exchange is evident at many levels, from physical postures to metaphors of power or release. These can be read as representing Criseyde being pressurized or tricked into sex. In particular, the striking simile of the lark caught in the sparrowhawk's foot 'What myghte or may the sely larke seye, / Whan that the sperhauk hath it in his foot?' (III.1191–2) seems to imagine Criseyde as prey to male power (the sudden clasping of her in his arms by Troilus, and/or Pandarus's larger plan), and Chaucer also describes her as shaking 'as an aspes leef' (III.1200). Nevertheless, Criseyde still claims a form of agency and interpretation, reclaiming the moment of her 'yielding' as having already happened: 'Criseyde answerde thus anon, / "Ne hadde I er now, my swete herte deere, / Ben yolde, ywis, I were now nought heere!"' (III.1210–11).[52] Layering the dark allusions and intertexts that remind us of the overall system of obligations in which the narrative operates, then, are cross-threads of agency and exchange that complicate the pattern, frustrating any search for a unified sense of identity in the protagonists. This shifting quality can easily be turned against Criseyde, using a misogynist tradition of woman as changeable, but *Troilus and Criseyde* shows that for all the tropes of fortitude or passion that characterize Troilus as a male romance hero and lover, he too is constituted by a confluence of emotional and generic streams. His processes of thought and feeling immediately before taking Criseyde in his arms range from fear lest she realize that his jealousy is manufactured, to sorrow in case she is angry about his (invented) reasons; placing himself 'al in youre grace' as an act of obeisance but with undertones of desire; and then relief and 'blisse' at Criseyde's forgiveness and her answering request for forgiveness.

This subtly changing pattern of relations makes Troilus and Criseyde's exchanges always poised amongst the interests and obligations of the fictional narrative; the generic and textual field; and the perspectives of intra- and extra-diegetic audiences. It is both/ and rather than either/or, and this series of exchanges, in which the protagonists work through their constraints within a larger set of obligations and expectations, opens up some of the complexity with which Chaucer shapes the scene and invites his audience(s) to bring their own experience of love and sex to the narrative. The exchange of love quickly moves to the reception, curation and modification of the story from *auctor* to the current text and thence to the audience: 'And if that ich, at Loves reverence, / Have any word in eched for the beste, / Doth therwithal right as yourselven leste' (III.1328–30). The story then returns to the exchange of lovers' gifts:

> Soone after this they spake of sondry thynges,
> As fel to purpos of this aventure,
> And pleyinge entrechaungeden hire rynges,
> Of whiche I kan nought tellen no scripture;
> But wel I woot, a broche, gold and asure,
> In which a ruby set was like an herte,
> Criseyde hym yaf, and stak it on his sherte. (III.1366–72)

The motif of the gift of rings returns, but this time embedded in the lovers' relationship, mutual, and uncalculating. They seem to be posy rings with a motto or inscription ('scripture') that the narrator does not have access to, preserving some element of intimacy and unknowable selfhood between them, some moment of time suspended by joy.[53] This playful exchange rubs away some of the tarnish of cynicism that Pandarus brought to Criseyde's earlier attempt to give Troilus a ring, and reflects the possibility of uncalculating generosity in their relationship. The more public gift of the brooch, however, is set to return later, offering a narrative payback but confirming a breach of the lovers' bonds.

It is in Book IV that the manoeuvres of the war impinge more directly on the lovers. As with Chaucer's own ransoming, and Palamon and Arcite's capture in *The Knight's Tale*, a number of Trojan figures have been captured by the Greeks, and a truce is arranged to negotiate 'Hire prisoners to chaungen, meste and leste / And for the surplus yeven sommes grete' (IV.59–60). Calkas asks the Greeks to request his daughter Criseyde, and in a debate in the Trojan parliament, Hector links her status as a woman and her potential treatment as a kind of hostage or prisoner of war:

> 'Syres, she nys no prisonere,' he seyde;
> 'I not on yow who that this charge leyde,
> But, on my part, ye may eftsone hem telle,
> We usen here no wommen for to selle.' (IV.179–82)

This differs from the kind of classic traffic in women debated in Anthropology, in the sense that Criseyde's going to the Greeks is designed to settle an exchange, rather than foster an ongoing alliance; Hector's main objection is Criseyde should not be regarded like a prisoner, among other examples of (male) prisoner exchange. However, the shadow of woman-trafficking (Helen's seizure by Paris which precipitates the war) falls across this moment too, especially for anyone with foreknowledge of Criseyde's later relationship with Diomede. Here too, then, Criseyde's identity is multiplied – an exchanged hostage and a potentially trafficked bride – and her later failure to return is mingled with the future treachery of Antenor. The categories of gift, prisoner, commodity cannot at this point in the narrative be kept apart.

The disruption of what we could call Troilus and Criseyde's moment of the gift in Book III, and Criseyde's role in the prisoner swap, bring on other kinds of exchanges that are poor substitutes for the lovers' previous relationship, such as their letters. Early in Book V, Pandarus tries to alleviate Troilus's despair at being parted even temporarily from Criseyde by noting that both men and women often have to see their beloved married off to someone else, in an exchange governed by larger forces: 'How don this folk that seen hire loves wedded / By frendes might, as it bitit ful ofte / And sen hem in hire spouses bed ybedded?' (V.344–6). This attempt at consolation is, however, darkly proleptic. Meanwhile, Criseyde's relationship to Diomede is distilled into the transfer of gifts to her new lover – a rupture in the *hau* of obligation and relationship between her and Troilus that finds the narrative voice moving close to condemnation:

> And after this the storie telleth us
> That she hym yaf the faire baye stede
> The which he ones wan of Troilus;
> And ek a broche – and that was litel nede –
> That Troilus was, she yaf this Diomede.
> And ek, the bet from sorwe hym to releve,
> She made hym were a pencel of hire sleve. (V.1037–43)

Troilus sees a brooch – probably this one – on a 'cote-armure' (a tunic decorated with heraldic designs) torn from Diomede in battle, and reversing the generous spirit of the original gift, it becomes the sign of her infidelity:

> And whan this Troilus
> It saugh, he gan to taken of it hede,
> Avysyng of the lengthe and of the brede,

> And al the werk; but as he gan byholde,
> Ful sodeynly his herte gan to colde,
>
> As he that on the coler fond withinne
> A broch that he Criseyde yaf that morwe
> That she from Troie moste nedes twynne,
> In remembraunce of hym and of his sorwe.
> And she hym leyde ayeyn hire feith to borwe
> To kepe it ay! But now ful wel he wiste,
> His lady nas no lenger on to triste. (V.1655–66)

This corrupted gift is the tangible evidence that finally makes Troilus see the reality of their split. Chaucer pays close attention to Troilus's process of examination and discovery, reading the heraldic tunic like a narrative in itself, just as we are reading the poem ('taken …. hede'; 'Avysyng'; 'werk'; 'byholde'). In this tragic performance of a romance theme, the lover's gift becomes evidence of a broken promise – an unhappy speech act – and its own trajectory from Troilus to Criseyde and then Diomede focuses Troilus's despair at Criseyde's broken word.

Generations of readers of *Troilus and Criseyde* have wrestled with the question of Criseyde's 'character', whether criticizing her as fickle; describing her as pressurized by Pandarus and Troilus, circumstances or misogynist history; or some combination of these. Either end of this spectrum tends to rely on an idea of Criseyde as a unified entity, whose decisions are either driven by her desires, or constrained by others. I find readings more convincing that treat both Troilus and Criseyde (amongst the other protagonists) as figures made up of an interplay of desire, genre and history (personal, literary), constraint and agency. Though as readers or listeners we partly suspend disbelief in them as 'characters' in order to generate the emotional engagement that Chaucer's narrative demands, these powerful drivers of our connection (our *pite*) do not necessarily make each figure into a stable identity whose actions or thoughts may always be judged against that mark.

A.C. Spearing's discussion of 'the narrator' in *Troilus and Criseyde* is apposite here. Spearing shows how critics have adopted the idea of a personality called 'the narrator' (sometimes 'Narrator') as a convenient way to explain incoherence or difficulty in the text; to cite irony at moments when the poem does not accord with that critic's understanding of Chaucer; and potentially to avoid deeper questioning of the techniques of evoking subjectivity that Chaucer develops. Spearing comments that like other romances, *Troilus and Criseyde* sometimes uses a warmly personal narrative style; it also:

> incorporates more complex effects such as skillful summary and ironic exaggeration, but these too in their different ways create a diffused subjectivization quite opposite to any notion of 'pure narrative', if that implies objective neutrality. Yet on the other hand this pervasive and flexible personalizing does not necessarily imply impersonation of a narrator.[54]

Spearing's notion of 'diffused subjectivization' is informed by narrative theory, but I think it bears kinship with Strathern's models of person-hood, where persons can comprise the set of transactions and obligations in which they take part. Discussing Criseyde, Spearing reads her as Chaucer's nuanced version of numerous textual traditions: 'if we consider all the factors involved in the characters' inner as well as outer lives, we shall see that she was something far more complex and interesting than the stereotype of female deception in the versions his audience could have known'.[55] The exchange of bodies and of gifts in *Troilus and Criseyde* helps us to see that complexity without retreating from ethical engagement. The gift of a brooch; the exchange of a person between warring groups: these acts bring person, object and ethical entanglement close together. As Strathern comments of gift economies: 'things and people assume the social form of persons. They thus circulate as gifts, for the circula-tion creates relationships of a specific type, namely a qualitative relationship between the parties to the exchange. This makes them reciprocally dependent upon one another.'[56] Both Spearing's warnings against an ironized narrator and consistent characters in medieval fiction, and Strathern's description of people and things creating relations between parties as they are exchanged, remind us that the protagonists of romance are only fictionally separated from the objects that they handle, give and interpret. They too can be read as signs, exchanged as pledges, and can accrue meanings – sometimes variant or contradictory ones – in their path through the narrative. As narrative subjects, Troilus and Criseyde do not become smoothly coherent personalities, and readings of the poem that claim to find coherence or resolve these questions usually have to sweep a lot under the carpet. They are more plausibly read as themselves pathways of obligation and connection who travel through the narrative. As thinking subjects, they additionally question their own coherence, trajectory and status, as for example in Troilus's Boethian speech at the temple in Book IV, or Criseyde's anticipation of her later reputation in Book V, lines 1051–71. Strathern acknowledges the challenge for anthropologists in seeking access to how other peoples represent society to themselves, since they do not tend to do this in ways that a Western scholar might want to analyse: 'It would be like requiring characters linked by an author's plot to entertain the idea of that plot.'[57] Brilliantly and disturbingly, Chaucer portrays both Troilus and Criseyde moving towards that sense of their own emplottedness, especially in Troilus's idea that 'Whan I the proces have in my memorie / How thow [i.e. Cupid] me has wereyed on every syde, / Men myght a book make of it, lik a storie' (V.583–5). This reminds us not only that in reading *Troilus and Criseyde* we become alert to the fictional composites that its major protagonists represent, but also how we as its audience – figured sometimes as interested lovers, sometimes detached editors – are called upon to engage personally and historically with the material that those composites make in our minds.

Both *The Knight's Tale* and *Troilus and Criseyde* centrally deal with the exchange of people at time of war. Both texts may be read through the notion of the traffic in women, while the discrepancies between the choices available to (some) men and women are integral to their plots. However, reading them primarily through the exchange of women is limited, because both move beyond a paradigm of men being secure or fully agential persons and women being traded objects. Instead, flows of obligation and relationship pass through the protagonists and the text: they are, indeed, the stuff that the protagonists are made of. In *The Knight's Tale*, this results in a narrative whose romance ending is the explicit outcome of the gods' traffic in favours, otherwise inscrutable to humans, and accommodated but not controlled by any human agency. *Troilus and Criseyde* is also characterized by the accommodation of loss, set at a point in history where that loss cannot be revalued and restored through Christian faith inside the narrative fiction, despite the gestures towards this in the poem's final movement. Rather, it is the complexity of

Criseyde's inner life, her competing impulses, thoughts and constraints, that rivals Troilus's *wele* and *wo* as the major narrative and ethical engagement of the poem. Both she and Troilus are objects in the exchanges of Fortune and the gods; both are made up of textual, gendered and psychological threads that create their selves and actions; and the poem's readers make the text complete(r) but also more plural by their own interactions with the narrative. The work of literature being undertaken here is one characterized by plural selves with numerous sources and uncertain destinations,[58] and the knowledge that reading generates is locatable more in the exchange of or between persons than in lasting claims to knowledge or belief. In the next chapter, I shall examine a particular kind of exchange between people in Chaucer's work – specifically the exchange of promises and speech acts in *The Franklin's Tale* and *The Manciple's Tale*, asking how verbal exchange creates and modifies ties of obligation or gift, and how performative language presses at boundaries between language, things and persons.

Notes

1 The genre of both texts is complex and debatable. James Simpson ('Derek Brewer's romance') for example, building on positions taken by Derek Brewer, has argued that 'romance' should not be used for tragic texts such as *Troilus*. I see genres as more inherently mingled and open than this: see Nicholas Perkins and Alison Wiggins, *The Romance of the Middle Ages* (Oxford: Bodleian Library, 2012), ch. 1. Medieval names for and understanding of romance are discussed in Paul Strohm, '*Storie, spelle, geste, romaunce, tragedie*: generic distinctions in the Middle English Troy narratives', *Speculum* 46 (1971), 348–59; K.S. Whetter, *Understanding Genre and Medieval Romance* (Aldershot: Ashgate, 2008); Melissa Furrow, *Expectations of Romance: The Reception of a Genre in Medieval England* (Cambridge: Brewer, 2009). Here, the term 'romance treatments' tries to capture the blending or overlaying of romance elements with Classical epic or tragic traditions.

2 See *Chaucer Life-Records*, ed. Martin M. Crow and Clair C. Olson (Oxford: Clarendon Press, 1966), e.g. pp. 123–4.

3 Ibid., pp. 13–22. See now Marion Turner, *Chaucer: A European Life* (Princeton, NJ: Princeton University Press, 2019), pp. 43–69.

4 Crow and Olson (eds), *Life-Records*, pp. 26–8.

5 Ibid., p. 23; Turner, *Chaucer*, pp. 83–4.

6 Crow and Olson (eds), *Life-Records*, pp. 49–53; Derek Pearsall, *The Life of Geoffrey Chaucer: A Critical Biography* (Oxford: Blackwell, 1992), pp. 105–6. Stury (d. 1395) was one of the so-called Lollard knights, and knew Chaucer well. See Charles Kightly, 'Lollard knights', *ODNB*, https://doi.org/10.1093/ref:odnb/50540, accessed 3 March 2019; Pearsall, *Geoffrey Chaucer*, pp. 181–5.

7 Rémy Ambühl, *Prisoners of War in the Hundred Years War: Ransom Culture in the Late Middle Ages* (Cambridge: Cambridge University Press, 2013), p. 10.

8 See Chris Given-Wilson and Françoise Bériac, 'Edward III's prisoners of war: the Battle of Poitiers and its context', *English Historical Review* 116 (2001), pp. 802–33.

9 Froissart, *Chronicles*, trans. Geoffrey Brereton, rev. edn (London: Penguin, 1978), p. 143; see *Chroniques de Jean Froissart 5: 1356–1360*, ed. Siméon Luce, Société de l'Histoire de France (Paris: Renouard, 1874), pp. 60–1 (ch. 395).

10 On the relationship between medieval war, the paradoxes of chivalry, and their representation in literature, see e.g. Joanna Bellis and Laura Slater (eds), *Representing War and Violence* (Woodbridge: Boydell Press, 2016); Richard Kaeuper, 'The societal role of chivalry in romance: northwestern Europe', in Krueger (ed.), *Medieval Romance*, pp. 97–114; Corinne Saunders, 'Medieval warfare', in Kate McLoughlin (ed.), *The Cambridge Companion to War Writing* (Cambridge: Cambridge University Press, 2009), pp. 83–97; Richard Kaeuper, *Chivalry and Violence in Medieval Europe* (Oxford: Oxford University Press, 1999).

11 Ambühl, *Prisoners of War*, p. 3; cf. the much-debated claims about how fantasy and reality interacted in late-medieval chivalric culture in Johan Huizinga, *The Waning of the Middle Ages: A Study of the Forms of Life, Thought and Art in France and the Netherlands in the XIVth and XVth Centuries*, trans. F. Hopman (London: Edward Arnold, 1924). Ambühl's version of this interaction is more pragmatic and less morally freighted than Huizinga's, acknowledging that imaginative versions of chivalric practice are part of a feedback system with 'real' war; I suggest that literary versions are also part of this system.

12 Geoffrey Chaucer, *The Knight's Tale*, in *The Riverside Chaucer*, ed. Larry D. Benson (Oxford: Oxford University Press, 1988), I.1009–32. All quotations of Chaucer's works are from this edition.

13 For the treatment of the dead after medieval battles, including scavenging and burial practices, see Anne Curry and Glenn Foard, 'Where are the dead of medieval battles? A preliminary survey', *Journal of Conflict Archaeology* 11 (2016), 61–77.

14 See e.g. Turner, *Chaucer*, pp. 83–9 (at p. 87), noting that Chaucer changes details from Boccaccio to emphasize Theseus's implacability.

15 This line has been read in different ways by editors. I take it as 'owes them as much thanks as I do'; it makes less sense for Theseus to say that Emily owes them as much thanks as she owes him.

16 Carolyn Dinshaw, *Chaucer's Sexual Poetics* (Madison: University of Wisconsin Press, 1989), p. 106.

17 Gayle Rubin, 'The traffic in women: notes on the "political economy" of sex', in Rayna R. Reiter (ed.), *Toward an Anthropology of Women* (New York: Monthly Review Press, 1975), pp. 157–201.

18 Claude Lévi-Strauss, *The Elementary Structures of Kinship*, trans. James Harle Bell et al. (London: Eyre & Spottiswoode, 1969), p. 115.

19 Rubin, 'Traffic in women', p. 207.

20 See Neil Cartlidge, *Medieval Marriage: Literary Approaches, 1100–1300* (Woodbridge: Brewer, 1997); Isabel Davis et al. (eds), *Love, Marriage, and Family Ties in the Later Middle Ages* (Turnhout: Brepols, 2003).

21 Rubin, 'Traffic in women', p. 201.

22 Rubin's focus on the oppression of women as objects in exchange has itself been challenged, e.g. in Karen Newman, 'Directing traffic: subjects, objects, and the politics of exchange', *differences* 2.2 (Summer 1990), 41–54. See also Carol Parrish Jamison, 'Traffic of women in Germanic literature: the role of the peace pledge in marital exchanges', *Women in German Yearbook* 20 (2004), 13–36, who discusses Rubin and Newman. My readings of Chaucer are in some ways distant from Jamison's of early medieval Germanic texts, but share an interest in the scope for action available to women, notwithstanding their agency being constrained.

23 Chaucer precisely dramatizes this kind of response, for example in the Host's (textually problematic) reaction to *The Clerk's Tale*, IV.1212a.

24 McDonald, 'A polemical introduction', p. 15; Derek Attridge, *The Work of Literature* (Oxford: Oxford University Press, 2017), e.g. pp. 24–37, in which Attridge debates these relationships. See also Jacques Derrida, 'Structure, sign and play in the discourse of the human sciences', in his *Writing and Difference*, trans. Alan Bass (London: Routledge & Kegan Paul, 1978), pp. 278–93, for the notion of play in a system as a way to de-monumentalize human discourse, including literary texts.

25 Sarah Kay, 'The lady and the gift', published in Italian as 'Le donne nella società feudale: la dama e il dono', in Piero Boitani et al. (eds), *Lo spazio letterario del Medioevo. 2: Il Medioevo volgare, vol. 4: L'attualizzazione del testo* (Rome: Salerno, 2004), pp. 545–72, at p. 553. I am very grateful to Sarah Kay for discussing these issues with me when we were both based at Girton College, Cambridge, and for

sharing her essay before publication. I quote from her English text, with page references to the published version. See also Kay, *'Chansons de geste'*, chs 1, 7.

26 Kay, 'Le donne', pp. 557, 558: 'non è solo un bene, ma anche una persona, capace quindi di donare a sua volta'.

27 Alongside *Gender of the Gift*, see also e.g. *Before and After Gender: Sexual Mythologies of Everyday Life* (Chicago, IL: Hau Books, 2016), first written in the 1970s; 'Partners and consumers: making relations visible', in Schrift (ed.), *The Logic of the Gift*, pp. 292–311; and 'Gifts money cannot buy', *Social Anthropology*, 20 (2012), 397–410. I am very grateful to Marilyn Strathern for valuable conversations about gifts between 2001 and 2004 at Girton College, and for lending me crucial reading material at an early stage in my thinking.

28 Strathern, *Gender of the Gift*, p. xi.

29 Ibid., p. 145.

30 Ibid., p. 13: 'Far from being regarded as unique entities, Melanesian persons are as dividually as they are individually conceived. They contain a generalized sociality within. Indeed, persons are frequently constructed as the plural and composite site of the relationships that produced them.' Without the word 'Melanesian', this description could be an acute reading of, say, *Piers Plowman* or many medieval romances.

31 Strathern, *Gender of the Gift*, p. 331. See also Strathern, *Before and After Gender*, p. 233: 'Constructing a contrast between an object, who is, and a person, who does, belongs to a rather specific tradition of thought.'

32 David Lipset comments that Strathern's book offers for feminist theory 'a radical critique of western frameworks of gender': 'What makes a man? Reading *Naven* and *The Gender of the Gift*, 2004', *Anthropological Theory* 8 (2008), 219–32. On subsequent developments in thinking about dividuality and subjectivity, see Karl Smith, 'From dividual and individual selves to porous subjects', *Australian Journal of Anthropology* 23 (2012), 50–64.

33 E.g. in the divided, sometimes competing entities making up the self in versions of faculty psychology, and the tradition of psychomachia. Mary Douglas, reviewing *Gender of the Gift*, suggests that Strathern characterizes Western ideas as more unified and unthinking than they really are; instead, Douglas finds affinities between the gift economies discussed by Strathern and ideas in Augustine and medieval political philosophy (Mary Douglas, 'A gentle deconstruction', review of Strathern, *The Gender of the Gift*, *London Review of Books* (1989), 17–18, at p. 18).

34 Strathern, *Gender of the Gift*, p. 344.

35 Jill Mann, *Feminizing Chaucer* (Woodbridge: Brewer, 2002), p. 142.
36 See V.A. Kolve, *Chaucer and the Imagery of Narrative: The First Five Canterbury Tales* (Stanford, CA: Stanford University Press, 1984), pp. 86–103, on the protagonists' position in relation to larger powers and constraints; and Jill Mann, 'Chance and destiny in *Troilus and Criseyde* and the *Knight's Tale*', in Piero Boitani and Jill Mann (eds), *The Cambridge Companion to Chaucer*, rev. edn (Cambridge: Cambridge University Press, 2003), pp. 93–111, at p. 108, for the Boethian perspective on the forces governing their choices and fate.
37 See Helen Cooper, 'The girl with two lovers: four Canterbury tales', in P.L. Heyworth (ed.), *Medieval Studies for J.A.W. Bennett* (Oxford: Clarendon Press, 1981), pp. 65–79 for variations on the story pattern of *The Knight's Tale*. As I suggested of Auchinleck texts, the *Canterbury Tales* might also be read as a system of overall prestations in which each text stands in relation to or exchange with others.
38 Robert Epstein, '"With many a floryn he the hewes boghte": ekphrasis and symbolic violence in the *Knight's Tale*', *Philological Quarterly* 85 (2006), 49–68, at p. 63 (citing Bourdieu, *Outline of a Theory of Practice*, p. 237).
39 Ibid., pp. 59, 60.
40 Georges Bataille, 'The notion of expenditure', in Bataille, *Visions of Excess: Selected Writings, 1927–1939*, ed./trans. Allan Stoekl (Manchester: Manchester University Press, 1985), pp. 116–29, at p. 118.
41 See Godelier, *Enigma of the Gift*, pp. 76–8; 154–7; and Alan D. Schrift, 'Introduction: why gift?', in Schrift (ed.), *Logic of the Gift*, pp. 4–6.
42 See Epstein, *Chaucer's Gifts*; and above, note 37.
43 On Chaucer's engagement with pagan narratives and culture, see A.J. Minnis, *Chaucer and Pagan Antiquity* (Cambridge: Brewer, 1982); and in particular on *Troilus and Criseyde* and *The Knight's Tale*, Lee Patterson, *Chaucer and the Subject of History* (London: Routledge, 1991), chs 2, 3. Patterson's exploration of Chaucer's deep engagement with historical process in *Troilus and Criseyde*, awareness of 'the failure of history, and of historical understanding', and the poem's 'refus[al] to offer any clear message' (p. 163) resonate with my reading of the multiple and competing obligations shaping the protagonists in both poems.
44 On responses to *The Knight's Tale*, see e.g. Scott-Morgan Straker, 'Deference and difference: Lydgate, Chaucer, and the *Siege of Thebes*', *Review of English Studies* 52 (2001), 1–21; Helen Barr, *Transporting Chaucer* (Manchester: Manchester University Press, 2014), ch. 5.
45 See Mann, 'Chance and destiny', and cf. Ch. 5's discussion of Lydgate's *Troy Book*, below. References to Fortune having a direct hand in events include the passage quoted above (I.138); her description as 'executrice

of wierdes' (III.617); the start of Book IV: 'But al to litel, weylaway the whyle, / Lasteth swich joie, ythonked be Fortune' (IV.1–2); and the description (added by Chaucer to Boccaccio's narrative) of Fortune being devolved the 'permutacioun / Of thynges' by Jove, and pulling out Troy's feathers (V.1541–7) – a striking image leading to the description of Hector's death. Fortune also appears in the protagonists' speeches as something between an actant and a metaphor.

46 Jeff Massey, '"The double bind of Troilus to tellen"': the time of the gift in Chaucer's *Troilus and Criseyde*', *Chaucer Review* 38 (2003), 16–35, quoting p. 26.

47 The complexity of responses to Criseyde and her agency is nowhere more apparent than in Robert Henryson's *Testament of Cresseid*, in which she is able to dictate her will and bequeath items to those that come after her, but she must also absorb physical affliction and moral responsibility. Troilus (and the audience) hears of her 'greit infirmitie, / Hir legacie and lamentacioun' (596–7) as an inextricably linked act/ event. I quote the *Testament* from *The Makars: The Poems of Henryson, Dunbar and Douglas*, ed. J.A. Tasioulas (Edinburgh: Canongate, 1999).

48 Cf. the discussion of *Tristrem* above, Ch. 2.

49 See Mann, *Feminizing Chaucer*, pp. 18–25, who describes the 'linked sequence of shifts and adjustments so small that they pass almost unnoticed at the time' (p. 19) in Criseyde's movement from rejecting Pandarus's initial intimations of Troilus's love, to her fully and joyously accepting Troilus. For Mann, this process parallels that of her turn away from Troilus, and the comparability of the two movements 'rescues the betrayal from an antifeminist reading' (p. 19). My purpose here is not to 'rescue' a reading of Criseyde or deny the antifeminist forces available to readers of her later role in the narrative (including Criseyde herself), but to show that both she and Troilus operate both under constraint and with agency.

50 See Cooper, *English Romance in Time*, ch. 3, on 'magic that doesn't work' and the need to deal with '[t]he collapse of wonder at the marvellous' (p. 138).

51 Paul Strohm, '*Troilus and Criseyde* as temporal archive', in Strohm, *Theory and the Premodern Text* (Minneapolis: University of Minnesota Press, 2000), pp. 80–96, at p. 82.

52 See Mann, *Feminizing Chaucer*, p. 86, who also perceptively draws out the 'minute and constant movement that constitutes the "process" of love' (p. 84) in the poem.

53 This matches the dynamic of this section of Book III, which is then turned to fear of loss and the awareness of time's inexorability from the crowing of the cock the next dawn (III.1415 onwards) and Troilus's

aubade. See above, p. 90, for posy rings as both conventional and highly personal objects expressing lovers' relations in the late medieval period.

54 Spearing, *Textual Subjectivity*, p. 94.
55 Ibid., p. 97.
56 Strathern, *Gender of the Gift*, p. 145, drawing on Chris Gregory.
57 Ibid., p. 9.
58 See Attridge, *Work of Literature*, esp. pp. 24–38.

4

Exchanging words and deeds: *The Franklin's Tale* and *The Manciple's Tale*

The Franklin's Tale ends with one of the best-known questions in medieval English literature:

> Lordynges, this question, thanne, wol I aske now,
> Which was the mooste fre, as thynketh yow?
> Now telleth me, er that ye ferther wende.
> I can namoore; my tale is at an ende. (V.1621–4)

This question is the culmination of a series of exchanges and releases going on throughout the narrative, and now opens up the tale into a *demande* to its audience, requiring them to become the tellers of this particular account: reckoning and reporting on its losses and gains. In that sense the tale's speaker both signals the closing of the story ('my tale is at an ende') and the story's material becoming a founding donation for those retellings ('Now telleth me'). The gift of narrative, in the sense of the Breton *lai* that has just been told by the Franklin, is set to initiate further stories on the part of the pilgrims, whether by discussing and debating this one, or telling their own. Since the text of *The Canterbury Tales* is incomplete here, we do not have Chaucer's performance of that debate as we have, for instance, with the pilgrims' responses to *The Knight's Tale* or (problematically) *The Clerk's Tale*, and the textual openness of *The Canterbury Tales* has facilitated further exchanges and counter-gifts by other readers, ranging from editorial and scribal decisions, to glossing, to whole further poems such as *The Tale of Beryn* and Lydgate's *Siege of Thebes*.[1] The Franklin's performance is also, of course, part of a storytelling competition, and his question about who was most 'fre' encourages the listeners to rank the protagonists. However, as with many medieval *demandes d'amour*, the answer is not straightforward, or even the same each time the story is heard; for these reasons, I view the end of the tale as opening rather than limiting the possibilities for future exchanges and stories.[2]

A further feature of this passage leads to the kinds of exchange (in and beyond the text) that I shall explore in this chapter. The final line of *The Franklin's Tale* contains two statements, which on the face of it look straightforward: 'I'm not able [to say] any more; my story is finished.' But each of these might be examined further. What does it mean for a fictional narrating voice to say 'I can't say any more'? It raises the question of the speaker's subjectivity at the same time as limiting it, reminding the listener or reader that this 'I' is voiced and/or inscribed, and its knowledge or ability is in important ways a product of the text of which it is a part. The second statement is also more than a simple description, seeming to become also a declaration that brings about what it is describing ('I hereby declare that my tale is at an end'), winking at its audience by placing 'ende' as the final word of the tale, or *envoi*.

The sort of statement that brings about a new state of affairs has, at least since the work of J.L. Austin, been known as a performative utterance or a speech act.[3] In this chapter I shall discuss other speech acts in *The Franklin's Tale* and *The Manciple's Tale* as part of their economies of exchange – between protagonists, from words to deeds or things, and out to their audience(s). That the exchange of speech, especially promising, can act as a form of gift exchange (with its performances, relational bonds, hierarchies, cruelties and generosities) is an idea embedded in many contemporary cultures. In this book I have argued that writing and telling can be understood as a form of gift-giving, and here I focus on ways that speaking acts as a gift in these tales. Perfomative utterances, in particular promises, bind the speaker (giver) and hearer (receiver) together in a relationship. They set up an expectation of further exchange, or consequential action. By doing things with words, they also deepen the relationship that Chaucer illuminates between word, action and physical things, including bodies. They create a surplus that gives momentum to the narrative. Performative language in these tales also presses the question of intention, too, for words once uttered are subject to others' interpretation and answering action. Finally, I suggest that the speech acts of these tales are synecdochal of the patterns of telling and quitting in the larger web of *The Canterbury Tales*.

The Franklin's Tale

Gary Lineker kept his promise and introduced the opening *Match of the Day* of the new season in his underpants.

Former England captain Lineker, 55, pledged to 'do the first MOTD of next season in just my undies' if former club Leicester won the Premier League.

'When I tweeted that silly bet back in December, I categorically knew there was zero chance of Leicester winning the league. Zero chance. It happened but was magical, it was great.'[4]

The narrative of *The Franklin's Tale* hinges around the promise that Dorigen (married to a long-absent and yearned-for husband Arveragus) makes to her importunate suitor Aurelius. She says that her final answer is a no. But then she says that she will give herself to him if he removes from the coast the rocks that threaten her husband's safe return:

'But now, Aurelie, I knowe youre entente,
By thilke God that yaf me soule and lyf,
Ne shal I nevere been untrewe wyf
In word ne werk, as fer as I have wit:
I wol been his to whom that I am knyt.
Taak this for fynal answere as of me.'
But after that in pley thus seyde she:
'Aurelie,' quod she, 'by heighe God above,
Yet wolde I graunte yow to been youre love,
Syn I yow se so pitously complayne.
Looke what day that endelong Britayne
Ye remoeve alle the rokkes, stoon by stoon
That they ne lette ship ne boot to goon –
I seye, whan ye han maad the coost so clene
Of rokkes that ther nys no stoon ysene,
Thanne wol I love yow best of any man;
Have heer my trouthe, in al that evere I kan.'
'Is ther noon oother grace in yow?' quod he.
'No, by that Lord,' quod she, 'that maked me!
For wel I woot that it shal never bityde.' (V.982–1001)

Given especially the generic context of the Breton *lai*, this rash promise is bound to lead to trouble, just as the Fairy King's promise to Orfeo enabled the harpist to secure Heurodis' release. Besides, Dorigen's promise is not simply hers to give.[5] She is bound by prior oaths that she made in marrying Arveragus:

> 'Sire, I wol be youre humble trewe wyf –
> Have heer my trouthe – til that myn herte breste.' (V.758–9)

> And therefore hath this wise, worthy knyght,
> To live in ese, suffrance hire bihight,
> And she to hym ful wisly gan to swere
> That nevere sholde ther be defaute in here. (V.787–90)

Moreover, Dorigen reinforces these oaths and obligations immediately before the promise to Aurelius, saying that she will never be an 'untrewe wyf'. The confirming formula 'In word ne werk, as fer as I have wit', is reminiscent of, for example, the exchange of oaths and gifts between Amis and Amiloun discussed in Chapter 2. Her conditional gift of her love to Aurelius is marked by being transacted 'in pley', believing that 'it shal never bityde' (as Gary Lineker would say: 'zero chance').

I will return to arguments about gifts and generosity in the tale, but first I would like to touch on the nature of Dorigen's promises as speech acts.[6] From an Austinian perspective, Dorigen's promise to Aurelius that she would grant him her love if he removes the rocks cannot work felicitously because she does not 'in fact have those thoughts and feelings'.[7] This does not mean that her promise to Aurelius is not a promise, but that if made in bad faith, it will not function happily.[8] Chaucer of course brilliantly characterizes the ethical ambivalence involved in Dorigen asking in play for something that might enable her husband to return, at the risk of devastating their marriage, but this does not mean that Dorigen seriously intends or wishes the outcome, since 'it shal never bityde'.[9] Her promise, complicated as it is by competing emotions, is all the more fraught with that slippage between desire and temporality: 'the promise is symptomatic of the noncoincidence of desire with the present'.[10]

While, then, we are told that Dorigen's promise is made in play, she cannot wholly control the power of its performative operation. Austin's investigation into the status and functioning of performatives pushes his audience not to take for granted the relationship between intention and speech (act). He accepts that performatives often go along with non-verbal acts, such as the giving of a gift; this possibility is accounted for in Austin's rules A.1 to B.2. He then picks up another possible objection – '[s]urely the words must be spoken "seriously" and so as to be taken "seriously"?', especially in the case of promises. He replies that this is 'though vague, true enough in general ... I must not be joking, for example, nor writing a poem'. Nevertheless, Austin wants us to moderate the role that intention plays, even when in general it is aligned with speech act; he warns against the trap of believing that speech acts are merely descriptive of inner feeling, and instead assigns more power to the utterance in its performative context.[11]

Austin seems to exclude non-serious utterances and poetry from functioning fully as performatives, and earlier he also sets these kinds of utterances aside:

> [A]s utterances, our performatives are *also* heir to certain other kinds of ill which infect *all* utterances. And these likewise, though again they might be brought into a more general account, we are deliberately at present excluding. I mean, for example, the following: a performative utterance will, for example, be *in a peculiar way* hollow or void if said by an actor on the stage, or if introduced in a poem, or spoken in soliloquy.[12]

Accounts of the literary performative have subsequently found productive ground in these very kinds of texts and utterances – though it should be noted that he only temporarily sets them aside: 'they might be brought into a more general account'.[13] Here, though, I want to return to Austin's careful weighing of outward and inward, and his proposal that instead of a sacramental model of intention and utterance, we should assess the power of the spoken word to do things in relation to but not merely subordinate to intention. This insight is relevant to Chaucer's reflections on the relations between language, act and intention. Just as gift-giving draws the participating persons into a relationship with one another that reaches out beyond the immediate moment of exchange, binds them into larger structures of relation, and may have consequences not antici-pated by either party, so Chaucerian speech acts provoke responses that reach beyond language and have visceral consequences. The relationship between speech, intention and act can vary or be at debate in different tales; style and genre also play an important part in how these elements of meaning and telling unfold. In *The Friar's Tale*, for example (as Jill Mann has discussed in a fine reading), intention becomes central to the question of whether an utterance has tangible effects. The devil's understanding of the speakers' intentions enables him to distinguish between a throwaway curse (the carter swearing at his horses) and a fully-intended gift (the old woman consigning her dish and the Summoner to the Devil).[14] In *The Franklin's Tale*, the *lai* environment and its romance-related understandings of word, *trawthe* and action, allow for a different relationship between speech, intention and act. Indeed, one of the most striking things about *The Franklin's Tale* is the way in which its narrative is shaped around significant verbal 'events', and how words are described as having specific and potentially physical effects in the world.

One example is the 'proces' by which Dorigen's friends eventually assuage her grief at Arveragus's departure:

> They prechen hire, they telle hire nyght and day
> That causelees she sleeth hirself, allas!
> And every confort possible in this cas
> They doon to hire with al hire bisynesse.
> Al for to make hire leve hire hevynesse.
> By proces, as ye knowen everichoon,
> Men may so longe graven in a stoon
> Til some figure therinne emprented be.
> So longe han they conforted hire til she
> Receyved hath, by hope and by resoun,
> The emprentyng of hire consolacioun,
> Thurgh which hir grete sorwe gan aswage. (V.824–35)

The friends' consolation is described as words ('prechen'; 'telle'), then 'confort' which they 'doon to' her – literally place or apply onto her, like a medicinal salve.[15] This moves to the analogy of carving a 'figure' on stone. The friends figuratively carve a text on Dorigen's body, or (re)form her as an image on stone. That imagery evokes conceptions of the physiology of language and memory, as Mary Carruthers in particular has explored.[16] Here, persuasive language is a material process that shapes the character of its auditor, making her the medium on which their telling and preaching carves a pattern.[17]

Despite their playfulness, Dorigen's words are granted power to enact physical consequences. Aurelius's claim that 'with a word ye may me sleen or save' (V.975) may seem like lovers' hyperbole, but after Dorigen has set her 'impossible' condition of removing the rocks, Aurelius feels that 'he may nat fro his deeth asterte' (V.1022). He prays to Phebus Apollo – prayer being a speech act that here tries to initiate another from the god. Aurelius translates the physical power that Phebus possesses in relation to the moon ('Youre blisful suster, Lucina the sheene' (V.1045)) to a plea that he 'Preye hire she go no faster cours than ye' (V.1066) so that the sea flows right over the rocks. Dorigen's promise, albeit not serious ('I must not be joking, nor writing a poem') has prompted a dynamic set of effects and obligations, whose energies will return to her eventually, like the *hau* of the gift that we discussed in Chapter 1. In this process, the power of words to do things has a central place. After Aurelius's prayer, he soon retires to bed 'Dispeyred in this torment and this thought ... Chese he, for me, wheither he wol lyve or dye' (V.1084, 1086). That is, Aurelius's apparently clichéd love-language, the direct connection he makes between language and physical effect, is part of the narrative process of the tale too, through its generic affinities as a Breton *lai*, and because of the gravitational force of the central speech act around which the tale orbits. In the world of this tale, words do things. In Shoshana Felman's exploration of the Don Juan legend via J.L. Austin, she brilliantly characterizes the central protagonist by saying that '[L]anguage, for Don Juan, is performative and not informative; it is a field of enjoyment, not of knowledge.'[18] While providing important kinds of knowledge as well as pleasure, I suggest that The Franklin's Tale, too, operates using language as a 'field of enjoyment' that has the capacity to shape its own fictional reality. As sceptical readers we might choose to resist this force, but The Franklin's Tale creates a distinctive atmosphere with its own mix of elements governing relations between word, thing and action.[19]

   These relationships are signalled even before the tale begins, when the Franklin praises the Squire's eloquence, and claims that he would rather that his own son had such 'discrecioun' than have 'twenty pound worth lond' (V.685, 683). While this exchange is open to a range of readings, the worth and power of language as both evidence of 'gentillesse' (V.694) and as constituting value in itself continues to be reflected on throughout the tale. It appears in the Franklin's *captatio benevolentiae*, aligning the colours of his rhetoric to those of nature (V.723–8) in a move that both raises and troubles the power of language to stand for or reproduce things in the world.[20] It also comes in the passage describing the clerk of Orleans and his ability to summon visions of forests, deer, hunting, and Aurelius dancing with Dorigen, marvellous illusions all made 'in his studie, ther as his bookes be' (V.1207). These illusions are created for us as listeners, too, by the tale's teller, as the apparent slippage of referent suggests in V.1203–4: 'he clapte his hands two, / And farewel! Al oure revel was ago'. They are a sign of the clerk's power of suggestion and figure in the tale as another form of poetic rhetoric, ratified by his book learning. Later, his 'magic' in making the rocks seem to vanish is equally down to calculation and the speaker's rhetoric. As Helen Cooper notes, 'nobody within the tale so much as goes to look';[21] this might seem like a trivial comment on the narrative, but in fact it reveals something more important, which is that the story is driven by and about the power of speech acts to create realities, to place people in debt, and to make and discharge obligations, and that in this *lai* environment, such speech acts are the focus of our attention: we suspend our scepticism to explore the consequences of speech that has performative, physical valence, and of a promise that, in this world, entails the obligations of a gift.

A promise may be an act, then, but it also implies or invites an answering act or acts; it is a spending of verbal resources that demands a payback later in the narrative, and thus shares characteristics with the gift, though the more specific its provisions and timescale, the more akin to a commodity exchange or debt agreement it becomes: 'A debt is just the perversion of a promise.'[22] Dorigen's promise invokes two physical actions: the disappearance of the rocks, and the sexual enjoyment of her by Aurelius, and *The Franklin's Tale* involves a number of other transformations and translations between words, the body, money and intangible ideas of value. We have already noted the verbal outlay that the tale makes in describing the clerk's persuasive fictions in Orleans, and the astrological details with which he aligns Aurelius's desires with the planetary positions. Once Aurelius has told Dorigen that he has removed the rocks and demands that she repay him with her 'grace' (V.1325), her impending submission to Aurelius weighs on Dorigen's mind but also on the linguistic expenditure of the poem, for instance in her elaborate catalogue of women who chose death rather than be raped or be unfaithful. The examples pile up comically, but are at odds with the drive towards generically comic resolution. They shadow the tale with a dark history of women's suffering, but at the same time invite impatience at Dorigen's prolixity. When we return to her present dilemma, though, and Dorigen admits all to Arveragus, her words have powerful verbal and physical consequences on him too:

> 'Ye, wyf,' quod he, 'lat slepen that is stille.
> It may be wel, paraventure, yet to day.
> Ye shul youre trouthe holden, by my fay!
> For God so wisly have mercy upon me,
> I hadde wel levere ystiked for to be
> For verray love which that I to yow have,
> But if ye sholde youre trouthe kepe and save. (V.1472–8)

'I would much rather be stabbed [or, pierced through; stabbed to death] for the true love that I have for you, than that you do not keep and preserve your *trouthe'*. Arveragus's 'ystiked' imaginatively takes into his body the consequences of Dorigen's speech act (with a dark, lurking analogy between his being pierced and her submitting to sex with Aurelius), and by doing so, attempts to figure this potential breach in her bodily integrity as in fact a way of protecting her *trouthe*. Dorigen's *trouthe* is treated by Arveragus as a kind of inalienable possession that must not be tarnished by being traded, despite the consequent effects of her submitting to Aurelius.

The tale precisely focuses on this clash of incompatible promises which must be repaid, and how their claims might be valued. Arveragus cannot fully acknowledge the implications of Dorigen's going to Aurelius, but the physical effects on him of the thought of her upholding her performative again emerge in the next few lines:

> 'Trouthe is the hyeste thyng that man may kepe' –
> But with that word he brast anon to wepe,
> And seyde, 'I yow forbede, up peyne of deeth,
> That nevere, whil thee lasteth lyf ne breeth,
> To no wight telle thou of this aventure'. (V.1479–83)

Trouthe – which in this case consists of matching word and action – is both a non-negotiable commitment in itself (*trouthe* must be kept, like a promise), and exacts a toll on the body, a breaching of bodily integrity: prospectively in the threat of adulterous sex; actually here in the act of bursting out in tears, remembering that Dorigen had earlier promised to be a 'humble trewe wif ... til that myn herte breste' (V.758–9). A tale that is sometimes read as somewhat distant and displaced from the physical or tangible world actually places bodily recompense at the centre of its narrative. However, that breaching or bursting is immediately displaced by another performative, 'I yow forbede', voicing Arveragus's fear that speaking about an act can destroy what doing the act might not – in this case, their reputation. As listeners, we are potentially collaborating in that breach and re-enacting the tale's own crisis of *trouthe*.[23]

The Franklin's Tale, then, traces a path from a point of congruity between speech, act, body, intention and value, and where exchanges of and between these things work effectively, through a moment of 'play' that disrupts this congruity, to a point where those categories and exchanges are in conflict, and what each is worth is set against its potential damage to the others. The subsequent explanations and 'releasing' performatives are ways of re-establishing a workable exchange between them, while also refusing an exact reckoning of value that would set clear limits around the generosity of the participants. When Aurelius meets Dorigen in the street and she tells him that she is on the way to the garden, their appointed place of assignation, 'My trouthe for to holde – allas, allas!' (V.1513), her words, and her report of another performative – the fact that Arveragus told her to keep her *trouthe* – are powerful enough to provoke a change in Aurelius's emotional state and his stance in the exchange:

> 'Aurelius gan wondren on this cas,
> And in his herte hadde greet compassioun
> Of hire and of hire lamentacioun,
> And of Arveragus, the worthy knyght,
> That bad hire holden al that she had hight,
> So looth hym was his wyf sholde breke hir trouthe;
> And in his herte he caughte of this greet routhe.' (V.1514–20)

The rhymes of 'compassioun / lamentacioun' and 'trouthe / routhe' underline the close relationship between word, deed and thought that, the tale suggests, enables generosity to heal conflict.

Aurelius's subsequent speech act releasing Dorigen from her promise is not, as J.L. Austin warned us, merely a description of his inner thoughts. It is aligned with them, but its formality and legal vocabulary represents (at the risk of edging into comedy) the value of what he is forgoing. Its embedded set of gestures recreate closely in the audience's mind the physical acts of giving and releasing that it both describes and performs, and its rhetorical framework also issues in other performatives, warning women to 'be war', and forming a judgement on Aurelius's speech/act as 'a gentil dede':

> 'I yow relesse, madame, into youre hond
> Quyt every serement and every bond
> That ye han maad to me as heerbiforn,
> Sith thilke tyme which that ye were born.
> My trouthe I plighte, I shal yow never repreve
> Of no biheste, and heere I take my leve,
> As of the treweste and the beste wyf
> That evere yet I knew in al my lyf.
> But every wyf be war of hire biheeste!
> On Dorigen remembreth, atte leeste.
> Thus kan a squier doon a gentil dede
> As wel as kan a knyght, withouten drede.' (V.1533–44)[24]

When Aurelius retells the story to the clerk of Orleans, his words (that is, his speech act releasing Dorigen, and implicitly, his retelling of the story) act as payment of his debt, and allow the clerk to claim that he too can perform a 'gentil dede' (V.1611):

> 'Sire, I releesse thee thy thousand pound,
> As thou right now were cropen out of the ground,
> Ne nevere er now ne haddest knowen me.
> For, sire, I wol nat taken a peny of thee
> For al my craft, ne noght for my travaille.
> Thou hast ypayed wel for my vitaille.
> It is ynogh, and farewel, have good day!'
> And took his hors, and forth he goth his way. (V.1613–20)[25]

In these final exchanges, the releasing or quitting of debts and obligations might seem to bring the tale not under the sign of the gift, but of commodity exchange, since neither Aurelius and Dorigen nor Aurelius and the clerk of Orleans are imagined to have an ongoing relationship. In that sense, are the speech acts and promises

more like offers of payment than the building up of generous relationships, and does the edifice of generosity become a film-set frontage
that scarcely hides commodification, particularly of Dorigen?
This is one of the approaches taken by a number of readers of
The Franklin's Tale. In these readings, the tale becomes, in Britton
J. Harwood's words, part of 'a competition among non-gifts that
fills the end of the fragment'. Taking up Derrida's apparent querying
of the very notion of the gift, Harwood wants to limit generosity
in the tale; the gifts are 'not gifts at all, since reasons for them can
be given'. He likewise critiques the actions of Arveragus as a 'tragic
knight *manqué*', a failure because in being concerned for his status
and reputation as well as Dorigen's *trawthe* 'he leaves us uncertain
whether "trouthe" is indeed "the hyeste thing that man may keep"'.[26]
Likewise, Kyle Mahowald focuses on the supposed impossibility of
the true gift to downgrade or replace generosity with economic
calculation in the tale: 'More extensive analysis of *The Franklin's
Tale* reveals that Chaucer sees economic exchange pervading even
the most seemingly legitimate generosity.'[27] However, as I discussed
in Chapter 1, Derrida's account both underplays the flexibility of
Mauss's own understanding of gifts as part of a broader system,
and itself allows for the possibility of an opening of the circle of
giving to re-energize the gift's power.[28] Gifts come in many shapes
and sizes, and under the constraints of many relationships. They
can reproduce and foster discord, hatred and inequity. They can be
integral to competition as well as to collaboration. Motivations for
giving can be varied, ambivalent and yet not disable the gift from
exerting power or shifting the parameters of those relationships. As
with speech acts, intention is also not the sole arbiter of the operation
of a gift. This is one reason why I find Harwood's speculations on
the protagonists' motivations and intentions unconvincing. Equally,
the setting of *The Canterbury Tales* at the intersection of devotional
practice, social interchange and economic competition does not
exclude the possibility that gifts can create value, or can reshape
relationships, and so I would not follow Mahowald in his claim
that economic exchange 'pervad[es]' and (therefore) undermines
apparent generosity.

Recently, Robert Epstein has on the contrary made a convincing
case for allowing the 'possibility of generosity' in *The Franklin's
Tale*. Reviewing anti-gift or sceptical readings of the tale, which

range from D.W. Robertson to Harwood and Mahowald, Epstein wryly notes that 'when exegetical and Derridean readings converge, it may be time to re-evaluate our hermeneutic assumptions'. Instead of disallowing generosity, Epstein argues that 'the central conflict in the *Franklin's Tale* is not between or among sets of values, but rather between modes of determining value', and that protagonists who start out as committed to ideals become 'locked in positions of contractual obligation and monetary debt'.[29] Epstein's reading draws on the work of David Graeber and neo-Maussian scholars who seek to dislodge an unhelpful binary between the supposed self-interest of the market and the (imagined, but unrealistic) complete altruism of the gift; they instead want to find a place for the gift as a productive and flexible site for social relations.[30] My reading of the tale is cognate with Epstein's, in that he wishes to 'recognize the agency in the characters' concluding choices in the tale, and the validity of their generosity'.[31] He sees Aurelius as recognizing a superfluity both in Dorigen's suffering and in Arveragus's shame, and he turns to the language of *gentillesse* to resolve the impasse. I see Epstein's approach as complementary to this chapter's focus on the performative's power to unmake and remake relationships, and to induce physical effects on its speakers and audiences. The act of telling by Dorigen, and the physical power of the emotional charge that accompanies her speech, unlocks Aurelius's generous response, the basis of which is not described as calculating (there is no suggestion at this moment that he will be forgiven his debt to the clerk); it is not a taking back but an opening out.[32] This does not erase the conflicts of gender, honour or power embedded in the tale, nor the shading of class competition between men that is part of the denouement. It does not simply offer a bland idealism, but it does suggest how powerful acts of generosity can be to unlock situations and relationships that seem intractably blocked.[33]

At the end of *The Franklin's Tale*, then, we are left with more than we started with: as with the gift of telling that helped energize *The Romance of Horn* and prompt answering acts both of material giving and retelling, here the telling of a story is seen not only to cancel an obligation but to provide a surplus that seeds further responses and retellings. Dorigen's moment of excess and 'pley', itself akin to a gift, leads to a whole series of narrative and ethical repayments, including the way in which matching emotion and language in retelling (Dorigen to Arveragus; Dorigen to Aurelius; Aurelius to the clerk; and all of them and the narrating voice out to the tale's wider audience) has outcomes beyond a simple reckoning of value or calculation of benefit (her 'lamentacioun' unlocking his 'compassioun'). This added value flows over beyond the tale into the debate that its final lines invite. The tale's generic affiliation with *lai* encourages this reading of the narrative as one where conflict may both be initiated by a speech act (in this case, a rash promise) but is also healed by reciprocal generosity in language or body. Chaucer's retelling of the story allows for the power of the promise as gift to be felt both as destructive, pressingly physical, and also potentially generative of forgiveness, and of retelling. In the next part of the chapter, I shall discuss *The Manciple's Tale*, whose story pattern of an unfaithful wife bears some outward similarity to *The Franklin's Tale* but whose generic and linguistic environment turns away from the generosity of speech acts to focus instead on the dangers and losses of matching word and deed.

The Manciple's Tale

This story appeared in *The Times* newspaper on 17 January 2006, and describes an event that had recently taken place in a flat in Headingley, Leeds:

> When Chris Taylor's best friend repeatedly mentioned the name Gary, his suspicions were aroused. He didn't know a Gary.
>
> And, when the best friend made slurpy kissing noises every time he heard the name Gary on television, Chris wondered if Ziggy [the parrot] was trying to tell him something ... The penny dropped when, one romantic evening, as Mr Taylor cuddled his girlfriend Suzy Collins on the sofa, Ziggy blurted out: 'I love you, Gary'.
>
> What gave the game away was that Ziggy spoke the fatal phrases in Ms Collins' voice. Even by the standards of African Grey parrots, Ziggy is a mimic and a half [who could exactly imitate Chris's friends, sing and dance to David Bowie's 'Let's Dance', and convincingly impersonate the doorbell, microwave and alarm clock.] [F]rom his cage in the corner, he had heard every bill and coo of a secret love affair.[34]

In the light of *The Manciple's Tale*, it is a relief that Chris Taylor did not kill Suzy Collins, nor turn Ziggy the parrot black, though he did have to part with him because 'it was torture hearing him repeat that name over and over again'. 'It really broke my heart to let Ziggy go', Mr Taylor is quoted as saying (Ms Collins understandably had a different attitude: 'I couldn't stand Ziggy, and it looks now the feeling was mutual'). This modern exemplary tale does, however, underline the visceral or material effect of words spoken or repeated in particular circumstances. The event of Suzy's declaring her illicit love for Gary has turned into a statement of evidence about her infidelity, whose meaning in this new context is sealed by its mimicking of her vocal signature: 'Ziggy spoke the fatal phrases in Ms Collins' voice.'

In my reading of *The Franklin's Tale* I suggested that some of its speech acts operated similarly to gifts, in establishing relationships and provoking further acts and exchanges. Even the final speech acts of release, though closing or rebalancing those relationships, were prompted by affective rhetoric and themselves sparked future description and debate. In *The Manciple's Tale*, there is a telling investigation of the power of speech acts and the exchange between words, body and actions, but the tale's environment, far from exploring the (generically) comic rebalancing of obligations, instead is one of threat, loss, and retreat into silence. This darker set of relations, in which generosity and forgiveness are replaced by lust and anger, provides a powerful counterbalance to *The Franklin's Tale*.

After Dorigen's playful but fateful promise to Aurelius, the woebegone lover prays to the sun-god, Phebus Apollo, pleading for help: 'Do this miracle, or do myn herte breste' (V.1056). Later, an old, pale Phebus, 'hewed lyk laton' (V.1245) – dulled into an alloy – presides over the tale's December-time denouement. Phebus's potential to intervene in the natural world is again alluded to at the start of *The Manciple's Tale*, where the god's singing, we are told, far surpasses that of Amphion, who, according to Classical myth, built a city with his song:

> Certes the kyng of Thebes, Amphioun,
> That with his syngyng walled that citee,
> Koude nevere syngen half so wel as hee. (IX.116–18)

This allusion to a mythical speech act with such huge, generative power in the material world provides a gauge against which to measure the destructive language in the rest of the tale, and its eventual retreat to self-preserving silence. While Amphion walled a city with his song, the tale's speaker reminds us later that:

> God of his endelees goodnesse
> Walled a tonge with teeth and lippes eke,
> For man sholde hym avyse what he speeke. (IX.322–4)

The defences of this body (politic) are turned against a threat from within.[35] In this final section of the tale, speaking is repeatedly imagined through its organ, the tongue, eliding verbal and physical, at that dangerous border of the body, the mouth:

> Right as a swerd forkutteth and forkerveth
> An arm a-two, my deere sone, right so
> A tongue kutteth freendshipe al a-two. (IX.340–2)

This tradition of the violent, excessive tongue, and the word as dangerous weapon, has a trajectory through penitential traditions against idle speech and the sins of the mouth which re-emerges in *The Parson's Tale*.[36] We could see similarities in this powerful imagery with what Shoshana Felman, writing on the interdependence of word and body in the Don Juan legend, describes as the 'scandal' of the performative:

> The act, an enigmatic and problematic production of the speaking body, destroys from its inception the metaphysical dichotomy between the domain of the 'mental' and the domain of the 'physical', breaks down the opposition between body and spirit, between matter and language … 'There is indeed a vague and comforting idea in the background that, after all, in the last analysis, doing an action must come down to the making of physical movements with parts of the body; but this is about as true as that saying something must, in the last analysis, come down to making movements of the tongue.'[37]

In a literary text, not only are speech acts performed by a speaking body in the narrative, but physical actions – gift-giving, sex, killing – are brought into existence by language.[38] Working both with those didactic traditions that figure the tongue as dangerous weapon, and through his close attention to the physical effects of language through affective and other responses, Chaucer's work frequently investigates the problematic relationship between body, word and action; *The Manciple's Tale* foregrounds that relationship in an acute and challenging way.[39] Between the extremes of verbal construction and constriction that the images of walling a city and walling up the mouth give us at the beginning and end of the tale, the limits of what alongside speech-act theory we could call word–deed theory are investigated. *The Manciple's Tale* contains both the theoretical possibility of a matching relationship between the spoken word and the material world, but also the repeated evidence of their failure to correspond in political, social and gendered spheres. The tale contains one of Chaucer's best-known voicings of this philosophical commitment:

> The wise Plato seith, as ye may rede,
> The word moot nede accorde with the dede.
> If men shal telle proprely a thyng,
> The word moot cosyn be to the werkyng. (IX.207–10)

The tale's narrating voice then goes on to defend the word 'lemman' or 'wenche' (IX.220) as a description of Phebus's adulterous wife, though a more socially acceptable term for a high-born woman involved in an affair would be 'lady' (IX.218).[40] The narrating voice then states that a 'titlelees tiraunt' and 'an outlawe or a theef erraunt' (IX.223, 224) are no different, except for their 'force of meynee' (IX.228), which leads one to be called a captain, and the other a thief or outlaw. While their actions deserve the same name, then, power intervenes and effectively people use a speech act to say 'I name this thief a captain.'

This brief but sharp analysis embedded in the tale suggests that language and power interact to create new realities. The gift of naming is also a performative act, a linguistic event that has real-world consequences. And for all the narrative voice's desire to match language and thing, the context and audience of an utterance can overflow any straightforward gauge. Returning to the story, the white crow has witnessed Phebus's wife and her lover *in flagrante*. As if egged on by the narrating voice's urging to call a spade a spade, the crow cries 'Cokkow' to Phebus and then spells out exactly what he has seen:

> 'By God,' quod he, 'I synge nat amys.
> Phebus,' quod he, 'for al thy worthynesse,

> For al thy beautee and thy gentilesse,
> For al thy song and al thy mynstralcye,
> For al thy waityng, blered is thyn ye
> With oon of litel reputacioun,
> Noght worth to thee, as in comparisoun,
> The montance of a gnat, so moote I thryve!
> For on thy bed thy wyf I saugh hym swyve.' (IX.248–56)

The crow underlines his description '[b]y sadde tokenes and by words bolde' (IX.258), mingling physical evidence and vivid description tantamount to re-enacting the crime for Phebus. Here, a supposed matching of words and deeds ('I synge nat amys') helps generate the excess of Phebus's violent wrath, killing his wife and then breaking his bow and musical instruments, which had previously seemed to hold in balance the potential for destruction and creation through language.

We can read this outcome through the relationships between giver and receiver, word and deed in the tale. At first sight, *The Manciple's Tale* might seem to contrast the sort of generous rhetoric of *The Franklin's Tale* (where the giver creates a surplus and provokes a generous response from the receiver) with a more commodified environment. In that arena, each deed may be valued and equated with a matching word – the apparent goal of the narrative voice's Platonic aside. However, this attempt to fix the exchange rate between word and deed instead leads to another kind of emotional surplus, this time a destructive one. *The Franklin's Tale* and *The Manciple's Tale* repeatedly show how speech has effects, creates acts, relationships and obligations beyond the reporting of facts or intentions. They also focus our minds on how the reception of an utterance is part of its meaning. Speech as gift can set into train the series of debts and repayments of the earlier tale, but can also provoke the violence of the later one. A glimpse of this potential is given in *The Manciple's Prologue*, where the Manciple's goading of the drunken Cook under the guise of plain language ('Of me, certeyn, thou shalt nat been yglosed' (IX.34)) leads to the Cook falling from his horse. The Host warns the Manciple that a reckoning might come in the form of the Cook accusing him of financial malpractice, and the Manciple heads off this possible feud by plying the Cook with a gift of yet more wine.

In *The Manciple's Tale* itself, claims that '[t]he word moot nede accorde with the dede' are equally shown to be loaded, and 'words having a certain conventional effect' in Austin's terms constantly remake human as well as linguistic relationships. This repeated making and remaking of action, relation and obligation is a significant feature of *The Canterbury Tales* as a whole, if, like the Auchinleck Manuscript, we can envisage its operating as a system of linguistic prestations. It is also one of the further implications of the Austinian performative discussed by Jacques Derrida:

> Rather than oppose citation or iteration to the noniteration of an event, one ought to construct a differential typology of forms of iteration, assuming that such a project is tenable and can result in an exhaustive program, a question I hold in abeyance here. In such a typology, the category of intention will not disappear; it will have its place, but from that place it will no longer be able to govern the entire scene and system of utterance [*l'énonciation*]. Above all, at that point, we will be dealing with different kinds of marks or chains of iterable marks and not with an opposition between citational utterances, on the one hand, and singular and original event-utterances, on the other. The first consequence of this will be the following: given that structure of iteration, the intention animating the utterance will never be through and through present to itself and to its content. The iteration structuring it a priori introduces into it a dehiscence and a cleft [*brisure*] which are essential. The 'non-serious', the *oratio obliqua* will no longer be able to be excluded, as Austin wished, from ordinary language.[41]

Derrida's proposal for understanding utterance as chains of iteration, refusing the separation of event-utterances from citational utterances, can help us understand Chaucer's treatment of speech as gift, and speech as act, in a number of ways: the suggestion that (human) speech is not originary (it is never outside the workings of iteration or textuality); gives something over and above that to which it refers (it is never simply constative); that intention does not always 'govern the entire scene' (it has its place, but so do genre, context, audience); and that iteration complicates an utterance's status and presence. A speech act in Chaucer (as for Derrida via Austin) is not merely a description of an inner feeling, but has consequences beyond those foreseen or intended by its speaker. Aurelius's 'se the teeris on my cheke' (V.1078); Dorigen's 'allas, allas' (V.1513); Arveragus's 'with that word he brast anon to wepe' (V.1480); Chris Taylor's 'it was torture'; the crow's 'Cokkow! Cokkow! Cokkow' (IX.243); and Phebus's 'thoughte his sorweful herte brast atwo' (IX.263) all indicate that linguistic exchange gives back more than the speaker bargains for, and stage that effect of splintering, folding, or trickery (all possible meanings of *brisure*) that Derrida envisages in the relation between intention, speech and context. In *The Franklin's Tale* the utterance's surplus becomes equivalent to a *hau* of speech-as-gift, whose value is returned to the giver as well as seeding further exchanges of speech. In *The Manciple's Tale*, in a much more pessimistic political, linguistic and generic environment, the violent consequences of linguistic acts continue in Phebus's denunciation of the crow as a 'false theef', and his speech acts that brutally pay back the crow's words, now also labelled 'false' (IX.292, 293):

> I wol thee quite anon thy false tale.
> Thou songe whilom lyk a nyghtyngale;
> Now shaltow, false theef, thy song forgon,
> And eek thy white fetheres everichon,
> Ne nevere in al thy lif ne shaltou speke. (IX.293–7)[42]

The concluding retreat into silence, placed in the mouth of the speaker's mother, paints a bleak picture of language that severs relations, and creates indebtedness rather than generosity: 'A tonge kutteth freendshipe al a-two ... He is his thral to whom that he hath sayd / A tale of which he is now yvele apayd' (IX.342, 357–8). The use of metaphors both of violence and of payment encapsulate the dangers of words expended in an environment lacking the generosity of *The Franklin's Tale*, or its generic drive to comic resolution.[43] Listening to the Parson after *The Manciple's Tale*,[44] it is no surprise that the close regulation of words and the potential harms of language, conceptualized as physical wounds, play a prominent part in his sermon, but it is also crucial that penitential speech can produce reform and salvation.[45] *The Parson's Tale* posits a standard of linguistic truth that challenges the capacity of fictional telling: 'Confessioun is verray shewynge of synnes to the preest ... Al moot be seyd, and no thyng excused ne hyd ne forwrapped' (X.318, 319). Equally, it allows for penitential words to unlock forgiveness: 'The hond of God is myghty in confessioun, for therby God foryeveth thee thy synnes' (X.987). This ideal relation, even imbrication, of act ('shewynge'; 'forwrapped'; 'hond') with word in a context of gift and grace may be an aspiration for readers of *The Canterbury Tales*, but neither it nor the speech act of the *Retraction* cancels out the messy, painful, but also generative way that the previous tales do things with words.

In this chapter I have compared a narrative where relationships are brought to crisis by a rash gift (a promise) and then rescued by a series of (re)tellings and speech acts, with a narrative in which a claim to exact correspondence between word and action precipitates disaster for all, closing down opportunities for redemptive or generous speech. Both *The Franklin's Tale* and *The Manciple's Tale* explore speech as gift, and the relationship between speech, act and body, but their perspectives on these allow for radically different responses. Both tales also involve female protagonists at risk of or in adulterous encounters. In the former, though, Dorigen's promises, actions, intentions and speech are at the heart of the action. Her mutually generous married relationship with Arveragus both provides the context for her rash promise and for her subsequent revelation to him of her predicament, enabling the series of healing speech acts to take place. This might itself seem an overly rosy reading of the tale, which could be interpreted much more sceptically as (yet) another story in which a woman is trapped by men's desires, only to be 'rescued' by becoming collateral to their competitive generosity. However, as with Criseyde in *Troilus and Criseyde*, I want here to emphasize the way in which Dorigen's decisions, while acutely constrained, are still explored as a form of agency-in-obligation, and how her acts of telling (to Arveragus and Aurelius) model the way that generous speech can unlock reciprocal actions. In *The Manciple's Tale*, by contrast, Phebus's wife is unnamed, and her only willed act in the story is to take a lover. She is described as equivalent to a bird, a cat, a she-wolf, who will always want to sate their desires, no matter how gilded their cage or delicious the diet on offer as a domestic pet.[46] The inequality of Phebus's household, in which his voice is like Amphion's while his wife is silent, and the crow is praised only for singing in the decorative (but dangerous) tones of a nightingale, disallows the kind of generative language that prompts *pite* as the surplus of speech as gift.

Placing these two Canterbury tales alongside one another sharpens our sense of how Chaucer's storytelling interacts with generosity, economics and the exchange of words and gifts; other tales (those of the Wife of Bath; the Shipman; the Squire; the Man of Law, for example) would extend and complicate this pattern. Since the tales are also loosely bound into an overall system of obligations (the tale-telling contest; but also any given manuscript instantiation of *The Canterbury Tales*), their genres, mode of narrating, allusions and appeals to their listeners will inevitably prompt answering gestures from their audiences, both within and beyond the fiction of the pilgrimage. *The Franklin's Tale* and *The Manciple's Tale* both embed that interaction into their conclusions: one by inviting debate, the other by volubly insisting on the danger of more talk. It might be tempting to read *The Manciple's Tale*, coming towards the end of the extant collection and in most manuscipt versions leading to the Parson's rejection of fictional narrative, as a more authentic expression of the costs of speech in the economy of late-medieval literary production, and to view *The Franklin's Tale* as a naïve and, finally, male-focused fantasy. However, as with the rejection of pagan stories at the end of *Troilus and Criseyde*, I do not think that this is an adequate way to read the contrast between these tales. *The Cantebury Tales'* open structure suggests that the bitter Ovidian metamorphosis and iterative *moralitas* of *The Manciple's Tale* is no more authoritative than *The Franklin's Tale*'s generous resolution, affiliated with romance and *lai*. Each explores the power and danger of speech as gift, and of speech as an attempt to fix relations between language and reality. Each invites ethical choices from its audience, and each leaves a surplus that demands a return from the pilgrims and ultimately from us as readers. In that sense, each makes its own gift to the audience in the form of a speech act, creating a changed world that must then be valued, debated and exchanged by its receivers.

In the next chapter, I shall return to narratives of exchange and the relationship between text, author and audience as one of giving and receiving. Focusing on John Lydgate's *Troy Book*, I will discuss how the Troy story itself is structured around acts of exchange, many of them vengeful or mistaken. I will also explore the role of objects, often gifts, that are accorded great power by the protagonists but whose role in the narrative is ambivalent, asking how

Lydgate as a Christian writer, and we as later readers, can view their status.

Notes

1 This is a burgeoning field, but for an example of discussion about scribal and editorial activity in early Chaucer manuscripts, see Simon Horobin, 'Thomas Hoccleve: Chaucer's first editor?', *Chaucer Review* 50 (2015), 228–50. On other texts as responses, see e.g. *The Canterbury Tales: Fifteenth-Century Continuations and Additions*, ed. John M. Bowers, TEAMS (Kalamazoo, MI: Medieval Institute Publications, 1992); John Lydgate, *The Siege of Thebes*, ed. Robert R. Edwards, TEAMS (Kalamazoo, MI: Medieval Institute Publications, 2001); Straker, 'Deference and difference'; Seth Lerer, *Chaucer and His Readers: Imagining the Author in Late-Medieval England* (Princeton, NJ: Princeton University Press, 1993); Kathleen Forni, *The Chaucerian Apocrypha: A Counterfeit Canon* (Gainesville: University Press of Florida, 2001); Barr, *Transporting Chaucer*, esp. ch. 2.

2 Jill Mann describes how Chaucer involves readers from the outset of *The Franklin's Tale*: 'the apparently casual insertion of "sires" in the first line is a deliberate preparation for the intensification of the narrative's claims on the reader'; 'Chaucerian themes and style in the *Franklin's Tale*', in Boris Ford (ed.), *Medieval Literature: Chaucer and the Alliterative Tradition*, New Pelican Guide to English Literature, vol. 1, part 1, rev. edn (Harmondsworth: Penguin, 1982), pp. 133–53.

3 J.L. Austin, *How to Do Things with Words*, 2nd edn (Oxford: Oxford University Press, 1976).

4 'Gary Lineker pants: Match of the Day presenter keeps Twitter promise'; BBC website, 13 August 2016, www.bbc.co.uk/sport/football/37074641, accessed 13 January 2019.

5 On Dorigen's promise in the context of late-medieval legal practice and rash promises in literature, see Richard Firth Green, *A Crisis of Truth: Literature and Law in Ricardian England* (Philadelphia: University of Pennsylvania Press, 1999), pp. 293–335. In an earlier article, Alan T. Gaylord views the promises as part of 'sophisticated' Chaucer's satire against the Franklin's 'fanatical literalism' in refusing to take intention into account: 'The promises in the *Franklin's Tale*', *ELH: A Journal of English Literary History* 31 (1964), 331–65, quoting pp. 347, 357. However, there are many problems with reading through the psychology of the tale teller. Leslie K. Arnovick reads the promises in the light of the tale's orality, and via John Searle's work on speech acts (though

I think Searle's stratified analysis is less helpful for reading Chaucer than Austin's playful approach); see 'Dorigen's promise and scholars' premise: the orality of the speech act in the *Franklin's Tale*', in Mark C. Amodio (ed.), *Oral Poetics in Middle English Poetry* (New York: Garland, 1994), pp. 125–47. Carol A. Pulham, 'Promises, promises: Dorigen's dilemma revisited', *Chaucer Review* 31 (1996), 76–86, discusses medieval views of marriage and expectations of promise-keeping in oral culture. Middle English vocabulary of promising is surveyed in Mari Pakkala-Weckström, '"No botmeles bihestes": various ways of making binding promises in Middle English', in Andreas H. Jucker and Irma Taavitsainen (eds), *Speech Acts in the History of English* (Amsterdam: John Benjamins, 2008), pp. 133–62.

6 Her promise to Aurelius could fall into the class of performative that Austin terms 'commissives' (including promise; undertake; shall; consent; swear; bet; intend) from his five 'very general classes'. The earlier statement mixes a confirmation or re-enactment of a previous commissive ('I shal'; 'Ne wol I') with the subsequent 'Taak this for fynal answere as of me' being an 'expositive' (affirm; deny; accept; agree; tell; answer; mean; argue); see Austin, *How to Do Things with Words*, pp. 151–2; 161–3.

7 Austin sets rules for the 'happy' functioning of performatives, including that they are part of an 'accepted conventional procedure' (rule A. 1); and that 'Where, as often, the procedure is designed for use by persons having certain thoughts or feelings, or for the inauguration of certain consequential conduct on the part of any participant, then a person participating in and so invoking the procedure must in fact have those thoughts or feelings, and the participants must intend so to conduct themselves', and further they 'must actually so conduct themselves' (rules G. 1 and G. 2); ibid., pp. 14–15.

8 For what Austin calls the happy or unhappy (felicitous or infelicitous) functioning of performatives, see e.g. ibid., pp. 12–24.

9 This statement turns out to be particularly freighted given that knowledge and manipulation of the tides to make the rocks appear gone is precisely what will occur later. See *MED* s.v. *tiden* (v); *tid(e* (n.), meanings 6–7.

10 Shoshana Felman, *The Scandal of the Speaking Body; Don Juan with J.L. Austin, or Seduction in Two Languages*, trans. Catherine Porter (Stanford, CA: Stanford University Press, 2003), p. 49 (*Le Scandale du corps parlant* (Paris: Éditions du Seuil, 1980)). Exploring Boccaccian and other analogues, Michael Calabrese argues that there are models of female rhetoric available to dampen a suitor's ardour, but which Dorigen does not employ; instead, Chaucer 'encode[s] danger' (291) in her playful promise. Calabrese also summarizes the debate over Dorigen's

agency and ethical positioning: 'Chaucer's Dorigen and Boccaccio's female voices', *SAC* 29 (2007), 259–92.

11 'But we are apt to have a feeling that their being serious consists in their being uttered as (merely) the outward and visible sign, for convenience or other record or for information, of an inward and spiritual act: from which it is but a short step to go on to believe or to assume without realizing that for many purposes the outward utterance is a description, *true or false*, of the occurrence of the inward performance' (Austin, *How to Do Things with Words*, p. 9; original emphasis).

12 Ibid., pp. 21–2; original emphasis.

13 The discussion of speech acts and literature is extensive; see e.g. Sandy Petrey, *Speech Acts and Literary Theory* (London: Routledge, 1990); Jacques Derrida, *Limited Inc*, trans. Samuel Weber and Jeffrey Mehlman (Evanston, IL: Northwestern University Press, 1988); J. Hillis Miller, *Speech Acts in Literature* (Stanford, CA: Stanford University Press, 2001). For initial guidance on speech acts more widely, see Mitchell Green, 'Speech Acts', *Oxford Bibliographies Online* www.oxfordbibliographies.com/view/document/obo-9780195396577/obo-9780195396577-0300.xml, accessed 23 February 2019.

14 See Jill Mann, 'Anger and "glosynge" in *The Canterbury Tales*', *Proceedings of the British Academy* 76 (1991), 203–23. For this passage of *The Friar's Tale* see *Canterbury Tales* III.1537–1641. In her edition of *The Canterbury Tales* (Harmondsworth: Penguin, 2005), Mann tellingly comments that '[i]n the world of the *Friar's Tale*, Dorigen would have had no problems' (p. xxxviii).

15 See *MED* s.v. *don* (v.1), meaning 5(a).

16 Mary Carruthers, *The Book of Memory*, 2nd edn (Cambridge: Cambridge University Press, 2008), chs 1–2.

17 On 'character' as carved sign, see Miller, 'Character', esp. pp. 30–3, 55–60.

18 Felman, *Scandal*, p. 27, here discussing Molière's *Don Juan*.

19 A similar claim might be made about *Troilus and Criseyde*, where the blend of love language with other generic elements gives a peculiar force to the relationship between word, body and action.

20 For larger debates over Chaucer's writing vis-à-vis realism and nominalism in philosophical and linguistic spheres, see e.g. Robert Myles, *Chaucerian Realism* (Woodbridge: Boydell & Brewer, 1994), and Hugo Keiper et al. (eds), *Nominalism and Literary Discourse: New Perspectives* (Amsterdam: Rodopi, 1997).

21 Helen Cooper, *The Canterbury Tales*, 2nd edn, Oxford Guides to Chaucer (Oxford: Oxford University Press, 1996), p. 239. Cooper rightly turns the focus away from speculating on 'whether it was sensible or right'

for Dorigen or Arveragus to act in the ways they do, noting that '[t]he rash promise is a condition of the story' (p. 238). She also aptly characterizes the tale's ending as requiring that 'a series of individuals should opt to yield up and give rather than take' (p. 240).

22 David Graeber, *Debt: The First 5,000 Years*, rev. edn (Brooklyn, NY: Melville House, 2014), p. 391. Graeber's work on the transformation of obligations into debt definable in monetary terms is incisively discussed in the context of *The Franklin's Tale* in Epstein, *Chaucer's Gifts*, pp. 183–9.

23 Colin Wilcockson notes how Arveragus's shift from 'yow' to the more intimate 'thou' signals to the audience his tender feelings to her at this moment of crisis: 'Thou and tears: the advice of Arveragus to Dorigen in Chaucer's "Franklin's Tale"', *Review of English Studies* 54 (2003), 308–12.

24 The Middle English verb *relesen* encompasses cancelling an obligation, remitting a debt, forgiving a sin, and easing pain; see *MED*, s.v. *relesen*, v.(1). Here and in its use by the clerk (quoted below), several of these meanings resonate. The *Riverside* edition presents all these lines as spoken by Aurelius, following the paragraph marks in manuscripts including Ellesmere and Hengwrt, but its explanatory note (p. 901) argues that lines V.1541–4 'seem more appropriate to the Franklin'. Mann likewise argues that it is not 'plausible' that Aurelius would boast about his *gentil* qualities, or deliver 'the finger-wagging admonition to wives' (*Canterbury Tales*, ed. Mann, p. 960). Whether we assign them to Aurelius or the narrating voice, they continue the speech's pattern of performative utterances, and the clerk echoes the boast about performing a 'gentil dede' in his own speech: V.1610–13.

25 Most editors assume that Aurelius has paid the clerk money to cover his expenses ('my vitaille'). This acknowledgement would underline the difference between a commodity payment that the clerk still expects, and the debt for performing his art, which has been cancelled by the verbal and ethical performances by other actors. Another reading (albeit more speculative) is that Aurelius's story itself constitutes that payment.

26 Britton J. Harwood, 'Chaucer and the gift (if there is any)', *Studies in Philology* 103 (2006), 26–46, at p. 45.

27 Kyle Mahowald, '"It may nat be": Chaucer, Derrida, and the impossibility of the gift', *SAC* 32 (2010), 129–50, quoting p. 143.

28 See above, pp. 46–8, and Derrida, *Given Time I*, e.g. pp. 6–8, 129–30; and see Epstein, *Chaucer's Gifts*, pp. 174–82.

29 Epstein, *Chaucer's Gifts*, pp. 171, 175, 183.

30 Ibid., pp. 183–5 and references there.

31 Ibid., p. 190.

32 See also Anne Scott, '"Do nu ase þu sedes": Word and Deed in *King Horn, Havelok the Dane*, and the *Franklin's Tale*' (doctoral dissertation, Brown University, 1988), pp. 138–53. Scott uses Grice's work on conversation to suggest that only in the tale's latter stages do the protagonists fully listen and understand one another's speech. She notes that 'the idea of reciprocity shines through the Franklin's very style, which exploits the additive, paratactic nature of traditional literature to create a language of "exchange" or "give-and-take"' (p. 147).

33 Cf. David Aers's description of Chaucer's 'profoundly reflexive art' in *The Franklin's Tale* and elsewhere, and his presentation of idea(l)s of marriage and love: 'His work included *both* cherished utopian aspirations, which constituted a fundamental perspective from which to develop a critique of the present, *and* his imaginative scrutiny of such aspirations as they might fare in the present': *Chaucer, Langland and the Creative Imagination* (London: Routledge & Kegan Paul, 1980), pp. 168, 161.

34 Alan Hamilton, 'How Ziggy the indiscreet parrot gave a cheating girlfriend the bird', *The Times*, 17 January 2006, p. 5. I am very grateful to Priscilla Martin for drawing my attention to this article at the time.

35 For *The Manciple's Tale* in the context of court politics and advice-giving, see e.g. V.J. Scattergood, 'The Manciple's manner of speaking', *Essays in Criticism* 24 (1974), 124–46; Louise Fradenburg, 'The Manciple's servant tongue: politics and poetry in *The Canterbury Tales*', *ELH: A Journal of English Literary History* 52 (1985), 85–118; and more broadly Robert W. Hanning, 'Chaucer and the dangers of poetry', *CEA Critic* 46 (1984), 17–26. Reading the crow as a figure for a court poet, Fradenburg sees the meanings of poetry made as a gift to the monarch being dominated by the sovereign's desires. I discuss *The Manciple's Tale* in this context, but qualify that reading of court poetry, in Nicholas Perkins, *Hoccleve's 'Regiment of Princes': Counsel and Constraint* (Cambridge: Brewer, 2001), pp. 5–49 (pp. 21–3 for *The Manciple's Tale*). Chaucer foregrounds the crow's status as songbird and servant of Phebus in his version: cf. *Sources and Analogues of 'The Canterbury Tales'*, ed. Robert M. Correale and Mary Hamel, 2 vols (Cambridge: Brewer, 2002–5), II.749–73.

36 See Edwin Craun, *Lies, Slander and Obscenity in Medieval English Literature: Pastoral Rhetoric and the Deviant Speaker* (Cambridge: Cambridge University Press, 1997), ch. 6.

37 Felman, *Scandal*, p. 94. Felman quotes J.L. Austin, *Philosophical Papers*, ed. J.O. Urmson and G.J. Warnock, 3rd edn (Oxford: Oxford University Press, 1979), p. 178; cf. Austin, *How to Do Things with Words*, p. 19.

38 On the creation of fictional worlds as part of the performative nature of literary writing, see Miller, *Speech Acts in Literature* and *Ethics of Reading*.

39 Britton J. Harwood contended over forty years ago that '[t]he subject of the tale is language': 'Language and the real: Chaucer's Manciple', *Chaucer Review* 6 (1972), 268–79.

40 There is not space here fully to explore the implications of word as 'cosyn' to 'werkyng' in Chaucer. The contexts of this passage in Classical and medieval texts are discussed by Paul B. Taylor, 'Chaucer's *cosyn to the dede*', *Speculum* 57 (1982), 315–27; Marc M. Pelen, 'The Manciple's "cosyn" to the "dede"', *Chaucer Review* 25 (1991), 343–54 and 'Chaucer's "cosyn to the dede": further considerations', *Florilegium* 19 (2002), 91–107, though I differ from his conclusion that Chaucer's intent is the 'systematic pursuit of an eternal salvation among the linguistic and iconographic confusions of his speakers' (104). For rich discussion of the *Roman de la Rose* in this context, see Alastair Minnis, *Magister Amoris: The 'Roman de la Rose' and Vernacular Hermeneutics* (Oxford: Oxford University Press, 2001), ch. 3; David F. Hult, 'Words and deeds: Jean de Meun's *Romance of the Rose* and the hermeneutics of censorship', *New Literary History* 28 (1997), 345–66.

41 Derrida, 'Signature event context', in his *Limited Inc*, pp. 1–23, at p. 18 ('Signature événement contexte', in *Limited Inc* (Paris: Éditions Galilée, 1990), pp. 17–51). *Brisure* is also a French heraldic term (in English, 'charge') for a mark that distinguishes the arms of different members of a family (the practice known as cadency); it thus signals repetition and difference. See *A New Dictionary of Heraldry*, ed. Stephen Friar (London: Alphabooks, 1987), s.v. *Cadency*, pp. 75–6.

42 The tale describes Phebus as also physically enacting these curses – 'pulled his white fetheres ... made hym blak ... refte hym al his song ... out at dore hym slong' (IX.304–6) – but as a god, his words hold as much power in the text as the actions: they all form part of a speech/act that is itself enacted for the audience in words.

43 The advice supposedly derives from the mouth of the Manciple's mother, but its proverbial status makes it generically iterative, and presses further the question of who is speaking.

44 The Parson speaks just after the Manciple in most manuscripts, but there is untidiness in the text and references to time here; see Cooper, *Canterbury Tales*, pp. 395–6.

45 On 'confession of the mouth' in *The Parson's Tale*, see e.g. Craun, *Lies, Slander, and Obscenity*, pp. 221–2.

46 Mann (*Feminizing Chaucer*, pp. 16–18) discusses the narrating voice's shift here to saying that the examples are about men, 'and nothing by wommen' (X.188), prompting attention to authorial intervention and the power of rhetoric. She later points out that Phebus's wife is 'not only the victim of male violence, but also the victim of male rhetoric' (p. 18) when Phebus lauds her supposed purity, having just killed her for her infidelity.

5

Things fall apart: the narratives of gift in Lydgate's *Troy Book*

Lydgate's *Troy Book* takes on in extended narrative form numerous dynamics that we have been discussing throughout this book. By tackling the history of Troy, perhaps the most resonant Classical legend in medieval chronicle, history and romance, Lydgate inevitably faces the question of narrative origins, of the *proces* of story making and of the Western tradition itself. In this way, the Troy story poses questions about action and reaction, gift and counter-gift, with the layered debts both personal, political and textual that this pattern implies. This chapter is a reading of Lydgate's poem that develops several of the strands of argument in previous chapters, examining how gift and exchange shapes narrative, how persons and things are constituted, and how verbal exchanges such as telling and promising take part in the dynamics of the gift. In addition, the *Troy Book* involves a network of action and obligations stretching beyond the human protagonists of the poem. How does it deal with the competing claims to authority or destiny at work in historical or romance storytelling? And, to use terms drawn from recent materialist accounts, how does it distribute agency in and around its narrative? The story of Troy raises problems of responsibility, intention and interaction between human and non-human actants, whether they be Classical gods or the Trojan Horse. Further, the *Troy Book*'s relationship with materiality extends beyond its poetic narrative to the forms in which it is presented. By reading the poem using a particular fifteenth-century manuscript copy and by analysing Lydgate's paratextual writing, a further set of engagements emerges between actors, agents and objects in a network of ongoing literary making, giving and exchanging.

As a path into these ideas I shall start with the early sections of Book I, which describe a series of relationships of agency and exchange. I shall then focus on sections of the poem that bring to the fore the problems that meaningful things embed in the Troy story. In one passage – the funeral of Hector and the preservation of his body – it seems on the face of it that the poem provides a model of human ingenuity that can alter or arrest the changeableness and restlessness both of human actors and of narrative itself. In a later section – the betrayal and destruction of the city – things that might provide comfort or power to human actors (a statue of a god that supposedly guarantees the safety of the city; a gift made apparently to seal peace and close the circle of revenge) instead prove fallible or untrustworthy. Alongside these forces, Lydgate's role as a Christian writer representing Classical antiquity places him in a complex position concerning motivation and agency. Since this chapter is concerned with the reception and interpretation of texts and (or as) gifts, I will discuss a particular copy of the *Troy Book*: Manchester, John Rylands Library MS English 1. This magnificently illustrated book is a fine example of a presentation or gift manuscript. How do the dynamics of the gift affect its relationship with the text it contains? How does the series of illustrations relate to the experience of reading Lydgate's poem, and how does this particular performance of the *Troy Book* provide a meeting point for a number of forces, intentions, materials, agencies and trajectories? Finally, I shall reflect on Lydgate's positioning of himself and his text in the flow of obligations and returns that constitute both the literary tradition with which he works, and the relations of writer, text and patron that move through and beyond the poem.

'cause ... causeles'

When Lydgate embarks on his mammoth undertaking of translating Guido delle Colonne's late thirteenth-century prose *Historia destructionis Troiae* into Middle English verse, he has to start somewhere, but Book I's opening movements describe an ending. Having very briefly introduced the Myrmidons of Thessaly, ruled by their king, Peleus, Lydgate relates their destruction. This people

> Were brou3t echon to destructioun
> With sodeyn tempest and with fery levene
> By the goddys sent down from þe heuene;

> For they of Ire, with-oute more offence,
> With the swerde & stroke of pestilence
> On this yle whylom toke vengaunce,
> Lyche as it is putte in remembraunce.[1]

Harking back to the Prologue's invocation to Mars as 'Irows and wood and malencolyk' (Prol. 9), the Myrmidons' downfall is explained by divine displeasure. However, this cause is immediately complicated. It is born from anger, not offence; a disposition, not an act. Of course, any late-medieval description of pestilence such as this carries echoes of the Bible and of plague in Europe. The reference to vengeance falling on 'this yle' (I.19; see also I.7) may have had an uncomfortable resonance for Lydgate's English audience (its textual antecedents 'Thesalye ... Salonye' come many lines previously, in lines 1–2). Lydgate shortens Guido's introduction of names and context to the story, to focus on a core element of his narrative: that the gods may act without apparent motivation, giving and taking away.[2] Immediately after this, King Peleus, the sole survivor of his people, is depicted more as a romance hero, 'þe whiche went allone / In-to a wode for to make his mone' (27–8). Partly by means of these generic markers in the narrative, the relationship between humans and gods is reconfigured here. Instead of the initial presentation of inscrutable and irous 'goddys' who sent down destruction on the Myrmidons, here an individual believer prays for grace, makes the appropriate sacrifice and is heard by one powerful deity:

> Iubiter herde his orisoun,
> And hath swiche rowth on hym at þe laste,
> That he anoon fulfilled his requeste. (I.52–4)

In these opening encounters, Lydgate shifts between the presentation of historical narrative, of symbol and fable, and then of scepticism and scholarship about that fable. Twenty lines after relating this story of Peleus and the ants turning to people, the poem's authenticating voice recasts the narrative as an origin story for the hard-working Myrmidon people:[3]

> Whiche for wisdam & prudent aduertence,
> Besy labour and wilful dilligence,
> By for-seynge and discrecioun,
> As I suppose in myn opinioun,
> That this fable of amptis was contreued. (I.71–5)

The *Troy Book* must make a number of these starts: exploring origins, weighing up the value of differing forms of narrative, genre and authority, and setting up systems of debt, obligation and return, as a way for the story to proceed. In the case of the Myrmidons, we arrive at a position where their reputation for industry, known from the more recent past (Lydgate cites a life of St Matthew for evidence) may have brought their origin story into existence. How do we then (re)read the narrative from twenty-five lines earlier? Were the Myrmidons really created from ants, or is this simply a 'fable of amptis'? Is it the power of Jupiter or of analogy that creates this connection? What then is the status of the claim to history in the poem? The shifting ground of authority and point of view are signalled here by the line 'As I suppose in myn opinioun', and we could argue that this is a just-so story that then settles down into more serious historical narrative.[4] However, this point exemplifies some of the challenges that Lydgate faces as the story of Troy unfolds, and we shall see that he has to manage numerous competing claims about exchanges of things and people in the Troy story, the sources of action, and the interaction between human and non-human actants. Early in Book I, he is already tugged between a 'gifted' opening in which protagonists arrive as if unmotivated, as in some of the romances we have read, and a calculated one, in which historical precedents and prior obligations are accounted for, however implausible it is to do this completely.

As Book I of the *Troy Book* continues, it describes a series of unfortunate events in which exchange and revenge, and the movement of people and objects, create narrative movement and expectation. Returning to Peleus, the story details his jealous attempts to send his nephew Jason to his destruction by tempting him to capture the golden fleece without mentioning the mission's formidable dangers. Having accepted the challenge 'with-out avisement' (I.513), Jason and his Argonauts happen to land near Troy to rest. But Fortune is here enlisted as the precipitating force giving impetus to the circle of narrative exchange:

> But þe ordre of Fortunys myȝt
> Hath euere envy þat men lyue in ese,
> Whos cours enhasteth vnwarly to dissese.
> For sche was cause, God wotte, causeles,
> Þis gery Fortune, þis lady reccheles,

Þe blynde goddesse of transmutacioun,
To turne her whele by reuolucioun
To make Troyens vniustly for to wene
That Grekys werne arived hem to tene. (I.750–8)

The shifting between 'cours' and 'cause ... causeles' reminds us of the problematic relationship between narrative direction and causation. Lydgate's language and recourse to Fortune attends to the difficulty of disentangling exchange relationships and finding the 'make believe of a beginning'.[5] The wheel of Fortune is well understood in the context of royal power, or of History's shifting patterns of reward and decline. In a Boethian context Fortune may be accommodated as the experience of contingency, misrecognized as fixed or decisive in human happiness.[6] Here, though, Fortune's Wheel additionally seems to contemplate narrative beginning itself.

In MS Eng. 1 fol. 28v, a striking illustration shows Fortune with her wheel (Figure 3). Fortune is labelled as 'The quene of fortune'. She is the second royal patron depicted in the manuscript after Henry V himself receiving the *Troy Book* in the presentation picture on fol. 1r (Figure 2). But unlike that picture of a throne room with carefully balanced and ordered hierarchical elements, here balance and movement come from the robed or crowned figures petitioning to mount her wheel on one side, and on the other being violently cast down from it. Though the *Troy Book* calls her a 'blynde goddesse', in the illustration Fortune looks at the figures on their way up, showing her face to them, either in surprise or sorrow at human folly, or perhaps representing the proverbial idea that she shows a kindly face at first, and an ugly or cruel one behind. Her spectacular gold wheel dominates the image. In this manuscript, dwelling on the wheel of Fortune and its ruined contemporary figures prompts the viewer to contemplate the relationships between this Classical narrative and the onward cycles of rise and fall that medieval tragedy and *de casibus* texts retell. The wheel reaches out of the story, linking the historical moment of the narrative with the time of the audience; it is a representation of time as repeated pattern analogous to Lydgate's mingling of continuous present and past in his narration.[7] Karen Elaine Smyth has described Lydgate's handling of time in the *Troy Book* as more varied and inventive than has previously been assumed, noting his interest in different kinds of time referents and forms of

Figure 2 Manchester, John Rylands Library MS English 1, fol. 1r

measurement, from liturgical hours to natural rhythms.[8] Here I
think that the presiding figure of Fortune destabilizes the idea that
historical process is a set of balanced, explicable exchanges, but
also places historical narrative in a larger cyclical pattern. The
narrative is thus swayed by chance events or encounters, but still
adheres to a process of rise and fall, one that MS Eng. 1's illustration
foregrounds. Chaucer's *Troilus and Criseyde* of course makes this

Figure 3 Manchester, John Rylands Library MS English 1, fol. 28v

interplay between contingency and process a central part of its method;[9] Lydgate's concern with pattern and chance are less immediately evident but nonetheless crucial to the *Troy Book* as well.

Fortune thus 'turne[s] her whele by reuolucioun' and King Lamedon reacts 'of wilfulnesse / With-out[e] counsail or avisenesse / To hast[i]ly' (I.957–9), sending an aggressive message to Jason and the Argonauts who have landed nearby.[10] Jason replies with a sarcastic tone to the messenger's speech. The exchange of threatening speeches, as in *The Battle of Maldon*, precipitates conflict by their pointed readjustment of the expected dynamics of gift and exchange. There, of course, Byrhtnoth says that his people will 'to gafole garas syllan' [give spears as tribute].[11] Here Jason's speech imagines the (non-existent) welcoming 'gifts' presented by the messenger:

> 'My frende,' quod he, 'I haue wel vnderstande
> Þe massage hool, þat þou toke on honde;
> Of þi kyng to bryng[en] vn-to vs
> Riȝt now vnwarly; & syth it standeth þus,
> Þat I haue his menyng euerydel
> From point to point, & vnderstonde it wel—
> For word by worde I haue it plein conseived,
> And þe ȝiftes þat we han resseived
> On his by-halue in our gret[e] nede,
> I wil remembre, and take riȝt gode hede
> To euery þing þat þou hast vs brouȝt.
> For trust[e] wel þat I forȝete it nouȝt,
> But enprente it surly in my mynde. (I.1095–1107)

By picking out 'þe ȝiftes þat we han resseived', Jason turns King Lamedon's words into an ironic gift in place of the expected welcome, but also places the absence of gift objects at the centre of the dispute. This echoes Lydgate's earlier paradox of a 'causeles' cause for the conflict, governed by Fortune's turning wheel. The 'euery þing' that Jason will 'enprente' in his mind both points to a lack of the expected physical objects of courteous exchange, and also represents words as exchangeable things. The messenger's response (to Hercules' further threats) positions him as a commentator or marginal glossator as well as a participant in the narrative, somewhat removed from the exchange of bravado and bombast. He reproaches Hercules for his angry words: 'For it sit not vn-to ȝour worthines, /Yffe ȝe take hede be weye of gentilnes, / Of manassyng swiche arwes for to schete' (I.1181–3), eliding sharp words with weapons themselves. He then warns Jason's company of future harm, in language that reaches proleptically beyond the immediate situation and becomes a miniature commentary on the whole story:

> And for my parte, I saie vn-to ȝow alle,
> It were pite þat ȝe distroied were,

> Or any man hyndre schulde or dere
> So worþi persones, in any maner wise,
> Whiche ben so likly to be discret & wise,
> And list with wordis as now I do ȝou greue,
> I saye no more, I take of ȝow my leue. (I.1190–6)

The punning irony that this Trojan messenger pities the Greeks in case they are 'dis*troied*', adds an edge to the potential harm that he fears his words will do. These sorts of effects, in which individual exchanges of words, objects or people seem to play out in microcosm the larger patterns of the narrative, create a particularly telling dynamic for the recursive energies of a Trojan poem.

If space permitted, we could keep tracking the *Troy Book*'s narrative, finding more examples of how ideas of gift and exchange are both integral to the plot and give Lydgate's poem a broader sense of patterning. Jason's exchanges with Medea, for example, in which Medea demands that he swear an oath of loyalty before giving him a series of gifts: a protective image of silver; written directions; fireproof ointment; an invisibility ring; a phial of liquid to throw down the throats of the fire-breathing bulls. Yet these gifts are overwhelmed by her losing control of the relationship when she gives up her virginity to him. In a dark replay of the romance scenario celebrated in *The Romance of Horn* – where Horn and Rigmel's exchanges remain charged with potential until the romance brings home the repayments, allows the lovers to marry, and sets up the ongoing story of the next generation – Jason's currency of exchange is in false promises, while everything else flows in the opposite direction:

> But first ȝe schul þe ordre & maner se
> How sche wrouȝt after he was swore:
> Þe same nyȝt, allas, sche hathe forbore
> Hir maidenhed, and þat was grete pite. (I.2936–9)

We could also look more broadly at the currency of women in the *Troy Book* as both symbols of exchange between Greeks and Trojans and actual bodies moving between the camps, being traded, examined, their worth valued.[12] These could be read in the light of Chapter 3's discussion of gender and personhood in *Troilus and Criseyde*, though Lydgate's commitment to a more historical and moralizing narrative is one factor limiting his poem's scope for reflection on constraint and agency, as I argued Chaucer developed. Instead, however, I shall read the problematic status of exchange, persons and objects alongside Lydgate's concerns with agency in two later sections of the poem, taking into account recent debates over agency and matter. As we have seen throughout this book, thinking about gifts and objects also encourages us to scrutinize the boundaries between people and things. *The Troy Book* encounters these questions in the stark context of war and the breakdown or subversion of what Hyde terms gift communities and gifts of peace.[13] First I shall examine the problematic attempt by Priam to constitute Hector's dead body as a resonant object that will still give hope to the Trojans.

'Like as it were quyk in existence'

Towards the end of Book III, the death of Hector provokes grief and anger throughout the city of Troy. King Priam orders an oratory to be built, in which Hector's body is to be preserved through the most modern techniques available:

> To telle pleynly how kyng Priamus
> In herte was inly desyrous
> To caste a weie, in his entencioun,
> Þe cors to kepe from corrupcioun,
> Whiche naturelly, but men take hede,
> Corrupte muste, riȝt of verray nede:
> For, of kyndly disposicioun,
> Þer may be made noon opposicioun,
> Aboue þe grounde ȝif þe body lie,
> Þat of resoun it mvt putrefie,
> But ȝif crafte be a-boue nature,
> Vncorrupte it myȝt[e] nat endure.
> Wherefore, þe kyng shope him to ordeyne
> To preserue it hool fro þinges tweyne:
> From odour and abomynacioun,
> And þer-with eke, by crafty operacioun,
> Þat it in siȝt be not founde horrible,
> But þat it be lifly and visible
> To þe eye, as be apparence,
> Like as it were quyk in existence. (III.5579–98)

The 'craftiest maisteres of þe toun' are employed to preserve Hector's body in this lifelike state, and place it inside a richly equipped oratory, next to a golden statue of Hector. The body itself is set standing upright, 'By sotil crafte, as he were lyvynge' (III.5657):

> For on his hede, like as it is tolde,
> Þoru3 smale pipes wrou3t & made of gold,
> Þat be mesour wern enbowed doun
> To an entre makyd in his crown,
> Be grete avys and subtylite,
> To eche party and extremyte
> Of his body lyneally porrect,
> Þoru3 nerfe & synwe driven & direct,
> By secre poris craftely to extende,
> Wherby þe licour my3t[e] doun discende
> To kepe hym hool fro corrupcioun,
> With-outen any transmutacioun
> Of hyde or hewe, in any part to tourne.
> And at his hede of gold was an ourne,
> Þat was filde with bawme natural
> Þat ran þoru3 pipes artificial,
> Þoru3 nekke & hed in-to many place,
> Penytrable by veynes of þe face,
> Þat þoru3 vertu & force of þe lycour
> He was conserued lifly of colour,
> Fresche of hewe, quyke, & no þinge pale,
> So my3tely þe bawme did avale—
> Comparysownyd, as it were semblable,
> To a sowle þat were vegetable,
> Þe whiche, with-oute sensibilite,
> Mynystreth lyf in herbe, flour, and tre,
> And, sembla[b]ly, in-to euery veyne
> Of þe cors þe vertu dide atteyne,
> By brest and arme spredynge enviroun. (III.5663–91)

This extended ekphrasis provides a climax for Book III of the poem, highlighting Hector's importance both as a military bulwark for the Trojans, and as an embodiment of chivalric qualities for the poem's audience. Now Hector's status is at question, and Priam's actions seek to control or mitigate the natural processes of decay into which his corpse would otherwise pass. Hector at this point exists as something between person, body, relic, reputation and sign. This in-between state is answered by the mingled materials for which his body is now the field of assembly: metal pipes and 'bawme' that flows through them, emanating into the otherwise lifeless limbs. Lydgate's description also anatomises Hector's body, speaking not only of its wholeness ('body'; 'cors') but also of its parts: 'hede'; 'crown'; 'party'; 'extremyte'; 'nerfe & synwe'; 'nekke & hed'; 'veynes'; 'brest and arme'. At some points it is hard to distinguish which parts are fleshly and which are engineered, as with the 'secre poris' by which the embalming liquid extends throughout his body.

Numerous studies of materiality have emphasized the ways in which non-human actants play a part in dynamic processes. In the work of some advocates of 'vibrant materiality', the *Troy Book*'s reflection on the mingling of human and (other) materials might spark particular interest and discussion. Hector is at this moment completed or constituted from non-human objects or powers, in the hope that these will act on those seeing his body, that in this state his body will be a thing that has power in the story. In *Vibrant Matter*, Jane Bennett poses the question:

> [What happens when we] take seriously the vitality of (non-human) bodies? By 'vitality' I mean the capacity of things—edibles, commodities, storms, metals—not only to impede or block the will and designs of humans but also to act as quasi agents or forces with trajectories, propensities, or tendencies of their own ... Vital materialists will thus try to linger in those moments during which they find themselves fascinated by objects, taking them as clues to the material vitality that they share with them.[14]

Bennett's work might encourage readers to decentre human powers or will as the focus of literary debate, and look to assemblages of things that distribute and decentralize agency.[15] Certainly Lydgate's understanding of the actants working in his narrative imagines human will or power as constrained by other forces both outside and within the body; by processes of history and governance opaque to human protagonists; and by textual currents with which he as translator or teller must steer. Lydgate's description also involves us in the qualities and affordances of the materials from which Hector is now made, mingling flesh and technology.[16] All these have significant implications for our reading, but I want to resist a complete decentring of human agency or the shimmer of independent material trajectories, which also risk leading us away from questions of ethics or intention.[17] In this passage of Lydgate I will instead focus more on the 'quasi' of Bennett's proposition: that is, in the political and creative will that shapes Hector's cyborg form, and the effects that presenting his body as if alive has on the Trojan viewers and Lydgate's readers.[18]

Later in the chapter, I will return to questions of agency and the overlapping trajectories at work in, through, and around the *Troy Book*. For now, I shall pursue the questions raised by this episode within the narrative environment of the poem. The description treads a careful line between stressing Hector's liveliness – 'He was conserued lifly of colour' – and the acknowledgement that this life, or force ('vertu') is external. In death, the vibrancy of Hector as a mingling of human and non-human is depicted as a persuasive argument for his continuing presence or inspiration to the Trojans. But on the other hand, such persuasion is the function of rhetoric, and the medium of the description (while carried on animal skin, and written with vegetable ink) is also language. Lydgate's description celebrates the craft of the makers – their skill in presenting a corpse as lively, and of its power to move others.[19] In praising their ingenuity, I argue that he places his own verbal craft in the same field of operation. The focus on 'crafte', 'engyn', in this passage crosses over from the craftsmen at work on Hector's corpse, to the author at work on his corpus. The echoes in this passage of the opening of Chaucer's *Canterbury Tales* (the 'vertu' of this 'licour' in the context of animating human bodies and linking them with natural processes of regeneration) are another reminder of how poetry can create that sense of liveliness and thing-ness through its craft, evoking the rhythms and power of the natural world, but in a well-wrought verbal form.[20] The *Troy Book*'s description of Hector's subtly enlivened body is an ekphrasis of an ekphrasis: this metekphrastic passage of poetry with its rhetorical control of aureate language is analogous to the golden pipes carrying liquor through Hector's otherwise decaying cadaver. In this regard, Hector's preserved body becomes a site not only of material assemblage but of linguistic aureation, echoing Lydgate's conjuring of Chaucer's spirit but with a different narrative context and trajectory.[21] The 'vibrancy' of Hector's corpse is, in Lydgate's account, all the time being infused by human craft, other materials, and a political and religious will. Such an interplay of material, person(s) and agency is something that Lydgate is reckoning with at various points in the *Troy Book*.

Paul Strohm reads Hector's posthumous irrigation system in relation to the problem of regulating the waste of a medieval city. A well-ordered city must have efficient ways of clearing away waste; this was a significant political and practical issue, and Strohm reminds us that kings had a serious interest in promoting good sewage disposal. In his reading, the careful preservation of Hector's body is likewise an index of royal authority, with the power to preserve and extend life (or the appearance of life), and Lydgate's detailed description is a signal of his ideological backing for such royal power:

> For death—whether of subjects or cities—threatens authority unless properly euphemized and managed, unless shown to be nonarbitrary and subject to royal control. What is required is nothing less than a dramatization of what Bloch calls the 'victory of order over event itself ... so that death can be represented as part of a repetitive social order.'[22]

For our purposes here, one of the significant things about this understanding of the episode and its relation to Bloch's arguments is the way that negotiating the relations between things and time is also at the heart of anthropological understandings of the gift.[23] To use the terms of reference I have employed during this study, Hector's body has continuing value as a participant in exchange, and as an exchangeable object itself (for example, in binding together the Trojan people through their belief in his prowess and his physical exchanges with the Greeks). Lydgate is well known for his willingness to write verse on all sorts of practical, socially debated and political topics. Elaborating a dream of power, in which the value of military heroes can extend beyond the grave as an inspiration to others and as a signal of royal control is an attractive reading of this passage, and Strohm connects it with his assessment of Lydgate as attempting to preserve Chaucer's memory but retain control over him/it, as opposed to the more ambivalent and volatile representations of power that, Strohm argues, Chaucer creates. Strohm's reading is consistent with his understanding of Lydgate as an author concerned to shore up royal authority and ideology: 'Unhindered by practical considerations, Lydgate's material imaginings are more fully bent to fulfilment of the sovereign behest.'[24]

The question of social order and prudential action is discussed by Colin Fewer, who argues that Priam's construction of Hector's shrine 'is an attempt to reaffirm human powers in the face of the entropic forces of nature and history'. Like Strohm, Fewer posits that '[t]he shrine reasserts control over the tragic death and its trivial causes by asserting a kind of control over the natural "corrupcioun" of Hector's body, incorporating him into the architectural design that maintains the coherence of Trojan society'.[25] There are numerous strengths to Fewer's reading of the *Troy Book* as emphasizing human opportunities to exercise prudential judgement at moments of crisis or decision making. It accords with an understanding of Lydgate's text both as a historical narrative and a set of regiminal lessons or challenges, which readers themselves, including Lydgate's royal patrons, can relate to their own political and military dilemmas. Fewer further connects Hector's assimilation into the fabric of Troy with contemporary moves to promote Henry V as a chivalric hero: 'the effects of power are disseminated by the prudential design of the city itself, and in Hector's tomb this new ideology quite literally replaces Hector and the feudal values he represents'.[26] My reading of Lydgate's approach both to objects and to the sovereign behest differs somewhat from this. While the *Troy Book* does at times celebrate chivalric ideology, myths of political authority and national identity, I would argue that Lydgate's commitment to prudential judgement helps create an ambivalence that darkens moments of civic celebration or ideological spectacle. Priam is shown as sponsoring a performance of Hector's chivalry that can stave off the effects of decay or history. However, Priam's lack of judgement elsewhere, and his celebrated fate at the fall of the city, militate against a wholly celebratory function for this passage. I suggest that Hector's body is more a rhetorical construction which represents functions both of epic narrative – the lively portrayal of the past, lest it decay and be lost – and of political assertion within the narrative: Hector is dead, Priam's actions claim, but by creating this apparently inalienable monument of Hector's preserved body, the Trojans will misrecognize it as still alive and exerting agency, believing that he will protect Troy. Such creative misrecognition is important not only to political symbols but to gift exchange.[27] In either of these readings, Hector's value as a vibrant object relies on the persuasive power of the ingenious makers. Without their skill, he would quicky fall apart – both physically, and in his capacity as resonant thing to shore up

Priam's legitimacy amidst crisis: 'Things fall apart; the centre cannot hold.'[28] In the longer sweep of the Trojan story, in which the exchange of (and refusal to exchange) gifts, tokens, persons and blows constitutes the narrative itself, this attempt to stop time, to refuse exchange and transformation, and to cling to the past by pretending that an idol has not fallen, is a kind of anti-narratorial gesture, ultimately doomed to failure. The material realities of Hector's dead body, tending towards change and decay, must constantly be fictionalized as both preserved and lively by Priam's craftsmen. As readers, we may be impressed by the craft involved, but we know that this state of affairs will not last for ever.

In this passage, then, Lydgate describes the Trojans' beliefs about Hector's power even after death; reveals Priam's role as sovereign in attempting to maintain the fiction of Troy's stability through this ekphrastic vision of chivalry; and perhaps also shows that these acts of power staged by the king are part of and reliant on a kind of mythmaking that aligns the roles of monarch and of storyteller or poet.[29] The poem does not, I believe, straightforwardly endorse the idea of sovereign power as the creator of ideological storytelling for the people, creating a myth of chivalric action that works as well as reality. Instead, elements of chivalric celebration, prudential history, moral commentary and the intrusion of Fortune into romance-style narration create a patchwork of competing positions and possible responses from readers, none of which overwhelms the others.[30] It is in this sense that concepts of distributed agency or assemblage – here especially generic expectations, styles and possible responses – are valuable in reading the *Troy Book*.

A telling instance of how Hector's shrine creates unexpected readerly effects comes later in Book IV, when a truce is held on the anniversary of Hector's death. Mourning rites take place and people 'Pleyne and wepe, & also preie and rede / For her frendis þat a-forn were dede' (IV.533–4). Achilles decides to pay a visit, 'With-oute wisdam or discrecioun' (IV.548). The body of Hector is still 'lifly ... as any rose newe' (IV.567–8), and this focus on the powerful liveliness of his corpse bleeds into the immediately subsequent description of Polyxena:

> But trowe ȝe (as Guydo list to telle)
> Þat Polycene, in al hir woful rage
> I-chaungid hath vp-on hir visage
> Hir natif colour, as fresche to þe siȝt

As is þe rose or þe lillye whiȝt?
Ouþer þe freshenes of hir lippes rede,
For al þe terys þat she gan to shede
On hir chekis, as any cristal clere? –
Hir heer also, resemblyng to gold wyre,
Whiche lay abrood like vn-to þe siȝt
[Of] Phebus bemys in his spere briȝt,
When he to vs doth his liȝt avale.
And ay she rent with hir fyngeris smale
Hir golden here on hir blake wede,
Of whiche þing Achilles toke good hede. (IV.582–96)

In a scene shot through with the texture of Troilus's first sight of
Criseyde in Chaucer's poem, Achilles is wounded by a combination
of the 'percyng stremys of hir eyen two'; 'Cupides brond'; and 'þe
arwe of þe god Cupide' (IV.603, 604, 609), the last of which enacts
a kind of martyr's wound, which 'Percid hym evene þoruȝ þe syde
/ To þe herte' (IV.610–11). The mingling of metaphorical and literal
wounding, sickness and complaint so familiar from *Troilus and
Criseyde* has a powerful impact here, coming so far into a story of
repeated, reciprocal violence.

This temple scene also seems to emphasize the power of objects
that carry narrative with them. As I have argued above, Hector's
preserved body can be read as a piece of poetic, aureate making.
Here, that analogy is transferred onto the blazon of Polyxena: pale
skin, red lips, crystal tears, gold hair, black clothes, turning her too
into an irresistible text that Achilles reads against the grain: as an
object of desire, not a mourning subject.[31] His love is an unwelcome
gift that turns out to be fatal poison. Having shocked the Trojans
(and the narrating voice) by the cruel way in which he killed Troilus,
Achilles is lured back to the temple of Apollo by Hecuba with a
promise of discussing marriage with Polyxena, and he is killed there
by Paris and others. This set of exchanges – of looks, blows, love,
(mis)reading, and bloody wounds – interlocks with the larger systems
of exchange in the poem. At the moment of Achilles' death, Lydgate
is also especially taken up with his own give and take with Chaucer's
Troilus. In a passage referencing Chaucer's poem, Lydgate dwells
on revenge as economic transaction, payment for payment:

Þus was þe fraude & þe falshede quit
Of Achilles, for his hiȝe tresoun:

As deth for deth is skilfully guerdoun
And egal mede, with-outen any fable,
To hem þat be merciles vengable.

* * *

Loo! here þe ende of falshed and vntrouþe,
Loo! here þe fyn of swiche trecherie,
Of fals deceit compassid by envie!
Loo! here þe knot and conclusioun,
How God quyt ay slauȝter by tresoun!
Loo! here þe guerdoun & þe final mede
Of hem þat so deliten in falsehede. (IV.3196–200; 3210–16)

This passage adapts Pandarus's comment to Criseyde that 'love for love is skilful guerdonynge' (*Troilus and Criseyde*, II.392). His pressure on Criseyde to understand relationships as economic transactions is transposed here to the rhetorically balanced but ethically hollow proposition that 'deth for deth' is equal payment, placed in the minds of 'hem þat be merciles vengable'. The subsequent eruption of 'Loo! here' utterances raises different questions about voice and tone from *Troilus* V.1849–55, which they invoke. There, the whole edifice of pagan myth and service to the gods is (apparently) condemned in one stanza. The audience is invited to think of Troilus's fate (or the description of it, perhaps including Chaucer's poem itself) as a self-defeating 'guerdoun' for service to the old gods: 'Lo here, the fyn and guerdoun for travaille / Of Jove, Appollo, of Mars, of swich rascaille!' (V.1852–3). Lydgate's equivalent comes in the condemnation of pagan gods and idols at the end of Book IV of the *Troy Book*. But the lines in *Troilus* are complexly voiced, allowing for several kinds of effect, especially since a five-book poem has just been devoted to exactly the pleasures and pains of this kind of 'travaille', 'guerdoun' and 'rascaille'. Read at an angle, the final couplet of Chaucer's stanza – 'Lo here, the forme of olde clerkis speche / In poetrie, if ye hire bokes seche' (V.1854–5) – could even constitute an invitation to explore as much as to despise ('Look, here is some of the [irresistible] material to be found in old writers' work, if you want to seek out their books'). By the time Lydgate was writing the *Troy Book*, Chaucer's status in the company of 'olde clerkis' was becoming established (partly through Lydgate's promotion of him), and Chaucer's work takes

its place in a continuing exchange of authority and textual matter
with the next generation of writers.[32] Lydgate's Troilean language,
'in-eched' at the moment of Achilles' death, deepens the sense of
déjà vu that this history of violence continues to provoke, but also
shifts its ethical lens, eventually making the unconvincing claim
that the story shows 'How God quyt ay slauȝter by tresoun'.[33] The
Troy Book cannot ignore questions of payment, reward, revenge,
desert – they are the substance of its narrative. However, the poem
cannot easily resolve them: this is not a self-contained romance in
which repayments can be made and gifts returned to bring the story
to satisfying wholeness. The energies of exchange and revenge are
instead jostled between Classical paganism and Christian history,
and powerfully resonant things such as Hector's lively corpse,
Polyxena's aureate beauty and the bloody remains of Troilus
continue to generate further movements across the city boundaries
and further breaches of the bodily integrity of the *Troy Book*'s
protagonists.

So far in this chapter, I have argued that Lydgate's *Troy Book*
provides an especially extended and acute lesson in the flow of
people, bodies and objects. Lydgate, like other writers on the Trojan
War, is faced with a challenge in presenting this narrative with a
set of coherent actors who shape or control events, or a framework
of action that pays attention to large-scale historical forces, to the
intervention of the gods, to human prudence and folly, and to chance
happenings. Reading the *Troy Book* through its flow of gifts, bodies
and obligations can, I think, help us to uncover how the poem
tackles those challenges. The example of Hector's death and bodily
preservation crystallizes the issues, linking a rhetorical or artistic
vision of chivalry within the narrative, with the act of telling the
Trojan story as a whole. This form of kingly rhetoric might prompt
readers to be cautious of Priam's attempt to preserve a vibrant dream
of chivalry – to hold the centre, in Yeats's terms – within the cadaver
of its most shining example. Readings that see Lydgate's poem as
squarely aligned with a project of celebrating Lancastrian kingship,
military adventure and English nationalism underestimate, in my
view, the set of conflicting currents that muddy these waters, and
paying attention to the movement of things in the text can also help
us to appreciate the *Troy Book*'s own ambivalent materials, both

physical and textual. Tellingly, while Hector's embalmed body does not in the end shore up Troy's defences, its presence both draws Achilles to the temple and colours his reading of Polyxena as an irresistible text – his own Criseyde. In that sense, Polyxena is a doubly textual entity: already written into Trojan textual tradition, but also intertextually linked with Chaucer's Criseyde. Seeing cause and effect, person and object as part of a network or assemblage of forces and agencies in the poem, then, complicates our view of Lydgate as an author and his relationship to the constantly shifting energies of the Trojan narrative. Later, I will discuss Andrew Pickering's concept of 'dances of agency' as a possible aid in unpicking how forces and materials (not just of different scales but of different kinds) exert pressure on the narrative.[34] Nevertheless, I would resist a reading that sets vibrant things in play without reckoning on how craft and intention help shape those things, and how readers' own affordances remake them. I now want to focus on a section of the poem where the power of things comes under particular scrutiny.

Book IV: agency, reciprocity, materiality

Book IV of the *Troy Book* narrates the climax of the siege narrative. It incorporates the love of Achilles for Polyxena and his subsequent death, after he has killed Troilus; the plotting of Ulysses, Diomede and Antenor; the building of the Horse; the final invasion of the city; and a description of the fate of some of the Trojan women. In Book IV the flows of gifts, obligations, objects and powers are channelled towards Troy's destruction. I shall discuss four examples of this for what they tell us about agency, reciprocity and materiality in Lydgate's poem: the Palladium; Priam's death and the condemnation of pagan gods; the Trojan Horse; and the fate of Trojan women.

The Palladium is a marvellous statue that stands in the temple of Pallas and which the Trojans believe protects the city. After the traitor Antenor has plotted with Ulysses and Diomede over the Greeks' demands for money and for the banishment of Amphimachus, there is trouble in the city. The two Greeks challenge Antenor, suspicious that they themselves are being led into a trap. Antenor then relates the origins and supposed protective power of the Palladium:

> For þer cam doun from þe hiȝe heuene,
> By Pliades and þe sterris seuene,
> And þoruȝ þe eyr holdyng his passage,
> Like a fairy a merueillous ymage,
> Þat in þis world þouȝ men had[de] souȝt,
> Ne was þer noon halfe so wel [y-]wrouȝt. (IV.5583–8)

Antenor goes on to say that even Pygmalion, 'remembrid in the Rose' (IV.5590), would not have been able to make this statue, and that it was 'wrouȝt wiþ dilligent labour / By hond of aungil in þe heuenly tour, / Þoruȝ Goddes myȝt & devyn ordinaunce' (IV.5593–5). He claims that the gods have granted it such power ('vertu') that Troy will never be ruined or taken, 'Til þis relik stole be a-way' (IV.5611).[35]

The Palladium, then, like the preserved body and statue of Hector, is a resonant object, but this time is a gift from the gods, whose power extends over the city and the narrative. It has acquired the characteristics of an inalienable possession.[36] Its status is reinforced by stringent access controls, meaning that only the temple priest may touch it. And like Hector's body, it apparently gives protection to Troy:

> [Minerva] I-graunted hath, in bokes as I lerne,
> Þoruȝ hir power whiche [þat] is eterne,
> Þis holy relik for a memorial
> To hir temple of bildyng most royal,
> It to conserue from al assaut of drede,
> And to socour in euery maner nede
> Ageyn her foon vn-to Troye toun,
> While it is kept with deuocioun. (IV.5635–42)

But things in the *Troy Book* – as in other romance and epic narratives of the flow and counterflow of obligations, goods and people – rarely last like this. Antenor's descriptions hint at what is to come in temporal clauses that qualify the statue's powers: 'Til þis relik stole be a-way' (IV.5611); 'While it is kept with deuocioun' (IV.5642). Indeed he proposes to remove it himself by bribing the temple priest Thonant. When he meets Thonant, Antenor's guileful speech plays on the counterbalancing of two kinds of goods: money for the statue, and the assigning of blame away from the two of them and

onto Ulysses, so that Antenor and Thonant shall 'goon al quyte'
(IV.5782). Lydgate's description of the priest's response, moving in
fifteen or so lines from adamant refusal to willing complicity, is
skilfully constructed to show the motion and effects of gold on the
will, also metaphorically invading the body:

> And first þis prest gan hym to with-stonde
> Ful myȝtely, and seide, for no þinge,
> Nouþer for praier nor for manacinge,
> For gold nor good, ne no maner mede
> He nolde assent to so foule a dede!
> (Þus he answered at þe prime face.)
> But ofte sithe it happeth men purchase
> By ȝifte of good, to speke in wordis pleyn,
> Þat trouþe in pouert myȝt neuer atteyne:
> For mede more by falshede may conquere
> Þan title of riȝt, þat men in trouþe lere;
> And ȝiftes grete hertis can encline;
> And gold, þat may no stele & marbil myne,
> Þis prestis hert hath so depe graue,
> Þat Anthenor shal his purpos haue,
> For to possede þe Palladioun. (IV.5806–21)[37]

This passage plays variations on a well-known topic of avarice and
the power of money. Here, the physical capabilities of gold are
cross-referenced with its persuasive power. Thonant's heart finally
becomes a pliable surface on which a false text can be engraved,
or a pattern worn away by a mark of gold, but those images mingle
with ones presenting the heart or mind of the priest as like a besieged
city or building, which gifts can make to lean and fall ('ȝiftes grete
hertis can encline'), mingling the literal and figurative meanings of
'encline'. Gold here has more agency than Thonant's malleable body
and mind. With this proleptic capture of a Trojan citadel through
his 'ȝiftes grete' Antenor succeeds in removing the Palladium, and
the flow of resonant things can continue, leaving tantalizingly present
the idea that the statue might have protected the city, had it not
been removed by human greed.

The Palladium's removal enacts a set of questions about the powers
of gods, gifts and things in the narrative. At the end of Book IV,
these questions, which as we have seen have lurked around from
poem's start, erupt into an outburst against the whole pagan pantheon.

It is sparked by the comment that the gods take no vengeance for the killing of Hecuba and of Polyxena:

> Þat an evele chaunce
> Come [to] þeis false goddes euerychoon!
> And her statues of stokkes & of stoon,
> In whiche þe serpent & þe olde snake,
> Sathan hym silf, gan his dwellinge make;
> And fraudently folkes to illude,
> Ful sottily kan hym silfe include
> In ymagis, for to make his hold,
> Þat forged bene of siluer & of gold. (IV.6930–8)

Whereas the end of Book III saw Hector raised to godlike status for the Trojans, here Lydgate's narrating voice exposes the gods as either powerless, or inhabited by diabolical forces. They cannot guarantee an ethical return from this narrative, and instead its dark exchanges lead to further and larger acts of violence. The condemnation of 'ymagis … forged … of siluer & of gold' resonates not only with the false image of the Trojan Horse, but also with Priam's attempts to apotheosize Hector. As has been discussed by, for example, James Simpson and Shannon Gayk, the outburst against the gods reveals fissures in the texture of the poem.[38] It seems to protest too much, as if Lydgate is trying to banish the nagging concern that by relating this Classical story he is allowing pagan gods to have ongoing powers through his narrative process. The *Troy Book*'s passage speaks to the fifteenth-century image debate, its rhetoric against pagan gods sharing language with Wycliffite condemnation of images, while elsewhere in his work Lydgate mounts a layered reflection on idols and images 'as textual *loci* where multiple histories, figures, traditions, and sources of authority intersect'.[39] But this passage also exposes the unsettled status of how people, gods and things act in the narrative, something which we saw to be at work at the start of the poem, with that question about whether the Myrmidons were really sprung from ants, or whether this was a just-so story to explain their productive nature. More proximately, it is part of the mix of pathos and distance surrounding the death of Priam. In this moment, the Trojan king is portrayed as a martyr, sacrilegiously murdered in a temple. But Priam's fate is also the culmination of his acts of folly and political misjudgements that have undermined his authority. He is a victim to be pitied, an exemplum of political grandeur but also lack of prudence, and a demonstration of the folly of pagan belief:

> [Pyrrhus] To-fore þe autere shad[de] þere his blood,
> Þat þe stremys of his woundys rede
> So hiȝe rauȝt, boþe in lengþe and brede,
> Þat þe statue of gold bornyd briȝt
> Of þis Appollo, for al his grete myȝt,
> For al his power and his sterne face,
> Defouled was, and pollut al þe place –
> Only by deth of þis worþi kynge
> By Pirrus slayn while he lay knelynge,
> Of olde hatrede & envious pride. (IV.6408–17)[40]

These plural understandings of Priam are at work in the generic texture of Lydgate's writing, but they are also bound up with his role in the movement of objects, persons, words and things into and out of Troy.

The scene of Priam's death forms the culmination of a series of entries into the city, and especially that of the most infamous gift object in the history of Western culture: the Trojan Horse. If ever there were a piece of vibrant matter, an object that acts in narrative, it should be this one. But it too is complex. It is an artefact of human ingenuity and construction, both compassed by people and containing people, but also a figure for human failure, lack of insight and inability to control destinal forces. Lydgate reminds us of the human skill that went into making it. It is an object freighted with meaning; a sign that is also a deception; a thing that is also a vessel for human soldiers; a work of art so persuasive that its audience pulls down the walls of their city to let it in:

> And of assent þei dide make a stede,
> Large and wyde, of coper & of bras,
> By crafte of Synoun, þat contrived was
> Þat it myȝt resseive large and wel
> A þousand knyȝtes armed briȝt in stel, –
> Þoruȝ þe sleiȝte and þe compassynge,
> Þe sotil wit & merveillous werchinge
> Of þis wyse and crafty Greke Synoun, –
> Whiche, þoruȝ his castynge and discrecioun,
> Parformed haþ þis riche stede of bras. (IV.6052–61)

Lydgate describes the Horse as a skilfully crafted piece of making (in the physical sense and, I believe, in the Middle English sense of poetic making). The description here focuses not on what it looks like, but what it contains and even more on the artistry of its designer. Synon's craft provides an envelope structure to the passage itself ('crafte of Synoun ... crafty Greke Synoun'). The other words denoting the Horse's artistry insistently come back to his design and cunning: 'sleiȝte'; 'compassynge'; 'sotil wit'; 'merveillous werchinge'; 'wyse and crafty'; 'castynge and discrecioun'. The Horse is 'parformed', primarily meaning 'constructed'; 'completed'; but carrying a potential meaning of putting into practice or carrying out a promise or plan.[41] In this passage of the poem, interconnecting trails of give and take, exchange and movement of persons and things come together. Exits and entrances from Troy include the allies that are now leaving Priam and the city, because they believe that the terms of peace have been settled:

> Whan þei saw how Priam be couenaunte
> Vn-to Grekis haþ outterly made graunte
> Al hast possible to paien his ransoun,
> Þei toke leve, and went oute of þe toun. (IV.6091–4)

Another set of debts is apparently paid by the return of Helen and transfer of money and goods by the Trojans, and the oaths sworn by both sides. Lydgate's often-criticized syntax wraps itself sinuously around the reciprocal movements of the plot and of bodies and words in this passage:[42]

> And þus whan alle were fro Troie gon,
> Þe morwe next Priamus anon
> With his lordis rood oute of þe toun,
> As was þacord for confirmacioun
> Of þes final vp-on ouþer syde.
> And in þe feld Grekis hym abide;
> And, on relikes openly y-born,
> Þer þei wen on ouþer parti sworn,
> On þe forme to ȝow a-fore recorded,
> As Anthenor with Grekis was accorded. (IV.6105–14)

The two sides come together over the relics that sanctify their oath-swearing, though it is another Greek–Trojan interchange, that between Antenor and his co-conspirators, that underlies and undermines the reciprocity of this one. Lydgate reminds his readers that God knows all, and can see through perjury: 'For God, þat knoweþ þe entencioun, / Demeth þe herte, & þe word riȝt nouȝt' (IV.6146–8).[43] However, this is one of those moments in the *Troy Book* where moral commentary bumps up against the claims of historicity in the story. The Greeks swear falsely and yet do succeed in sacking Troy. The Horse too is part of this structure of oath-exchange, linking peace between the warring parties with a gift to Pallas. The Horse, the Greeks claim, will be an offering to the goddess to atone for the theft of the Palladium from Pallas's temple: 'To make a-seth [recompense, restitution] by oblacioun / For þe þefte of Palladioun' (IV.6177–8). In this sense, its narrative trajectory is both fitting and all the more subversive, piling a false oath on top of the theft. Like an insincere speech act in Austinian terms, the Horse is still a gift, but an unhappy one, which both symbolizes and exemplifies the darker cycles of vengeance that characterize the Trojan story.

The coming home of these long-laid-down exchanges gives direction to the final sections of Book IV of the *Troy Book*, pointed especially through the fate of women and their responses to Troy's fall. The Greeks claim that they will be retreating to Tenedon to protect Helen, since some Greeks want to kill her:

> For she was grounde & gynnynge of her wo,
> Þe verray rote and the cause also
> Of þe slauȝtre of many worþi man. (IV.6259–61)

With 'woman as the cause of strife' embedded as an explanatory model for the conflict and loss, questions of how to describe or value female protagonists recur in these sections of the *Troy Book*. In addition, Lydgate uses the fate of the Trojan women to intensify the affective description of the fall of the city; to license the focus on individual suffering or on things falling apart (bodies, the city); and to provide a countering set of propositions which, though swept aside by the onrush of events and male action, nevertheless give an alternative perspective on epic history.[44]

Once the Greek soldiers have been let out of the Horse by Synon to sack the city, the story is focalized for a time through Priam's reaction, waking to the noise and realizing that he has been deceived: 'But þo he wist þat þer was tresoun / Falsly compassid vn-to his cite / By Anthenor and also by Enee' (IV.6316–18). The passage that follows takes Priam's initial perspective and broadens it to invoke the workings of vices including 'þe galle of conspirac[i]oun', 'fraude', 'envie and contrived hate', 'deceit & olde conspiracie' (IV.6321; 6325; 6329; 6331), turning the historical narrative into a moral one, peopled by these abstractions become active things. The allegorical narrative mode here serves as a meditation on distributed agency within the person. After a further savage description of the despoiling of the city buildings, and leaving Priam awaiting his death in the temple of Apollo, it is through the Trojan women that Lydgate details the bodily impact of the destruction, ironically using the trope of *occupatio* to lead into the most close-up, material depiction:

> And in her dool þer y lete hem dwelle;
> For alle her sorwes ȝif I shulde telle
> In þis story, and her wo descrive,
> Mi penne shuld of verray routhe rive,–
> Rehersinge eke how in euery strete,
> Her cloþes blake, rodi, moiste, and wete,
> As þei, allas! bothen oon and alle,
> On her lordes doun a-swone falle,
> With her blod be-dewed & y-spreint,–
> Wher men may seen þe cristal teris meynt
> Of her wepinge in þer woundes grene,
> Þay lay and bledde ageyn þe sonne shene,
> With dedly eyen castinge vp þe whyte:
> It were but veyne al her wo to write,
> Nor þe maner of her mortal sorwe. (IV.6373–87)

This passage is added to Guido's very short observation that 'The rest of the women remained in the palace of the king with much weeping' (p. 224), and Lydgate changes Guido's account by placing the women he writes about with Cassandra in the temple of Minerva. The broken body parts of the killed are mixed here with the lamenting bodies of the women, tears and blood mingling and disturbing the borders between living and dead, person and object. But the effect of transference is not only from bleeding bodies of 'her lordes' to the women. The passage is framed in the subjunctive, using blood, tears, clothes, wounds, eyes synecdochally as a gauge of the impossibility of writing in full about the horror of what happened. A sense of displacement is generated from the narrating voice's claim that his pen would break ('rive') if a full account were given, but then opening the door to this very description by imagining '[r]ehersing' these very horrors. Imagining an account then becomes the account itself. Female lament in its full force would disrupt the male pen and force the narrative to a halt. The story only continues by re-sourcing it with a reference to what 'Guydo writ' (IV.6388). This passage licenses Lydgate's descriptive language in particular by associating it with the experiences of the women of Troy, their tears and their menfolk's blood as a kind of supplementary ink for the writing of the poem, at a point where the male, clerical, moralizing and prosthetic 'penne' cannot continue.[45]

Women's voices and the exchange of women continue to have prominence for the remainder of Book IV's narrative. Hecuba rails against Aeneas, but also appeals to him to have pity on Polyxena, and he hides her, 'mevid of pite' (IV.6506). Andromache and Cassandra are taken into the custody of Ajax, and Menelaus receives Helen. Subsequent arguments over the fate of the women become a signal of the operation of pity and the possibility of restitution even after the destruction of Troy. These women-as-objects slide in the narrative between possessions, symbols of the defeated city, and persons with their own interests, sometimes accruing more than one category and making themselves assemblages of multiple interests in and through the narrative.[46] Polyxena in particular signals these plural qualities in a speech she makes just before being killed by Pyrrhus. Its initial address to the gods approaches the language of Egeus in *The Knight's Tale*, encompassing their knowledge of every 'þing', its creation and material processes, but then focuses on her soul and her body as the conduits through which that attention should be directed:

> O ȝe almyȝti, that þis world gouerne,
> And euery þing considren & discerne,
> By whom þis world, so huge, large & rounde,
> Boþe eyr & see, heuene & eke þe grounde
> At ȝoure devis with a word was wrouȝt,
> And sothfastly knowen euery þouȝt,
> Riȝt as it is, of euery maner wyȝt,
> With-oute lettinge, so percynge is ȝoure siȝt,
> Þat no þing is conseled nor y-wrye
> From þe beholdyng of ȝoure eternal eye,
> And euery þing may attonis se, –
> Vp-on my soule hath merci and pite! (IV.6731–42)

Drawing attention to her virginity as a measure of physical integrity alongside her innocence of Achilles' death, and in a kind of reversal of the artificial preservation of Hector's body, her martyr's speech already draws attention to her self as a collection of parts: physical, psychological and spiritual, including 'soule'; 'wo'; 'woful spirit'; 'maydenhede'; 'port and chere, and in countenaunce'; 'clere & pure'; 'wil, dede, word, nor þouȝt'; 'my blood'; 'breth'; 'My tendre hert'.[47] The end of her speech likewise conjures the gods to take into their care her 'dredful goost' (IV.6847), before closing her speech and life simultaneously with 'and þus an ende I make' (IV.6848). This attention to Polyxena as assemblage of parts is emphasized with bitter irony immediately afterwards, as Pyrrhus 'Dismembrid haþ with his sharpe swerde / Þis maide ȝonge' (IV.6853–4), realizing externally and horrifically the logic of person as assemblage that Polyxena's speech worked with. It could be argued, of course, that this is a familiar medieval way of thinking about self. While not making undue claims for its originality, at this point in the poem and given Lydgate's depiction of persons as collections of tangible matter and intangible qualities, I think that it does important work, channeling through this female body at the moment of its break-up the ethically charged attributes that personhood comprises.

We have seen how the Troy Book's narrative is characterized by exchanges of gifts and persons, words and blows. In that sense, it bears similarities to the structures of exchange embedded in romances such as The Romance of Horn. However, Lydgate's poem is also committed to an understanding of historical writing that must use the past for ethical lessons to the present, and maintain some distance from the pagan narrative it retells. The framework of agency in which the narrative operates is strained by these competing generic and political motivations, and at times there is clear conflict between them. The things of the poem – Hector's cyborg corpse, for example – likewise have moments of suggestive power or persuasive presence. They can resonate, open narrative pathways and bind persons in relationships. But noticing their bulk, composition, their material presence or their narrative trajectory does not necessarily amount to their having agency in themselves in the story. They are as likely to be collaborations with or projections of human assemblage and human desire, and while their non- or posthuman materials provoke wonder or persuasion, Lydgate also wishes his readers to understand the weight of moral responsibility for action lying significantly with a different kind of assemblage: the force of qualities or emotions such as pity, wrath or hate. Lydgate's ambivalence – his admission of multiple entities, actants and sometimes competing claims to responsibility in the story – creates rifts in his narrative that sometimes burst open, as with the lengthy condemnation of the pagan gods at the end of Book IV, but they also create a sense of the layered, contingent and complex historical process that his audience was not only reading about, but living through in the early fifteenth century. A writer familiar with the material world, who catalogues and at times celebrates it in his work, Lydgate (as Lisa Cooper and Andrea Denny-Brown suggest) had a capacious understanding of 'matter' at different levels:

> 'Matter' for Lydgate is a term that stretches to encompass not only the details of many and various poetic projects but also the body that weights us down and holds us back; the objects, both necessary and less so, with which we furnish our everyday lives; and the intellectual and spiritual illumination that we urgently seek to find and strain toward when it seems within our grasp (and, quite often, even when it does not).[48]

In the *Troy Book*, matter encompasses the materials from which the city and its monuments are constructed and then broken apart, and the stuff from which the world is shaped. In Book I, for example, stories of Medea's power as a sorceress are challenged by the narrating voice, which reaffirms God's sole control over nature. Part of the misogynistic rhetoric accompanying this argument sees women described as matter in search of form ('as matere by naturel appetit, / Kynd[e]ly desyreth after forme' (I.1876–7)), and as a dangerous source of material instability in the world: 'of nature to mevyng þei be thewed' (I.1893). Overwhelmingly amongst its 98 uses, however, the word *mater* in the *Troy Book* denotes a subject of discussion within the narrative, or Lydgate's textual matter.[49] To take examples from Book IV, Agamemnon defends his leadership, claiming that 'no man hath mater to compleyne' (IV.202);[50] Priam urges Amphimachus to keep their plot against Aeneas and Antenor secret: 'late so be ordeyned / Þat þis mater cloos be kepte in mewe' (IV.4936–7); this plot is then revealed: 'þe mater whiche þei had on honde / Discured was' (IV.5042–3); Antenor describes the problem of the

Palladium to Ulysses and Diomede: 'Þer is o þing perturbeth þis mater' (I.5558). In these uses, the word means something like 'business', 'topic', but also potentially 'cause' or 'substance'. Lydgate's 'textual' uses of *mater* include 'And þus I leue hem siȝe and sorwe make ... While I turne to my mater ageyn' (III.5575, 5578), introducing the passage describing Hector's preserved body and oratory; and 'I can no more touchinge þis matere, / But write forþe, lik as ȝe shal here' (IV.2687–8), turning his text and our eyes away from the shocking details of the death of Troilus.

The *mater* of Troy, then, involves the raw materials from which the world is formed (both the world of the poem and ours); the plans and exchanges between protagonists, often overlapping with the verbal description of those matters; and the tradition of narrative history and romance into which Lydgate is inserting his poem. His re-creation of Trojan history is in some ways explicitly distanced, for example by the citing of Guido as *auctor*, or by his attacks on the pagan gods. But the trajectories of *mater* help to link the narrative's materials with the experience of its readers. Unlike Chaucer in *Troilus and Criseyde*, Lydgate does not use a small fragment of the conflict to reflect both minutely and epically on individual agency, trajectory and chance. Like Chaucer, however, and in the tradition of Trojan texts, the *Troy Book* does confront its readers with the relations between human choices, fortune, give and take, systems of belief and the alluring but troubling role of material things in these stories.

Andrew Pickering uses the term 'dance of agency' to describe the coming together or interplay of different materials in performance:

> Dances of agency have a *decentred* quality—they are zones of intersection where the non-human world enters constitutively into the becoming of the human world and vice versa. They cannot be accounted for by focusing either on the human or the non-human alone.[51]

In Lydgate, we can see some dances of agency at work, between human and non-human persons, things and materials; in the relationships between author, tradition, textual matter and manuscript performance; and in the *Troy Book*'s continuing life in the hands of its readers. Pickering draws on Bruno Latour's argument that 'modernity itself is characterized by an impulse somehow to make a clean separation between people and things'.[52] This is of course a contestable statement about modernity, but also leaves open questions about how other periods (dis)entangled things and people, especially since one of the fundamental observations in gift theory concerns the entanglement between persons and things. As we have seen in this book, each text and interaction between person and text is in the process of negotiating or reflecting on those entanglements. Pickering promotes what he calls 'mangling' as the effect of dances of agency: 'What is at stake in dances of agency? Everything. Everything one can think of is liable to open-ended transformation here, *mangling* as I call it.'[53] Pickering employs the term partly polemically to deny hierarchies or distinctions between agents, whereas in Lydgate and elsewhere I find it more convincing to think of the *interplay* of agency, tendency and affordance, with some kinds of agency more prominent or effective than others at certain moments. I will briefly discuss a moment from Book IV as it appears in MS Eng. 1, to reflect on these dynamics.

Interpreters and imagetexts

MS Eng. 1's pictures are at interplay with the text. They themselves constitute a narrative, they accompany the textual narrative and they compete with it for space and priority. One page of the manuscript that literally illustrates the shifting relationship between the materials that make up the poem is fol. 145v (Figure 4). It contains Book IV, lines 5969–6056, in which Cassandra tells the Trojans that Apollo is angry with them because of the killing of Achilles in his temple, and that they must light torches at his grave; she also says that an eagle flying away from Troy indicates that the city will be destroyed. For readers attuned to the flow of entrances and exits to the city, the eagle highlights this pattern. Meanwhile the Greeks take heart from the same sign, and Calchas proposes building the Horse to breach the Trojan defences. This passage of the poem begs the question of how far non-human actants have agency or predictive power. It describes and to an extent enacts a desire to read and be swayed by prognostications from the material world, but this desire is set at a remove from the audience. Cassandra and Calchas are both shown as interpreters and makers of the narrative, playing analogous roles to that of 'clerkes' in Lydgate's Prologue, who interpret history for

Figure 4 Manchester, John Rylands Library MS English 1, fol. 145v

current rulers. However, that clerkly interpretation is 'for to bere witnesse' (Prol. 185) to the truth. Clerkly roles in the narrative, especially of Calchas, are much more ambivalent, and this pressurizes the Prologue's claims that interpreting history allows clerks to speak truth to power. Significantly, in the Prologue the truth-telling element of historical writing is figured as retrospective: its own pressure on rulers is made by analogy and exemplum, and requires those rulers to be involved as good readers.[54]

The passage of the *Troy Book* represented on fol. 145v is shot through with such interplays of agency. While interpreting things at narrative level, Lydgate's 'matterful' writing is also evident in smaller scale, more rhetorical ways, for example in describing Calchas's future reputation as a traitor:

> [Calchas] Whom clerkis han putte in remembraunce
> In her bokis, wiþ lettris, olde and newe,
> To exemplifie no man be vntrewe:
> For þauȝ ȝeris passe faste a-weye,
> Ruste of sclaundir liȝtly wil nat deye;
> Þe fret þer-of is so corosif,
> Þat it lasteþ many mannys lyf,
> And is ful hard to arrace away. (IV.6026–33)

Reputation is presented here as written text.[55] It consists of 'lettris' on a page, and the reminder that 'clerkis' are responsible for this reputation echoes the Prologue's claims for clerkly authority. These lines also operate as a metaphor imagining reputation being corroded by condemnation ('sclaundir'), not a matter of chance or melting over time, as in Chaucer's *House of Fame*. The passage then mingles these closely related images of written text and rusting metal, noting the difficulty of 'arrac[ing]' condemnation once it is embedded.[56] Here, Calchas has merged into the trace he makes in the materials of written text and tarnished name.

The passage then describes the Horse's construction, made of copper and brass, housing a thousand knights 'armed briȝt in stel' (IV.6056). The imagery erodes distinctions between the Horse and the knights, both becoming parts of a war engine covered in or made from metal. However, it is still possible to distinguish between Horse as container and made object with resonance and power, signifying relations of revenge and violence, and the human actors inside who (while embedded in circumstance, narrative and equipment) should exercise ethical judgement. The page is immediately dominated by its four-part illustration. Moving from the left-hand margin and sweeping across the lower part of the page, it shows the Horse with its creator, Calchas; Greek troops led by a king (Agamemnon? name worn away) attacking Troy; the city walls breached and corpses falling from the ramparts or scattered around them, with the Horse now inside Troy and the Trojans being killed;

and the murder of Priam in a temple (the killer is labelled 'Rex Merion' but the text says that Pyrrhus killed Priam). The poem places the killing in the temple of Apollo, though the illustration is of a generic pagan temple, or one of Venus. This page, and the manuscript as a whole, works as a constantly shifting set of relationships between text, image, reader and listener, scribes and artists, author and sources, material as poetic 'matere' and material as the parchment page and what is used to cover it. To borrow W.J.T. Mitchell's influential terms, fol. 145v can be thought of as an imagetext, but that implies not simply a relationship of mutual support or interweaving, but of tension and interaction. Mitchell's conceptualization of the relationship bears similarities to the other relations of object and narrative, or text and reader, that we have been discussing in this chapter:

> We might summarize the predicates that link word and image with an invented notation like 'vs/as': 'word vs. image' denotes the tension, difference, and opposition between these terms; 'word as image' designates their tendency to unite, dissolve, or change places. Both these relations, difference and likeness, must be thought of simultaneously as a vs/as in order to grasp the peculiar character of this relationship.[57]

A relation of vs/as can characterize narrative exchanges, whether of gift object, or the exchange between languages and authors in translation and transmission of stories. The gift is both a representation of an obligation or of repayment, and is a mark of difference that creates new debts, new energies in transfer or accrual. It is both illustration and narrative. In MS Eng. 1, the pictures are at interplay with the text, in a relationship of give and take: they do not merely reflect a stable text, but tug at and rearrange the assemblage of materials that the manuscript's user experiences. In a detailed study of one of the most richly illustrated romance manuscripts of the Middle Ages, Mark Cruse similarly describes dynamic relations not only in its creation but use and adaptation:

> Bodley 264 is not a static or silent manuscript but the enabler of dynamic interaction between different individuals and communities: the authors of the works compiled in it, the manuscript's patron, scribes, illuminators, and those in England who, decades after its original creation, commissioned and executed the expansion of Bodley 264 into the book we know today.[58]

Talking about this interaction as an assemblage can raise useful questions about the distribution of agency and constraint amongst the persons and things involved in a manuscript's making, as long as this does not lead us to evade questions of ethics or responsibility, and I think can work alongside my proposal in Chapter 2 that we can think of the Auchinleck Manuscript as a system of overall obligations, in which exchanges of language, genre and ethics take place. Such an interplay of relationships has a claim on its fifteenth-century readers. As several studies have suggested, Troy is a contemporary subject for late-medieval English writing.[59] Its originary claims for British history make the Troy story both exemplum and precedent; its relationship to the present is both parallel and continuous. I am now going to read in the borders of MS Eng. 1's text, to explore how this *Troy Book* is enmeshed in such a temporal, imaginative and material fabric, dealing in exchange between writer and patron, past and present, text and audience.

Pretexts, patrons and *hors-texte*

On folio 1r, a rubric introduces the *Troy Book* with these words:

> Here begynneth the boke of the Sege of Troye, compiled by Daun John Lydgate monke of Bery atte excitacioun and steryng of the moost noble worthi and mighty Prynce kyng Henry the fyfthe. ffirste rehersyng the conquest of the golden flees acheued by the manly prowesse of Jason. Under the correccioun of euery prudent reder.

This signals some of the structures of affiliation and exchange in which the *Troy Book* operates. Lydgate is here a compiler of learned history. The impetus for the compilation has come from royal desire – 'excitacioun and steryng' – suggesting both a projection of the King's internal state, and an active movement on his part. Lydgate is (in more than once sense) performing royal desire. The rubric notes the major topic of Book I: Jason and the golden fleece. It then returns to questions of agency by placing the text under the correction of prudent readers. Prudential judgement is, of course, one of the key qualities that the Troy legend describes and tests. The rubric, then, encapsulates some of the assembly of materials and intersections that this manuscript brings together in embarking on reading the poem.

Above the rubric is a half-page picture, the first illustration in the manuscript (Figure 2). In an architectural setting showing a palatial building with turrets, roofs and casements cut away to reveal a tiled chamber, a king, enthroned and crowned, holds a sceptre in his left hand. His right hand is placed around a book, which a kneeling, tonsured figure in the black robes of a Benedictine monk appears to be presenting. To the king's right stands a bearded man bearing a sword, which overlaps the canopied space of the throne. Both this swordbearer and the king look down and (to the viewer's) left towards the kneeling monk. This scene of course depicts Lydgate presenting the *Troy Book* to Henry V. Kathleen Scott notes that an antelope, or sejant (Henry V's badge) is depicted on the building's cupola.[60] The scene binds this represented figure of Lydgate in a relationship of service and reciprocity with the King. Lydgate is drawn into a circle of honourable service and literary distinction: the book as product of his pen's compilations echoes and matches the sword and sceptre, symbols of Henry's power to create and act. The presentation picture also emphasizes gift exchange as at interplay with royal commissioning in the generation of literary texts.[61] This retrospective image of the beginning of the poem's public life imagines Lydgate as giver, as well as servant.

In the Prologue to the *Troy Book*, this give and take of obligation between author and monarch is signalled in the language describing Henry. However, the Prologue starts not with an English king but with an invocation to the god Mars. A seven-line initial for the opening 'O' of the poem is placed immediately under the rubric on fol. 1r, and intertwines with the floreate full borders of the page. Mars is '[t]he myghty lorde, the god armypotent' (Prol. 4), and 'the brydel lede / Of cheualry, as souereyn and patrown' (Prol. 6–7). He is 'causer … / Of werre and stryf in many sundry rewmys' (Prol. 17–18). The passage asks for Mars's aid in retelling the Trojan legend, not simply because of his intrinsic connection to the story, but because of his love for Venus and Bellona. Mars is called on to supplement Lydgate's lack and correct his pen:

> So be myn helpe in this grete nede
> To do socour my stile to directe,

And of my penne the tracys to correcte,
Whyche bareyn is of aureat lycour. (Prol. 28–31)

In a scenario reminiscent of the dead Hector being kept in the semblance of liveliness by Priam's craftsmen's 'licour', Mars's influence must help a barren author live through the gift of eloquence, before also calling on Othea 'goddesse of prudence' (Prol. 38) to make Clio Lydgate's muse; and on Calliope mother of Orpheus, so that 'of thy golde dewe lat the lycour wete / My dulled brest' (Prol. 55–6).[62]

   Lydgate's introduction of Henry, 'eldest sone of the noble kyng, / Henry the firþe, of kny3thood welle & spryng' (Prol. 95–6), interleaves his qualities with some of Mars's. The Prologue thus diversifies the origin, agency and impetus for the text's creation, aligning Mars, the muses and the prince; the author-compiler is then embedded in that system of exchange between power, narrative telling and reputation.[63] Lydgate says that his work of translation was undertaken 'For to obeie with-oute variaunce / My lordes byddyng fully and plesaunce' (Prol. 73–4), and describes Henry as wishing to 'remembre ageyn' (Prol. 76) the value of old chivalry in order to follow virtue and 'to eschewe / The cursyd vice of slouthe and ydelnesse' (Prol. 82–3). While the Prologue, then, ascribes power to Henry, it also places him in a series of exchanges between old virtue and contemporary vice, and it sites him both as a powerful prince and a young man willing to be taught how to avoid sloth, while making available the Trojan legend in English, 'By-cause he wolde that to hy3e and lowe / The noble story openly wer knowe / In oure tonge' (Prol. 111–13). The Prologue goes on to describe a pattern of balancing interests in which noble deeds performed by princes and others are celebrated by writers, while bad behaviour is censured. Elsewhere I have discussed the way in which this relationship pressurizes the princely reader to live up to the prudential advice contained in Lydgate's Classical narratives.[64] Here I shall simply note how this passage too connects past deeds, historical writing, and current politics and ethics in a system of overall obligations. In fact, while Lydgate's rhetoric projects the repayment of obligation and assessment of value back into the past and forward to future retellings, he is acutely aware of the entanglement of gift and commodity that his current project implies.[65]

At the end of the Prologue, this balancing act comes into play with Lydgate's praise of his main source, Guido delle Colonne. By a sort of alchemy of style, Lydgate claims, Guido retained the substance and meaning or ethical valence of Dares and Dictis, but transformed the story to make something new and rich:

Ther was an auctour of ful hiȝe renoun
That besied hym the tracys for to swe
Of Dite and Dares, & cast hym nat transmwe
In al the story a worde as in sentence,
But folweth hem by swyche convenience,
That in effecte the substaunce is the same;
And of Columpna Guydo was his name,
Whiche had in writyng passyng excellence.
For he enlvmyneth by crafte & cadence
This noble story with many fresche colour
Of rethorik, and many riche flour
Of eloquence to make it sownde bet
He in the story hath ymped in and set,
That in good feythe I trowe he hath no pere,
To rekne alle þat write of this matere,
As in his boke ȝe may beholde and se.
To whom I seie, knelyng on my knee:
Laude and honour & excellence of fame,
O Guydo maister, be vn-to thi name,
that excellest by souereinte of stile
Alle that writen this mater to compile. (Prol. 354–74)

As elsewhere in Lydgate's work where aureate style is both praised and employed, he makes a claim about Guido's (prose) work, while insinuating the qualities Lydgate claims for it into his own poetic. At the end of the Prologue, Prince Henry is no longer the royal figure in front of whom Lydgate kneels as patron; now it is Guido as 'maister', whose 'souereinte of stile' grants him an elevated status amongst writers.[66] The value judgements in this last passage turn the 'matere' of Troy into a currency that can be 'rekne[d]', and then passed on by Lydgate, who prays that 'it be vn-to the pay / Of hym for whom I haue vndertake / So as I can this story for to make' (Prol. 376–8). The 'hym' is in one sense Henry, who should find reward or benefit from the text, but because Henry is unnamed, Guido remains at the forefront of the reader's mind as a literary patron. Guido is also constituted by his writing: he is a text, or his text has come to embody or be animated as 'Guido'. As the *Troy Book* continues, Guido is Lydgate's name to conjure with: summoning him as authority; marking narrative transitions; citing in order to diverge from, move forward with or ground the story.[67] Guido has become 'matere' from which the Troy story emerges, as in turn will Lydgate.

A reader of MS Eng. 1, then, will have a field of exchanges, values, agencies and materials to encounter between the presentation picture and the close of the Prologue. But there is something else about the picture on fol. 1r that provides another layer to the dynamics at work here. At the left-hand side of the palace, there is an arched doorway from which two figures are emerging. One is a man in leggings and a red jacket/blouson, wearing a pink turban whose end he holds across his chest in his left hand while the other rests on his belt (Scott describes him simply as 'a man in aristocratic dress'). The other figure is much smaller, though no more distant from us, and appears to be a child. They look like they are setting off on a path that leads away from the viewer, through a gateway in a curtain wall and into the landscape beyond. The artist of MS Eng. 1's illustrations, whom Scott calls 'the Master of the Eng. 1 manuscript', characteristically achieves a sense of movement and dynamic action in his pictures. Here, the enclosed presentation scene has its own implied movement, layered by a number of enmeshed obligations and exchanges. It is focused on the book as the centre of the image: hands, eyes, sceptre and sword framing and directing our attention towards it as it moves from author to reader. The departing figures provide a contrasting sense of movement and incipient narrative. Are they derived from an episode in the *Troy Book* itself? Are they retained or adapted from a model in another presentation scene? Might a fifteenth-century viewer have interpreted them as representing the path of the reader in embarking on the major journey of the Troy story itself, a text that teaches adults and the young about chivalry, war, politics and fortune, as well as about the exchanges that constitute poetic narrative? I will now turn to the closing movements of the poem and manuscript, to trace where that path may lead.

After the bloody climax of Book IV, the final book of the *Troy Book* deals with the division of spoils, settling of debts, and journeys home, including that of Ulysses. As readers of MS Eng. 1, we also have moved physically through the manuscript and are nearing its conclusion; if reading continuously, our path maps that of the narrative, but manuscript books equally allow us to skip and delve into different parts of the story, or move from one picture to another. Lydgate too binds a sense of journey and expenditure into the final part of the poem, stating that exhaustion has nearly overtaken him, and that he will summon a last effort to describe Ulysses' death ('Of his ende þe surplus for to telle' (V.2914)), before he too is spent:

> For I shal now, lyk as I am wont,
> Sharpen my penne, boþe rude & blont,
> To descryue þe fyn of þi soiour,
> Vp-on þe boundis set of my labour:
> For almost wery, feint & waike I-now
> Be þe bestes & oxes of my plow,
> Þe longe day ageyn þe hil to wende.
> But almost now at þe londes ende
> Of Troye boke, ficche I wil a stake,
> Saue I mote spende a few lines blake
> Þe laste chapitle shortly to translate
> Of al þis werke. (V.2923–34)

In this transition passage, the confluence of Lydgate's expenditure on the text; the journey of the narrative and its protagonists; the coming home of debts and the payback of the story; and Ulysses' death as a surplus in/to the narrative, bring together a number of the currents that have guided the poem, here imagined in the rich metaphor of ploughing a furrow in a textual field.

The 'surplus' narrative of Ulysses' death is separated from his odyssey (where Lydgate leaves Ulysses and Penelope 'in Ioie and in solace' (V.2311)) by the death of Pyrrhus, following Guido's order of narration. When we return to Ulysses, we arrive in a romance-toned story of his dream of a beautiful woman whom Ulysses tries to embrace and pursue, but who escapes:

> And Vlixes, with hir loke supprysed,
> Gan hir beholde al-weie more & more,
> And in his slep for to siȝe sore,
> Presyng ay with ful besy peyne
> Hir tenbracen in his armys tweyne;

> But ay þe more he presed hir to se,
> Ay þe more from hym [she] gan to fle;
> And ay þe more [þat] he gan purswe,
> She ageynwarde gan hym to eschwe,
> So contrarie to hym was fortune! (V.2972–81)

Guido's description of Ulysses' dream sees him encounter a beautiful young man carrying a spear. When Ulysses asks to approach him 'so that I may perchance recognize you', the youth replies: 'oh, how unfortunate that union would be! For it is necessary that one of us die from such a union' (p. 259). In a reversal of the model of Aeneas's tantalizing encounter with Anchises in *Aeneid* VI, Ulysses here sees a vision of his son Telegonus, and their exchange suggests both the payback of Ulysses' bloody actions during the siege, and a transfer of power and masculinity from one generation to the next, symbolized by the spear with which Ulysses will later wound Telegonus without recognizing him, and which Telegonus returns with interest, giving Ulysses his mortal wound. Lydgate's version of the dream shifts the dynamic. It becomes a mini-allegory of unchecked male desire, echoing the dangers of mislooking that Paris and Achilles fell into. It also reproduces the characteristics of a dream of Fortune, where desire for power or wealth is figured as male sexual desire for an outwardly attractive but fickle woman. Here Lydgate's poem is drawn back to the destructive role of Fortune in the course of events that we noted early in this chapter, while the coming 'home' of Telegonus, the child seeking his absent father, is a familiar romance plot pattern whose structure foregrounds the repayment of debts and refashioning of relationships through telling. In the case of Ulysses, this exchange of telling and (for)giving comes too late to save his life ('He vn-to hym anoon for-gaf his deth / As he myȝt for want & lak of breth' (V.3259–60)), but the romance pull towards reintegration is satisfied by the alliance of Telemon and Telegonus after their father's death.

The final acts of Lydgate's narrative are the division of wealth between the brothers, followed by Telegonus returning to Circe, her joy at his return and subsequent death ('hir dette ȝalde vn-to nature' (V.3311)), and the two brothers' long reigns and eventual deaths. The contestive relationships between Ulysses and his sons are uncomfortably reminiscent of the strained relations between Henry V and his father, especially in the final period of the latter's reign just as Lydgate was embarking on the *Troy Book*.[68] Nevertheless, the poem ends with a direct address to Henry V, optimistically predicting that his hoped-for unification of England and France will lead to a stabilization of the polity after bloody conflict, comparable to the long reigns of Telemon and Telegonus. Henry has as it were grown up into kingship himself over the course of the *Troy Book*, having been described as 'eldest sone of the noble kyng' (Prol. 95) in the Prologue, and now 'Herry þe Fyfþe, þe noble worþi kyng / And protector of Brutis Albyoun' (V.3376–7).[69] After Henry's conquests in France, this passage imagines that his bride Katherine's arrival will bring with it 'Plente, welfare, and fulsom abundaunce' (V.3434) amongst a list of other benefits, and an absence of 'Meschef, pouert, nede, or indygence' (V.3437) with even 'ful cessyng of deth & pestilence' (V.3438).

These final sections of the poem mingle a number of conceptions of the relations between Lydgate, his work and his patrons. Praise and prayers for Henry V's security and prosperity rub up against Lydgate's monitory explanation of the Troy story, in which Fortune, in her 'cours mutable' (V.3547) has 'Lordes, princes from her royalte / Sodeinly brouȝt in adversite, / And kynges eke plounged in pouert' (V.3549–51). The list becomes darker, with

> Vnwar slauȝter compassed of envie,
> Mordre execut by conspirasie,
> Await[e] liggyng falshede and tresoun,
> And of kyngdammys sodeyn euersioun, –
> Rauysshyng of wommen for delyt,
> Rote of þe werre & of mortal despit. (V.3553–8)

The answer to mutability and violence is, as at the end of *Troilus and Criseyde*, to turn to Christ. Lydgate then addresses Henry again, praying that Christ will grant him a long reign and a place in the ninth sphere after his death. Henry becomes a Christianized Troilus who can enjoy both this world's goods, and a peaceful ascent to the heavens. However, the previous section established that this is dependent on escaping Fortune's clutches, 'For þer is nouþer prince, lord, nor kyng, / Be exaumple of Troye, like as ȝe may se / Þat in þis lif may haue ful surete' (V.3576–8).

Lydgate's introduction of the language of gift and grace, especially as he moves into the poem's envoy to Henry, and address to the book, signals his interest in this balance of reciprocal action between monarch/patron, and poet/adviser. The *Troy Book*, as a product of long labour and poetic heft, can then take part in a more equal transaction with King Henry. Returning the poem imaginatively to the scene depicted in the presentation picture on fol. 1r of MS 1, Lydgate asks:

> Late good wil my litel gift amende,
> And of þi mercy & renomed goodnesse
> Haue no disdeyn of my bareyn rudnesse,
> And, in makyng þouȝ I haue no mvse,
> Late trewe menyng þe surplus [al] excuse. (Envoy, 73–7)

The envoy closes with Lydgate's reminder that nobody has anything more than 'good hert' to give to God or someone else, and that he presents this to Henry. The final address to the book both calls to the reader's mind the text's physical presence and its ventriloquizing role in the author–patron relationship, and places responsibility on readers to 'amende' (Envoy, 107) the poem, which Lydgate claims is 'enlumined with no floures / Of rethorik, but with white and blak' (Envoy, 100–1). While of course these final movements in the poem's voice are highly stylized and rhetorically layered, they point to a social fact about the *Troy Book*'s production and reception, circulating in a system of exchange both as a valuable object in itself, and as a cultural artefact.

Lydgate's warning that Fortune is always liable to bring down the powerful, was, reading after Henry's death in 1422, all too accurate. The poem's shape and texture – its affordance for readers – can accommodate a sense of nostalgia or the absorption of Henry into the catalogue of past rulers felled by Fortune. This shifting capability does not rely on reading the poem as deliberately monitory rather than celebratory, though my own sense is that these and other currents are working alongside and sometimes against one another throughout the *Troy Book*. However, by the time the arms of the Carent family were depicted on fol. 173r of MS Eng. 1, probably in the 1440s or shortly afterwards, political tension, rivalry and incipient conflict in England had made Lydgate's address to the prince all the more telling, and during the second half of the fifteenth century, the *Troy Book*'s narrative of reciprocal violence was available as a reflection on civil war and familial conflict much closer to home.[70] At the foot of fol. 172r, after the end of the 'Verba translatoris ad librum suum' the text hand has copied the popular rhyme 'Pees maketh plentee':

Pees makith plente	}	
Plente makith pride	}	
Pride makith plee	}	And therfore
Plee makith pouert	}	
Pouert makith pees	}	
Grace growith aftir gouernaunce		

This verse fills the last six lines of the page, and so gives it a look of completeness and unity. It also immediately offers a supplement to Lydgate's already massive project. The verse is a simple but powerful statement on the circularity of Fortune, the causes and consequences of war, and on one of Lydgate's major interests in the *Troy Book*: that of prudence and governance, both personal and political.[71]

This particular Troy book, then, accrued meanings different from those available to a reader of the poem in 1420. As both a literary form and a collection of performances in manuscripts with a developing set of connections and histories, Lydgate's poem interacted with scribes, readers and owners in an interplay of interests and agencies. Likewise MS Eng. 1 started its own trajectory as a presentation or gift book, resting at times with new owners as the result of donation or inheritance. Later it formed part of the stock of collectors and dealers, before being purchased by Enriqueta Rylands from the Earl of Crawford in 1901, and thence given to the John Rylands Library as a contemporary form of inalienable property whose value rests in its contribution to institutional reputation, to scholarly activity, to cultural reimagination, and to potential commercial reproduction. In this chapter, I have argued that the *Troy Book* can be read through the exchanges and paybacks of its plot, and that Lydgate pays attention to those moments when shifts in the balance of payments (through Fortune, battle, desire, deceit) call for answering payments or commitments. I have read some of the things described in the narrative as having effects, most often in relation to the desires of human protagonists, the agency of craftspeople, and ongoing flows of obligation and exchange. The *Troy Book*, that is, does not easily license us to think of Hector's aureate body as a piece of vibrant matter apart from the networks of agency and intention that made, view and describe it, even if the fiction of the text sees Trojan citizens believe in its own power. Further, I have suggested that thinking of these moments as dances of agency, or agency in interplay, can also be extended to the way that Lydgate negotiates the demands of Classical gods, the Christian God, the 'matere' of his sources, the power of exemplary analogy, and the direction of his text out to networks of patrons and readers. In a manuscript such as MS Eng. 1, we can see not only how these demands are managed synchronically in a particular performance of the poem, interacting with its cycle of illustrations, but also how this gift develops value and meanings diachronically through its own continuing itinerary. This *Troy Book* is both a gift book, embeds relations of giving and service in its text, describes multiple acts of exchange, and is part of an ongoing system of obligations stretching from Lydgate's textual predecessors to future readers and owners.

Notes

1 John Lydgate, *Troy Book*, ed. Henry Bergen, EETS e.s. 97, 103 and 106 (1906–10; reprinted as one vol., Woodbridge: Boydell & Brewer, 1996), Book I, lines 14–20. Quotations will be from this edition.
2 Compare the arguments about Theban texts, including Lydgate's *Siege of Thebes*, in James Simpson, 'Human prudence versus the emotion of the cosmos: war, deliberations and destruction in the late-medieval Statian tradition', in Stephanie Downes et al. (eds), *Emotions and War: Medieval to Romantic Literature* (Basingstoke: Palgrave Macmillan, 2015), pp. 98–116.
3 Cf. Stanley B. Greenfield, 'The authenticating voice in *Beowulf*', *Anglo-Saxon England* 5 (1976), 51–62. I do not have space to discuss in detail the narrating voice and its relationships, but in saying 'Lydgate writes' I do not mean to mask the complexities at work.
4 For discussion of the Troy Book's genre and claims to historical author-ity, see e.g. C. David Benson, *The History of Troy in Middle English Literature: Guido delle Colonne's 'Historia Destructionis Troiae' in Medieval England* (Cambridge: Brewer, 1980); Robert R. Edwards, 'John Lydgate and the remaking of classical epic', in Rita Copeland (ed.), *The Oxford History of Classical Reception in English Litera-ture, volume 1: 800–1558* (Oxford: Oxford University Press, 2016), pp. 465–83, at pp. 466–72.

5 See above, p. 47.

6 See e.g. Mann, 'Chance and destiny'.

7 For Fortune and temporality, see Simona Cohen, *Transformations of Time and Temporality in Medieval and Renaissance Art* (Leiden: Brill, 2014), pp. 73–9. The iconography of Fortune's Wheel in the MS Eng. 1 illustration matches the understanding of the Wheel as social and moral commentary, rather than being related to the Ages of Man, an idea assimilated in some later examples that she discusses.

8 Karen Elaine Smyth, *Imaginings of Time in Lydgate and Hoccleve's Verse* (Farnham: Ashgate, 2011), p. 59.

9 For the complex layering of time in Chaucer's Theban and Trojan texts, see especially Patterson, *Chaucer and the Subject of History*, chs 1 and 2.

10 As with Jason's hastiness in accepting Peleus's challenge, here Lydgate highlights Lamedon's imprudent action and lack of counsel. For prudential judgement and the importance of advice in Lydgate, see Benson, *History of Troy*, pp. 116–20, 124–8, John Lydgate, *Troy Book: Selections*, ed. Robert R. Edwards, TEAMS (Kalamazoo, MI: Medieval Institute Publications, 1998), 'Introduction', http://d.lib.rochester.edu/teams/text/edwards-lydgate-troy-book-introduction, accessed 20 February 2018; Nicholas Perkins, 'Representing advice in Lydgate', in Jenny Stratford (ed.), *The Lancastrian Court* (Donington: Tyas, 2003), pp. 173–91; Colin Fewer, 'John Lydgate's *Troy Book* and the ideology of prudence', *Chaucer Review* 38 (2004), 229–45; Scott-Morgan Straker, 'Propaganda, intentionality, and the Lancastrian Lydgate', in Larry Scanlon and James Simpson (eds), *John Lydgate: Poetry, Culture and Lancastrian England* (Notre Dame, IN: Notre Dame University Press, 2006), pp. 98–128.

11 *The Battle of Maldon*, in *The Cambridge Old English Reader*, ed. Richard Marsden, 2nd edn (Cambridge: Cambridge University Press, 2015), line 46.

12 A prime example of this would be Paris answering Hector's advice about securing peace with the Greeks, by proposing that instead he carries off a Greek woman (II.2305–68) in order to exchange her later for Hesione; and Helen's subsequent capture, reception in Troy and marriage to Paris. See also Nicola McDonald, '*The Seege of Troye*: "ffor wham was wakened al this wo"?', in Putter and Gilbert (eds), *Popular Romance*, pp. 181–99 on the valuing and exchange of women in another Middle English Troy narrative.

13 Hyde, *The Gift*, pp. 76–94; 59–60.

14 Jane Bennett, *Vibrant Matter: A Political Ecology of Things* (Durham, NC: Duke University Press, 2010), pp. xiii; 17. See also Diana Coole

and Samantha Frost, 'Introducing the new materialisms', in Diana Coole and Samantha Frost (eds), *New Materialisms: Ontology, Agency, and Politics* (Durham, NC: Duke University Press, 2010), pp. 1–43. On things and literary forms, see e.g. Leah Price, *How to Do Things with Books in Victorian Britain* (Princeton, NJ: Princeton University Press, 2012); Bill Brown, 'Thing theory', in *Things*, ed. Bill Brown (Chicago, IL: University of Chicago Press, 2004), pp. 1–22. See also two valuable essays by Kellie Robertson, reviewing approaches to materialism and medieval studies: 'Medieval things: materiality, historicism, and the premodern object', *Literature Compass* 5/6 (2008), 1060–80; and 'Medieval materialism: a manifesto', *Exemplaria* 22 (2010), 99–118. I discuss ways of reading romances materially in Perkins, 'Materiality of medieval romance'. Graham Harman, 'The well-wrought broken hammer: object-oriented literary criticism', *New Literary History* 43 (2012), 183–203, critiques literary study from the perspective of object-oriented philosophy, part of the movement called speculative realism. He challenges literary scholars to scrutinize and demote 'the Human agent' (p. 193) as central to their study. However, Harman tends to caricature critical positions, while the 'suggestions' for novel approaches fold down towards a search for 'how the literary object cannot be fully identified with its surroundings or even its manifest properties' (p. 202); this is an unobjectionable goal, but not something unique to object-oriented criticism. For a survey-cum-critique of materialism in the literary sphere, see David Hawkes, 'Against materialism in literary theory', in Paul Cefalu and Bryan Reynolds (eds), *The Return of Theory in Early Modern English Studies: Tarrying with the Subjunctive* (Basingstoke: Palgrave Macmillan, 2011), pp. 237–57.

15 See also Bruno Latour, e.g. *Reassembling the Social: An Introduction to Actor-Network-Theory* (Oxford: Oxford University Press, 2005). Daniel Miller debates the issues, especially questions of agency, in 'Materiality: an introduction', in Daniel Miller (ed.), *Materiality* (Durham, NC: Duke University Press, 2005), pp. 1–50; and see Christopher Pinney, 'Things happen: or, from which moment does that object come?', in Miller, *Materiality*, pp. 256–72.

16 The use of 'affordance' in this context to mean properties that an object possesses and how they might shape its use stems partly from the work of James J. Gibson, e.g. *The Ecological Approach to Visual Perception* (Boston, MA: Houghton Mifflin, 1979). See discussion in Lambros Malafouris, 'At the potter's wheel: an argument *for* material agency', in Carl Knappett and Lambros Malafouris (eds), *Material Agency: Towards a Non-Anthropocentric Approach* (New York: Springer, 2008), pp. 19–36. Malafouris argues that '*while agency and*

intentionality may not be properties of things, they are not properties of humans either: they are the properties of material engagement, that is, of the grey zone where brain, body and culture conflate' (p. 22, original emphasis).

See also Lambros Malafouris and Colin Renfrew, 'The cognitive life of things: archaeology, material engagement and the extended mind', in Lambros Malafouris and Colin Renfrew (eds), *The Cognitive Life of Things: Recasting the Boundaries of the Mind* (Cambridge: McDonald Institute, 2010), pp. 1–12. My stance differs somewhat from theirs, though their concen to stress the imbrication of things with subjects and minds bears a productive relation to ideas of personhood that I discuss in Chs 2 and 3. Their position is that 'very often, what we call an "object" is part of what we call a "subject". In short, things *are* us or can *become* us' (p. 4). In reading Lydgate's poem I want to delineate both Lydgate's concern with the possibilities and limits of human agency and intention in relation to other subjects and to things, and my (also conflicted, conditional) position, both via Lydgate as author and through those copying, illustrating and reading the *Troy Book*. For a critique of using affordance too loosely, or not accounting sufficiently for how people learn and use objects, see Martin Oliver, 'The problem with affordance', *E-Learning* 2 (2005), 402–13. Some of these questions are reviewed in Andrew M. Jones and Nicole Boivin, 'The malice of inanimate objects: material agency', in Hicks and Beaudry (eds), *Handbook of Material Culture Studies*, pp. 333–51.

17 For critiques from medievalist perspectives, see e.g. Andrew Cole, 'The call of things: a critique of object-oriented ontologies', *minnesota review* 80 (2013), 106–18; and Bruce Holsinger, 'Object-oriented mythography', *minnesota review* 80 (2013), 119–30. Cole points to medieval philosophical traditions that anticipate and challenge recent claims, and warns of the tendency to reinscribe the philosopher (and by implication, critic) as an authority who can 'hear the call of things and ... speak *to* and *for* them' (p. 107, original emphasis); see also above, Ch. 1, note 24. Anne E. Lester and Katherine C. Little debate different approaches in 'Introduction: medieval materiality', *English Language Notes* 53 (2015), 1–8, a journal issue exploring these ideas.

18 On the cyborg, see Donna Haraway, 'A cyborg manifesto: science, technology, and socialist-feminism in the late twentieth century', in Donna Haraway, *Simians, Cyborgs and Women: The Reinvention of Nature* (New York: Routledge, 1991), pp. 149–81. Haraway's trajectory is towards feminism, late-twentieth-century technologies and the body – all apparently far from the preserved Hector – but this work is influential in querying the 'leaky distinction ... between animal-human

(organism) and machine' (p. 152), and the themes of gender, distinction, identity and ideology are all raised by the *Troy Book* episode. For medieval prosthesis and reading bodily adaptation, see Katie L. Walter, 'Fragments for a medieval theory of prosthesis', *Textual Practice* 30 (2016), 1345–63. My thanks to Hannah Ryley for discussing this aspect of the *Troy Book* passage with me.

19 On artworks as projecting agency, and the desire for viewers to imagine the source(s) of that agency, see Alfred Gell, *Art and Agency: An Anthropological Theory* (Oxford: Clarendon Press, 1998), briefly discussed in Miller, 'Materiality', pp. 12–14; Jones and Boivin, 'Malice of inanimate objects', p. 340.

20 For a different reading of those Chaucerian connections, see Paul Strohm, 'Sovereignty and sewage', in Lisa H. Cooper and Andrea Denny-Brown (eds), *Lydgate Matters: Poetry and Material Culture in the Fifteenth Century* (New York: Palgrave Macmillan, 2008), pp. 57–70, at 66–7. My thanks to Paul Strohm for discussing this passage with me.

21 On Lydgate and aureation, see Lois Ebin, *Illuminator, Makar, Vates: Visions of Poetry in the Fifteenth Century* (Lincoln: University of Nebraska Press, 1988). For readings of revenant Chaucer in fifteenth-century texts, see e.g. James Simpson, 'Chaucer's presence and absence, 1400–1550', in Boitani and Mann (eds), *Cambridge Companion to Chaucer*, pp. 251–69, and references there; Nicholas Perkins, 'Haunted Hoccleve? *The Regiment of Princes*, the Troilean intertext, and conversations with the dead', *Chaucer Review* 43 (2008), 103–39; Barr, *Transporting Chaucer*.

22 Strohm, 'Sovereignty and sewage', p. 62.

23 See above, pp. 44–8.

24 Strohm, 'Sovereignty and sewage', p. 68.

25 Fewer, 'Ideology of prudence', pp. 238, 239.

26 Ibid., p. 240.

27 Cf. Bourdieu's idea that 'méconnaissance' is fundamental to the gift relationship, discussed above, Ch. 1. Hector's preserved body does not, however, ultimately provide Troy with the protective powers imagined for it.

28 W.B. Yeats, 'The Second Coming', line 3, in *The Collected Poems of W.B. Yeats*, 2nd edn (London: Macmillan, 1950).

29 For late-medieval and early modern courts as sites of staging and spectacle, see Barbara A. Hanawalt and Kathryn Reyerson (eds), *City and Spectacle in Medieval Europe* (Minneapolis: University of Minnesota Press, 1994); Seth Lerer, *Courtly Letters in the Age of Henry VIII: Literary Culture and the Arts of Deceit* (Cambridge: Cambridge University Press, 1997).

30 Cf. Andrew Lynch, '"With a face pale": melancholy violence in John Lydgate's Troy and Thebes', in Bellis and Slater (eds), *Representing War and Violence*, pp. 79–94. Lynch's thoughtful essay suggests that Lydgate uses 'both chivalric and clerkly discourses of war, but ... seems to bring them to the point of fatal compromise and collapse' (p. 80).

31 MS Eng. 1's illustration here shows a temple, but with Venus as presiding goddess, and women not in mourning robes (fol. 115r). Given how the generic mix of this passage has shifted towards romance, it is notable that Achilles is depicted in the MS illustration as a young man, whereas earlier, when wounded in his tent (fol. 112r) and surrounded by his troops, he is shown as old with a white beard.

32 For Lydgate's relationship with Chaucer's work, see e.g. Lerer, *Chaucer and His Readers*, esp. ch. 1; Christopher Baswell, '*Troy Book*: how Lydgate translates Chaucer into Latin', in Jeanette M.A. Beer (ed.), *Translation Theory and Practice in the Middle Ages* (Kalamazoo, MI: Medieval Institute Publications, 1997), pp. 215–37; Simpson, 'Chaucer's presence and absence'; Edwards, 'Remaking of classical epic'. Focusing on *The Siege of Thebes* but posing relevant arguments is A.C. Spearing, *Medieval to Renaissance in English Poetry* (Cambridge: Cambridge University Press, 1985), esp. pp. 59–88.

33 For 'in-eched' as a way to describe Chaucer's additions to *Il filostrato* in *Troilus and Criseyde*, see *Troilus and Criseyde: The 'Book of Troilus' by Geoffrey Chaucer*, ed. B.A. Windeatt (Harlow: Longman, 1984), pp. 7–9.

34 See below, pp. 214–15.

35 On Antenor's curious reference to *The Romance of the Rose*, see Philip Knox, '*The Romance of The Rose* in Fourteenth-Century England' (doctoral dissertation, University of Oxford, 2015), p. 234.

36 See Weiner, *Inalienable Possessions*, and above, Ch. 2.

37 In line 5818 Bergen emends London, British Library MS Cotton Augustus A. iv to read 'þat may in stele'. I think that the manuscript reading makes more sense, and so I have reverted to it here.

38 James Simpson, *Under the Hammer: Iconoclasm in the Anglo-American Tradition* (Oxford: Oxford University Press, 2010), ch. 2; Shannon Gayk, *Image, Text, and Religious Reform in Fifteenth-Century England* (Cambridge: Cambridge University Press, 2010), pp. 84–122.

39 See Simpson, *Under the Hammer*, p. 59; the quotation is from Gayk, *Image, Text, and Religious Reform*, p. 86.

40 Lydgate's phrasing echoes the crow's words to Phebus (Apollo) in *The Manciple's Tale* (IX.249–52).

41 *MED*, sv. *performen* (v.). The meaning of performing a part in a play, or reciting a poem, for example, is first noted by the *OED* (sv. *perform* (v.)) in the mid-sixteenth century, but the word is used for the construction

or completion of a building or decorative structure from the fourteenth century.

42 On Lydgate's syntax see Phillipa Hardman, 'Lydgate's "uneasy" syntax', in Larry Scanlon and James Simpson (eds), *John Lydgate: Poetry, Culture and Lancastrian England* (Notre Dame, IN: Notre Dame University Press, 2006), pp. 12–35.

43 Lydgate expands this from a brief reference in Guido to the proverb 'Who swears falsely, perjures falsely': Guido delle Colonne, *Historia destructione Troiae*, trans. Mary Elizabeth Meek (Bloomington: Indiana University Press, 1974), p. 222. Subsequent quotations from this translation will be cited in the text by page number.

44 See my discussion of Emily and Criseyde, above, Chapter 3.

45 On medieval texts' play with the intersections of blood, tears and ink, see Martha Rust, 'Blood and tears as ink: writing the pictorial sense of the text', *Chaucer Review* 47 (2013), 390–415.

46 For prisoners as both possessions and persons, see above, pp. 000–000.

47 IV.6742, 6744, 6746, 6751, 6753, 6765, 6771, 6778 and 6796, 6818, 6823.

48 'Introduction', in Cooper and Denny-Brown (eds), *Lydgate Matters*, pp. 1–11, at pp. 2–3; cf. Robertson, 'Medieval materialism', pp. 110–15.

49 See *A Lemmatized Concordance to Lydgate's 'Troy Book'*, ed. Hiroyuki Matsumoto (Tokyo: Shohakusha, 2007).

50 An identical line occurs in Agamemnon's speech about the division of spoils: IV.6559.

51 Andrew Pickering, 'Material culture and the dance of agency', in Hicks and Beaudry (eds), *Handbook of Material Culture Studies*, pp. 191–208, at p. 196. I am grateful to Katherine O'Brien O'Keeffe for discussing Pickering's work in relation to pre-Conquest manuscripts, in her lectures in Oxford in 2017, and in conversation.

52 Ibid., p. 197. This is Pickering's summary, citing Bruno Latour, *Science in Action: How to Follow Scientists and Engineers through Society*, trans. Catherine Porter (Cambridge, MA: Harvard University Press, 1987), and Latour, *We Have Never been Modern*, trans. Catherine Porter (Cambridge, MA: Harvard University Press, 1993).

53 Pickering, 'Material culture', p. 196. See also the term 'meshwork', employed by Malafouris and Renfrew, 'Cognitive life of things' (e.g. p. 4, 'meshworks of material engagement'), influenced by the work of Deleuze and Guattari.

54 On kings as readers in fifteenth-century regiminal texts, see Perkins, *Hoccleve's 'Regiment'*, ch. 2.

55 For Lydgate's concern with fame and reputation, see Mary Flannery, *John Lydgate and the Poetics of Fame* (Cambridge: Brewer, 2012).

56 See *MED*, sv. *aracen* (v.), meaning 3(b), giving examples from Chaucer and Lydgate of rubbing out or blotting away that bring metaphorical erasure close to textual correction.

57 W.J.T. Mitchell, 'Word and image', in Robert S. Nelson and Richard Shiff (eds), *Critical Terms for Art History* (Chicago, IL: University of Chicago Press, 1996), pp. 51–61 at p. 53. See also Roland Barthes, 'Rhetoric of the image', in his *Image Music Text*, trans. Stephen Heath (London: Fontana, 1977), pp. 32–51, esp. p. 47: 'The language of the image is not merely the totality of utterances emitted ... it is also the totality of utterances received: the language must include the "surprises" of meaning.'

58 Mark Cruse, *Illuminating the 'Roman d'Alexandre': Oxford, Bodleian Library, MS Bodley 264: The Manuscript as Monument* (Cambridge: Brewer, 2011), p. 181.

59 See e.g. Benson, *History of Troy*; Sylvia Federico, *New Troy: Fantasies of Empire in the Late Middle Ages* (Minneapolis: University of Minnesota Press, 2003); Marion Turner, *Chaucerian Conflict: Languages of Antagonism in Late Fourteenth-Century London* (Oxford: Clarendon Press, 2007), chs 2–3.

60 Kathleen L. Scott, *Later Gothic Manuscripts, 1390–1490*, 2 vols (London: Harvey Miller, 1996), II.259. On author illustrations and authority in Lydgate's *Fall of Princes*, see Lerer, *Chaucer and His Readers*, pp. 40–4. For a survey of *Troy Book* illustration, see Lesley Lawton, 'The illustration of late medieval secular texts, with special reference to Lydgate's "Troy Book"', in Derek Pearsall (ed.), *Manuscripts and Readers in Fifteenth-Century England: The Literary Implications of Manuscript Study* (Cambridge: Brewer, 1983), pp. 41–71.

61 See McGrady, *The Writer's Gift or the Patron's Pleasure?*, p. 9, describing presentation scenes and dedicatory addresses as 'sites of negotiation', with writers aiming to 'define their relationship with the political elite as a partnership built on the free circulation of intellectual riches'. My thanks to her for discussing these issues with me in Colorado.

62 The classic study of the strategic deployment of dullness is David Lawton, 'Dullness and the fifteenth century', *ELH: A Journal of English Literary History* 54 (1987), 761–99.

63 For a valuable reading of the Prologue cognate with mine, but emphasizing Lydgate's laureate ambitions and celebration of Henry, see Robert J. Meyer-Lee, *Poets and Power from Chaucer to Wyatt* (Cambridge: Cambridge University Press, 2007), pp. 65–75. Meyer-Lee argues that the poem has 'two idealized agents at its center': the prince and the translator, and that '[a]long with being a "memorial" to Henry, the poem ... will be a memorial to itself' (p. 68).

64 Perkins, 'Representing advice'.
65 Cf. McGrady, *The Writer's Gift or the Patron's Pleasure?*, p. 16.
66 For a comparable sense of clerkly authority and genealogy in a manuscript of Lydgate's *The Fall of Princes*, see Lerer, *Chaucer and his Readers*, pp. 40–4.
67 As e.g. with the bloody description of the sacking of Troy discussed above, pp. 210–11.
68 See e.g. Gerald Harriss, *Shaping the Nation: England 1360–1461* (Oxford: Clarendon Press, 2005), pp. 501–6.
69 Cf. Chaucer's description of Henry IV as 'conquerour of Brutes Albyon' in *The Complaint of Chaucer to his Purse*, line 22.
70 On the Carent arms and the manuscript's ownership, see J.J.G. Alexander, 'William Abell "lymnour" and fifteenth-century English illumination', in Artur Rosenauer and Gerold Weber (eds), *Kunsthistorische Forschungen: Otto Pächt zu seinem 70. Geburtstag* (Salzburg: Residenz Verlag, 1972), pp. 166–72, at p. 169; Kathryn Warner, 'The provenance and early ownership of John Rylands MS English 1', *Bulletin of the John Rylands Library* 81 (1999), 141–54; Scott, *Later Gothic Manuscripts*, p. 262; and MS Eng. 1's description at https://archiveshub.jisc.ac.uk/data/gb133-engms1. One candidate for commissioner or early owner is William Carent (d. 1476), who had interests in Somerset and Dorset, and was at various times a Member of Parliament for those counties, an Escheator, Commissioner of Enquiry, and a Sheriff. See his biography in *The House of Commons 1386–1421*, ed. J.S. Roskell et al. (Stroud: Alan Sutton, 1993), via www.historyofparliamentonline.org/volume/1386-1421/member/carent-william-1476, accessed 10 February 2018. Carent seems to have been an able administrator for the Crown under Henry VI, and his brother-in-law John Stourton had a trusted position in the royal household, becoming Lord Stourton. Carent was also linked to John Beaufort, Duke of Somerset. These connections with influential figures, and his services for the Crown (for which he received substantial documented rewards), would be a potential means by which Carent may have commissioned or been given MS Eng. 1. The biography notes that 'During the crises of 1459–61 Carent seems to have … adopt[ed] an impartial stance as far as possible … and showed himself ready to offer his services to the Yorkist regime when the time came.' Carent's status and involvements make him just the kind of gentry reader whose ownership of regiminal texts signals a concern with questions of governance, ethics and exemplary action in fifteenth-century England; see Perkins, *Hoccleve's 'Regiment'*, pp. 171–7.
71 *DIMEV* 4354; *NIMEV* 2742. This verse survives in fifteen manuscripts, many of which also include major regiminal or Lydgatean texts, e.g.:

Oxford, Bodleian MS Digby 230 and Oxford, St John's College MS
6 (*Troy Book*); Chicago, University of Chicago Library MS 566;
Oxford, Bodleian Library MS Rawlinson poet. 140 and London, BL
MS Harley 629 (*Life of our Lady*); Cambridge, CUL MS Ff.1.6 (the
Findern Manuscript); Cambridge, Trinity College MS R.3.22 (*Life of our
Lady;* Hoccleve's *Regiment of Princes*); London, Society of Antiquaries
MS 34 (*Life of our Lady*; *Confessio amantis*; *Regiment of Princes*;
Walton's Boethius translation); Princeton, Princeton University Library
MS Taylor Medieval 5 (*Confessio amantis*).

Conclusion

Happily, everything is not yet classified exclusively in terms of purchase and sale.[1]

I have sought to do a number of things in this book. To start with, I hope to have furthered the case for reading narratives from medieval England alongside the stories, propositions and debates engendered by gifts and exchanges, including those in Anthropology and theory. I believe that this kind of interaction between imaginative writing and reflections on gift and exchange help to open more paths for reading medieval texts, here especially romances. I suggest that this happens not only because gift-giving, the exchange of objects, people, and language (such as promises or curses) is a topic or theme that these narratives employ – although it is, and is symbiotically connected with practices of exchange in medieval culture. I think that this kind of reading is productive in particular because thinking about the gift inevitably opens up new levels of analysis. Gifts give impetus to stories because at the point of giving they are usually imbalanced, providing a surplus, perhaps fostering pleasure, signalling virtue or power, and imposing an obligation to receive and return later in the narrative. Gifts embroil people with other people, and people with things. For that reason, paying attention to how exchanges happen and their consequences in these narratives leads onto questions not only about narrative process, surplus and resolution, but about the value and trajectories of persons and things in stories. I believe that romances and related texts provide welcome ground for those trajectories, because romances' focus on telling *as* meaning, and on objects as both part of the narrative and representative of (the) narrative, highlights how exchanges between people also involve the histories and obligations of other exchanges, in the past and future of the narrative. Implicit in my readings of these stories – some of them celebrated, some relatively understudied or regarded as humdrum by many readers – is that they explore complex ideas about relationships, value, agency, gender and linguistic exchange, and that their often conservative, sometimes designedly reductive, endings do not erase the contradictory or plural possibilities engaged in their narrative process. I have been thinking about them as a form of speculative Anthropology, that imagines other peoples in order to examine customs, desires, dilemmas, beliefs and other forms of interplay in the groups that they represent, while all the time these imaginative narratives are at interplay with their own under-standings and those of their audiences.

One way in which I have tried to extend this concern with gifts and exchange in the texts I have read, is by paying attention to how telling is also a form of giving. Horn's explanation to Hunlaf of his family history, debts and journey; Amourant's expenditure of loyalty to Amiloun by recounting the bond between his master and Amis; Orfeo's gift of song, which moves his audiences to generosity; Gawain's return to Arthur's court with a story in words, wound and silk; the pledges and prayers of Chaucer's Theban and Trojan protagonists; generosity of word and body in *The Franklin's Tale* and its obverse in *The Manciple's Tale*; the rhetorics of boast and curse; the claims made of and in Hector's body and the Palladium; the false story spun by the gift of the Trojan Horse; the carefully weighed language of deference, gift, advice and reciprocal obligation made by Lydgate's authorial persona; the way that many medieval books, including MS Eng. 1, are both gifts and storytelling objects: all these suggest the ability of linguistic events to create or shape obligation, either in the act of giving objects, or as speech acts themselves. This is not to say that by nominating them as gifts they cease to also be mingled with other processes of calculation, com-modification or power. Entanglements of these kinds are not simply evaded in the gift, and nor is there some straightforward line advancing from more gift-orientated cultures and texts to those more orientated around commodities and closed payments: the messiness and danger of dealing with gifts and commodities is clearly apparent in medieval texts. Nevertheless, I do not believe that the gift as process or idea is merely a comforting fiction or narrative MacGuffin in medieval texts – a shiny object that leads us through the narrative but in the end is empty or emptied of meaning. Its claims on receivers in stories and receivers of stories are powerful, sometimes disturbing. They stretch out beyond individual narratives to work across story collections, manuscript compilations, patrons and audiences: from the early listeners to *The Romance of Horn* to the *Gawain*-Poet's call that we too give some time to listen to his story. In a world where being generous with goods, time or by opening the self to others is often seen as quaint or naïve, that call, and those claims, still deserve our attention.

Note

1 Mauss, *The Gift*, p. 177; *Essai sur le don*, p. 219.

Bibliography

Manuscripts and facsimiles

Manchester, John Rylands Library MS English 1; Digital images available via https://luna.manchester.ac.uk/luna/servlet/view/search?q=reference_number=%22English%20MS%201%22

The Auchinleck Manuscript: National Library of Scotland, Advocates' MS. 19.2.1, intr. Derek Pearsall and I.C. Cunningham (London: Scolar Press, 1977)

The Auchinleck Manuscript, ed. David Burnley and Alison Wiggins, https://auchinleck.nls.uk/editorial/project.html

Published primary sources

Amis and Amiloun: Zugleich mit der Altfranzösischen Quellen, ed. Eugen Kölbing (Heilbronn: Henninger, 1884)

Amys e Amillyoun, ed. Hideka Fukui, ANTS Plain Texts Series 7 (London: ANTS, 1990)

Andreas Capellanus, *On Love*, ed./trans. P.G. Walsh (London: Duckworth, 1982)

The Battle of Maldon, in Richard Marsden (ed.), *The Cambridge Old English Reader*, 2nd edn (Cambridge: Cambridge University Press, 2015)

Klaeber's 'Beowulf', 4th edn, ed. R.D. Fulk, Robert E. Bjork and John D. Niles (Toronto: University of Toronto Press, 2008)

The Birth of Romance: An Anthology, trans. Judith Weiss (London: Dent (Everyman), 1992)

Camden, William, *Britannia* ... (London: [Eliot's Court Press], 1607), p. 185, via Early English Books Online, https://eebo.chadwyck.com/home

The Canterbury Tales: Fifteenth-Century Continuations and Additions, ed. John M. Bowers TEAMS (Kalamazoo, MI: Medieval Institute Publications, 1992)

Chaucer, Geoffrey, *Troilus and Criseyde: The 'Book of Troilus' by Geoffrey Chaucer*, ed. B.A. Windeatt (Harlow: Longman, 1984)

——, *The Riverside Chaucer*, ed. Larry D. Benson (Oxford: Oxford University Press, 1988)

——, *The Canterbury Tales*, ed. Jill Mann (Harmondsworth: Penguin, 2005)
Chaucer Life-Records, ed. Martin M. Crow and Clair C. Olson (Oxford: Clarendon Press, 1966)
Codex Ashmole 61: A Compilation of Popular Middle English Verse, ed. George Shuffelton TEAMS (Kalamazoo, MI: Medieval Institute Publications, 2008), https://d.lib.rochester.edu/teams/publication/shuffelton-codex-ashmole-61
Eliot, George, *Adam Bede*, ed. Carol A. Martin (Oxford: Clarendon Press, 2001)
——, *Daniel Deronda*, ed. Graham Handley (Oxford: Oxford University Press, 2014)
Froissart, Jean, *Chroniques de Jean Froissart 5: 1356–1360*, ed. Siméon Luce, Société de l'Histoire de France (Paris: Renouard, 1874)
——, *Chronicles*, trans. Geoffrey Brereton, rev. edn (London: Penguin, 1978)
Geoffrey of Monmouth, *The History of the Kings of Britain*, ed. Michael D. Reeve, trans. Neil Wright (Woodbridge: Boydell Press, 2007)
Gottfried von Strassburg, *Tristan; with the Tristran of Thomas*, trans. A.T. Hatto (Harmondsworth, Penguin: 1960)
Guido delle Colonne, *Historia destructione Troiae*, trans. Mary Elizabeth Meek (Bloomington: Indiana University Press, 1974)
Henryson, Robert, *The Testament of Cresseid*, in *The Makars: The Poems of Henryson, Dunbar and Douglas*, ed. J.A. Tasioulas (Edinburgh: Canongate, 1999)
Horn Childe and Maiden Rimnild: Edited from the Auchinleck MS, National Library of Scotland, Advocates' MS 19.2.1, ed. Maldwyn Mills (Heidelberg: Winter Universitätsverlag, 1988)
King Horn: An Edition based on Cambridge University Library MS Gg.4.27(2), ed. Rosamund Allen (New York: Garland, 1984)
King Horn, in *Four Romances of England: King Horn, Havelok the Dane, Bevis of Hampton, Athelston*, ed. Ronald B. Herzman et al., TEAMS (Kalamazoo, MI: Medieval Institute Publications, 1997), http://d.lib.rochester.edu/teams/publication/salisbury-four-romances-of-england
John of Salisbury, *Policraticus: Ioannis Saresberiensis episcopi Carnotensis Policratici; sive, De nugis curialium et vestigiis philosophorum, libri VIII*, ed. C.C.J. Webb, 2 vols (Oxford: Clarendon Press, 1909)
——, *Policraticus*, trans. Cary J. Nederman (Cambridge: Cambridge University Press, 1990)
'Lancelot of the Laik' and 'Sir Tristrem', ed. Alan Lupack, TEAMS (Kalamazoo, MI: Medieval Institute Publications, 1994), https://d.lib.rochester.edu/teams/publication/lupack-lancelot-of-the-laik-and-sir-tristrem
Lydgate, John, *Troy Book*, ed. Henry Bergen, EETS e.s. 97, 103 and 106 (1906–10; reprinted as one volume, Woodbridge: Boydell & Brewer, 1996)
——, *Troy Book: Selections*, ed. Robert R. Edwards, TEAMS (Kalamazoo, MI: Medieval Institute Publications, 1998), https://d.lib.rochester.edu/teams/publication/edwards-lydgate-troy-book-selections

——, *The Siege of Thebes*, ed. Robert R. Edwards, TEAMS (Kalamazoo, MI: Medieval Institute Publications, 2001)

Marie de France, *Lais*, ed. Alfred Ewert (London: Bristol Classical Press, 1995)

——, *The Lais of Marie de France*, trans. Glyn S. Burgess and Keith Busby (London: Penguin, 1986)

The Middle English Breton Lays, ed. Anne Laskaya and Eve Salisbury, TEAMS (Kalamazoo, MI: Medieval Institute Publications, 1995), https://d.lib.rochester.edu/teams/publication/laskaya-and-salisbury-middle-english-breton-lays

Les fragments du Roman de Tristan: poème du XIIe siècle, ed. Bartina H. Wind, 2nd edn (Geneva: Droz, 1960)

Sir Gawain and the Green Knight, in *The Works of the Gawain Poet: 'Sir Gawain and the Green Knight', 'Pearl', 'Cleanness', 'Patience'*, ed. Ad Putter and Myra Stokes (London: Penguin, 2014)

Sir Orfeo, ed. A.J. Bliss, 2nd edn (Oxford: Clarendon Press, 1966)

Sources and Analogues of 'The Canterbury Tales', ed. Robert M. Correale and Mary Hamel, 2 vols (Cambridge: Brewer, 2002–5)

Thomas, *The Romance of Horn*, ed. Mildred K. Pope, 2 vols (volume 2 revised and completed by T.B.W. Reid), ANTS 9–10, 12–13 (Oxford: Blackwell, 1955, 1964); also available via The Anglo-Norman On-Line Hub, www.anglo-norman.net

Yeats, W.B., *The Collected Poems of W.B. Yeats*, 2nd edn (London: Macmillan, 1950)

Reference works, online resources and news reports

Anglo-Norman Dictionary, via The Anglo-Norman On-Line Hub, www.anglo-norman.net

Digital Index of Middle English Verse, ed. Linne R. Mooney et al., www.dimev.net

Duff, E. Gordon, *Catalogue of Books in the John Rylands Library, Manchester, Printed in England, Scotland, and Ireland, and of Books in English Printed Abroad to the End of the Year 1640* (Manchester: Cornish, 1895)

[no author], 'Gary Lineker pants: Match of the Day presenter keeps Twitter promise', BBC website, 13 August 2016, www.bbc.co.uk/sport/football/37074641

Hamilton, Alan, 'How Ziggy the indiscreet parrot gave a cheating girlfriend the bird', *The Times*, 17 January 2006, p. 5

The House of Commons 1386–1421, ed. J.S. Roskell, Linda Clark and Carole Rawcliffe (Stroud: Alan Sutton, 1993), via http://www.historyofparliamentonline.org

A Lemmatized Concordance to Lydgate's 'Troy Book', ed. Hiroyuki Matsumoto (Tokyo: Shohakusha, 2007)

London, Victoria and Albert Museum online catalogue, http://collections.vam.ac.uk/

Manchester, John Rylands Library MS Eng. 1 description via the Archives Hub, https://archiveshub.jisc.ac.uk/data/gb133-engms1
Middle English Dictionary, ed. Hans Kurath and S.M. Kuhn (Ann Arbor: University of Michigan Press; London: Oxford University Press, 1952–), http://quod.lib.umich.edu/m/med/
A New Dictionary of Heraldry, ed. Stephen Friar (London: Alphabooks, 1987)
New Index of Middle English Verse, ed. Julia Boffey and A.S.G. Edwards (London: British Library, 2005)
Oxford Dictionary of National Biography, www.oxforddnb.com
Savernake Estate website, savernakeestate.co.uk

Secondary works

Abels, Richard, 'The historiography of a construct: "feudalism" and the medieval historian', *History Compass* 7 (2009), 1008–31, https://doi.org/10.1111/j.1478-0542.2009.00610.x
Aers, David, *Chaucer, Langland and the Creative Imagination* (London: Routledge & Kegan Paul, 1980)
Alexander, J.J.G., 'William Abell "lymnour" and fifteenth-century English illumination', in Artur Rosenauer and Gerold Weber (eds), *Kunsthistorische Forschungen: Otto Pächt zu seinem 70. Geburtstag* (Salzburg: Residenz Verlag, 1972), pp. 166–72
Algazi, Gadi, 'Introduction: doing things with gifts', in Algazi et al. (eds), *Negotiating the Gift*, pp. 9–27
Algazi, Gadi, Valentin Groeber and Bernhard Jussen (eds), *Negotiating the Gift: Pre-Modern Figurations of Exchange* (Göttingen: Vandenhoeck & Ruprecht, 2003)
Ambühl, Rémy, *Prisoners of War in the Hundred Years War: Ransom Culture in the Late Middle Ages* (Cambridge: Cambridge University Press, 2013)
Appadurai, Arjun (ed.), *The Social Life of Things: Commodities in Cultural Perspective* (Cambridge: Cambridge University Press, 1986)
——, 'Materiality in the future of Anthropology', in van Binsbergen and Geschiere (eds), *Commodification*, pp. 55–62
Arnovick, Leslie K., 'Dorigen's promise and scholars' premise: the orality of the speech act in the *Franklin's Tale*', in Mark C. Amodio (ed.), *Oral Poetics in Middle English Poetry* (New York: Garland, 1994), pp. 125–47
Ashe, Laura, *Fiction and History in England, 1066–1200* (Cambridge: Cambridge University Press, 2007)
——, *Conquest and Transformation*, Oxford English Literary History 1: 1000–1350 (Oxford: Oxford University Press, 2017)
Attridge, Derek, *The Work of Literature* (Oxford: Oxford University Press, 2017)
Atwood, Margaret, 'Introduction', in Lewis Hyde, *The Gift: How the Creative Spirit Transforms the World* (Edinburgh: Canongate, 2012), pp. vii–xi

Austin, J.L., *How to Do Things with Words*, 2nd edn (Oxford: Oxford University Press, 1976)
——, *Philosophical Papers*, ed. J.O. Urmson and G.J. Warnock, 3rd edn (Oxford: Oxford University Press, 1979)
Bahr, Arthur, *Fragments and Assemblages: Forming Compilations of Medieval London* (Chicago, IL: University of Chicago Press, 2013)
Bakhtin, Mikhail, 'Forms of time and of the chronotope in the novel', in Mikhail Bakhtin, *The Dialogic Imagination*, ed. Michael Holquist; trans. Caryl Emerson and Michael Holquist (Austin: University of Texas Press, 1981), pp. 84–258
Baldwin, Anna P., 'The notion of debt in medieval literature', in Hiro Futamura et al. (eds), *A Pilgrimage through Medieval Literature* (Tokyo: Nan'un-do, 1993), pp. 21–44
Barr, Helen, *Transporting Chaucer* (Manchester: Manchester University Press, 2014)
Barthes, Roland, 'L'effet de réel', *Communications* 11 (1968), 84–89
——, *Le plaisir du texte* (Paris: Éditions du Seuil, 1973)
——, 'Rhetoric of the image', in Roland Barthes, *Image Music Text*, trans. Stephen Heath (London: Fontana, 1977), pp. 32–51
Bartlett, Robert, *England under the Norman and Angevin Kings, 1075–1225* (Oxford: Clarendon Press, 2000)
Baswell, Christopher, '*Troy Book*: how Lydgate translates Chaucer into Latin', in Jeanette Beer (ed.), *Translation Theory and Practice in the Middle Ages* (Kalamazoo, MI: Medieval Institute Publications, 1997), pp. 215–37
Bataille, Georges, 'The notion of expenditure', in Georges Bataille, *Visions of Excess: Selected Writings, 1927–1939*, ed./trans. Allan Stoekl (Manchester: Manchester University Press, 1985), pp. 116–29
Bell, Kimberly K., and Julie Nelson Couch (eds), *The Texts and Contexts of Oxford, Bodleian Library, MS Laud Miscs. 108: The Shaping of English Vernacular Narrative* (Leiden: Brill, 2011)
Bellis, Joanna, and Laura Slater (eds), *Representing War and Violence* (Woodbridge: Boydell Press, 2016)
Bennett, Jane, *Vibrant Matter: A Political Ecology of Things* (Durham, NC: Duke University Press, 2010)
Benson, C. David, *The History of Troy in Middle English Literature: Guido Delle Colonne's 'Historia Destructionis Troiae' in Medieval England* (Cambridge: Brewer, 1980)
Bernasconi, Robert, 'What goes around comes around: Derrida and Levinas on the economy of the gift and the gift of genealogy', in Schrift (ed.), *The Logic of the Gift*, pp. 256–73
Bijsterveld, Arnoud-Jan A., *Do ut Des: Gift-Giving, 'Memoria', and Conflict Management in the Medieval Low Countries* (Hilversum: Uitgeverij Verloren, 2007)
Bjork, Robert E., 'Speech as gift in *Beowulf*', *Speculum* 69 (1994), 993–1022

Bliss, Jane, *Naming and Namelessness in Medieval Romance* (Woodbridge: Brewer, 2008)

Boitani, Piero, and Jill Mann (eds), *The Cambridge Companion to Chaucer*, rev. edn (Cambridge University Press, 2003)

Bossy, André Michel, 'Arms and the bride: Christine de Pizan's military treatise as a wedding gift for Margaret of Anjou', in Marilynn Desmond (ed.), *Christine De Pizan and the Categories of Difference* (Minneapolis: University of Minnesota Press, 1998), pp. 236–56

Bourdieu, Pierre, *Outline of a Theory of Practice*, trans. Richard Nice (Cambridge: Cambridge University Press, 1977)

——, *The Logic of Practice*, trans. Richard Nice (Cambridge: Polity Press, 1990)

——, 'Marginalia—some additional notes on the gift', in Schrift (ed.), *The Logic of the Gift*, pp. 231–41

Braunholtz, E.G.W., 'Cambridge fragments of the Anglo-Norman "Roman de Horn"', *Modern Language Review* 16 (1921), 23–33

Brewer, Derek, *Symbolic Stories: Traditional Narratives of the Family Drama in English Literature* (Harlow: Longman, 1980)

——, 'Introduction: escape from the mimetic fallacy', in Derek Brewer (ed.), *Studies in Medieval English Romances: Some New Approaches* (Cambridge: Boydell and Brewer, 1988), pp. 1–10

Brown, Bill, 'Thing theory', in Bill Brown (ed.), *Things* (Chicago, IL: University of Chicago Press, 2004), pp. 1–22

Burnley, J.D., 'The *Roman de Horn*: its Hero and its ethos', *French Studies* 32 (1978), 385–97

Burns, E. Jane, *Courtly Love Undressed: Reading through Clothes in Medieval French Culture* (Philadelphia: University of Pennsylvania Press, 2002)

——, (ed.), *Medieval Fabrications: Dress, Textiles, Clothwork and Other Cultural Imaginings* (New York: Palgrave Macmillan, 2004), pp. 137–46

——, *Sea of Silk: A Textile Geography of Women's Work in Medieval French Literature* (Philadelphia: University of Pennsylvania Press, 2009)

Burrow, J.A., 'Honour and shame in *Sir Gawain and the Green Knight*', in J.A. Burrow, *Essays on Medieval Literature* (Oxford: Clarendon Press, 1984), pp. 117–31

Calabrese, Michael, 'Chaucer's Dorigen and Boccaccio's female voices', *SAC* 29 (2007), 259–92

Camber, Richard, and John Cherry, 'The Savernake Horn', in Richard Camber (ed.), *Collectors and Collections: The British Museum Yearbook 2* (London: British Museum Publications, 1977), pp. 201–11

Campbell, Marian, *Medieval Jewellery in Europe, 1100–1500* (London: V&A Publications, 2009)

Cannon, Christopher, *The Grounds of English Literature* (Oxford: Oxford University Press, 2004)

Carruthers, Mary, *The Book of Memory*, 2nd edn (Cambridge: Cambridge University Press, 2008)

Cartlidge, Neil, *Medieval Marriage: Literary Approaches, 1100–1300* (Woodbridge: Brewer, 1997)

Chartier, Roger, *Forms and Meanings: Texts, Performances, and Audiences from Codex to Computer* (Philadelphia: University of Pennsylvania Press, 1995)

Chattaway, Carol M., 'Looking a medieval gift horse in the mouth: the role of the giving of gift objects in the definition and maintenance of the power networks of Philip the Bold', *Bijdragen en mededelingen betreffende de geschiedenis der Nederlanden* 114 (1999), 1–15

Clanchy, M.T., *From Memory to Written Record: England 1066–1307*, 3rd edn (Oxford: Wiley-Blackwell, 2012)

Cohen, Esther, and Mayke B. de Jong (eds), *Medieval Transformations: Texts, Power, and Gifts in Context* (Leiden: Brill, 2001)

Cohen, Simona, *Transformations of Time and Temporality in Medieval and Renaissance Art* (Leiden: Brill, 2014)

Cole, Andrew, 'The call of things: a critique of object-oriented ontologies', *minnesota review* 80 (2013), 106–18

Coole, Diana, and Samantha Frost, 'Introducing the new materialisms', in Diana Coole and Samantha Frost (eds), *New Materialisms: Ontology, Agency, and Politics* (Durham, NC: Duke University Press, 2010), pp. 1–43

Cooper, Helen, 'The girl with two lovers: four Canterbury tales', in P.L. Heyworth (ed.), *Medieval Studies for J.A.W. Bennett* (Oxford: Clarendon Press, 1981), pp. 65–79

——, *The Structure of the Canterbury Tales* (Athens: University of Georgia Press, 1983)

——, *The Canterbury Tales*, 2nd edn, Oxford Guides to Chaucer (Oxford: Oxford University Press, 1996)

——, *The English Romance in Time: Transforming Motifs from Geoffrey of Monmouth to the Death of Shakespeare* (Oxford: Oxford University Press, 2004)

Cooper, Lisa H., and Andrea Denny-Brown, 'Introduction', in Lisa H. Cooper and Andrea Denny-Brown (eds), *Lydgate Matters: Poetry and Material Culture in the Fifteenth Century* (New York: Palgrave Macmillan, 2007), pp. 1–11

Cowell, Andrew, *At Play in the Tavern: Signs, Coins, and Bodies in the Middle Ages* (Ann Arbor: University of Michigan Press, 1999)

Crane, Susan, *Insular Romance: Politics, Faith, and Culture in Anglo-Norman and Middle English Literature* (Berkeley: University of California Press, 1986)

——, *The Performance of Self: Ritual, Clothing and Identity During the Hundred Years War* (Philadelphia: University of Pennsylvania Press, 2002).

Craun, Edwin, *Lies, Slander and Obscenity in Medieval English Literature: Pastoral Rhetoric and the Deviant Speaker* (Cambridge: Cambridge University Press, 1997)

Cruse, Mark, *Illuminating the 'Roman d'Alexandre': Oxford, Bodleian Library, MS Bodley 264: The Manuscript as Monument* (Cambridge: Brewer, 2011)

Curry, Anne, and Glenn Foard, 'Where are the dead of medieval battles? A preliminary survey', *Journal of Conflict Archaeology* 11 (2016), 61–77

Da Rold, Orietta, et al. (ed.), *The Production and Use of English Manuscripts, 1060 to 1220* (2010, rev. 2013), www.le.ac.uk/english/em1060to1220

Damian-Grint, Peter, *The New Historians of the Twelfth-Century Renaissance: Inventing Vernacular Authority* (Woodbridge: Boydell Press, 1999)

Daniels, Inge, 'The "social death" of unused gifts: surplus and value in contemporary Japan', *Journal of Material Culture* 14 (2009), 385–408

Davies, Wendy and Paul Fouracre (eds), *The Languages of Gift in the Early Middle Ages* (Cambridge: Cambridge University Press, 2010)

Davis, Isabel, Miriam Müller and Sarah Rees Jones (eds), *Love, Marriage, and Family Ties in the Later Middle Ages* (Turnhout: Brepols, 2003)

Davis, Natalie Zemon, *The Gift in Sixteenth Century France* (Oxford: Oxford University Press, 2000)

Derrida, Jacques, 'Structure, sign and play in the discourse of the human sciences', in Derrida, *Writing and Difference*, trans. Alan Bass (London: Routledge & Kegan Paul, 1978), pp. 278–93

——, *Limited Inc*, trans. Samuel Weber and Jeffrey Mehlman (Evanston, IL: Northwestern University Press, 1988)

——, *Limited Inc* (Paris: Éditions Galilée, 1990)

——, *Given Time I: Counterfeit Money*, trans. Peggy Kamuf (Chicago, IL: University of Chicago Press, 1992)

——, *The Gift of Death* (Chicago, IL: University of Chicago Press, 1995)

——, 'Women in the beehive: a seminar with Jacques Derrida', *differences* 16.3 (2005), 138–57

Dickson, Morgan, 'Twelfth-Century Insular Narrative: *The Romance of Horn* and Related Texts' (doctoral dissertation, University of Cambridge, 1996)

——, 'Verbal and visual disguise: society and identity in some twelfth-century texts', in Judith Weiss, Jennifer Fellows and Morgan Dickson (eds), *Medieval Insular Romance: Translation and Innovation* (Cambridge: Brewer, 2000), pp. 41–54

——, 'Female doubling and male identity in medieval romance', in Phillipa Hardman (ed.), *The Matter of Identity in Medieval Romance* (Cambridge: Brewer, 2002), pp. 59–72

——, 'The role of drinking horns in medieval England', *AVISTA Forum Journal* 21 (2011), 42–48

Dinshaw, Carolyn, *Chaucer's Sexual Poetics* (Madison: University of Wisconsin Press, 1989)

Dolmans, Emily, 'Regional Identities and Cultural Contact in the Literatures of Post-Conquest England' (doctoral dissertation, University of Oxford, 2017)

Douglas, Mary, 'A gentle deconstruction', review of Marilyn Strathern, *The Gender of the Gift*, *London Review of Books* (1989), 17–18

——, 'Foreword: No free gifts', in Mauss, *The Gift*, trans. Halls, pp. vi–xviii

Driver, Martha, 'Medievalizing the classical past in Pierpont Morgan MS M 876', in Alastair Minnis (ed.), *Middle English Poetry: Texts and*

Traditions: Essays in Honour of Derek Pearsall (Woodbridge: York Medieval Press, 2001), pp. 211–39

Duffy, Eamon, 'Late medieval religion', in Richard Marks and Paul Williamson (eds), *Gothic: Art for England, 1400–1547* (London: V&A Publications, 2003), pp. 56–67

Ebin, Lois A., 'Lydgate's views on poetry', *Annuale Mediaevale* 18 (1977), 76–105

——, *Illuminator, Makar, Vates: Visions of Poetry in the Fifteenth Century* (Lincoln: University of Nebraska Press, 1988)

Edwards, Robert R., 'John Lydgate and the remaking of classical epic', in Rita Copeland (ed.), *The Oxford History of Classical Reception in English Literature, Volume 1: 800–1558* (Oxford: Oxford University Press, 2016), pp. 465–86

Eming, Jutta, Ann Marie Rasmussen and Kathryn Starkey (eds), *Visuality and Materiality in the Story of Tristan and Isolde* (Notre Dame, IN: University of Notre Dame Press, 2012)

Epstein, Robert, '"With many a floryn he the hewes boghte": ekphrasis and symbolic violence in the *Knight's Tale*', *Philological Quarterly* 85 (2006), 49–68

——, *Chaucer's Gifts: Exchange and Value in the 'Canterbury Tales'* (Cardiff: University of Wales Press, 2018)

Evans, Joan, *English Posies and Posy Rings* (London: Oxford University Press, 1931)

Federico, Sylvia, *New Troy: Fantasies of Empire in the Late Middle Ages* (Minneapolis: University of Minnesota Press, 2003)

Fein, Susanna (ed.), *Studies in the Harley Manuscript: The Scribes, Contents, and Social Contexts of British Library MS Harley 2253*, TEAMS (Kalamazoo, MI: Medieval Institute Publications, 2000)

——, (ed.), *The Auchinleck Manuscript: New Perspectives* (Woodbridge: York Medieval Press, 2016)

Felman, Shoshana, *Le Scandale du corps parlant* (Paris: Éditions du Seuil, 1980)

——, *The Scandal of the Speaking Body; Don Juan with J.L. Austin, or Seduction in Two Languages*, trans. Catherine Porter (Stanford, CA: Stanford University Press, 2003)

Fewer, Colin, 'John Lydgate's *Troy Book* and the ideology of prudence', *Chaucer Review* 38 (2004), 229–45

Field, Rosalind, 'Children of anarchy: Anglo-Norman romance in the twelfth century', in Ruth Kennedy and Simon Meecham-Jones (eds), *Writers of the Reign of Henry II: Twelve Essays* (Basingstoke: Palgrave Macmillan, 2006), pp. 249–62

——, 'Courtly culture and emotional intelligence in the *Romance of Horn*', in Nicholas Perkins (ed.), *Medieval Romance and Material Culture* (Cambridge: Brewer, 2015), pp. 23–40

Firth, Raymond, *Economics of the New Zealand Maori* (Wellington: Shearer, 1972)

Flanagan, Marie Therese, *Irish Society, Anglo-Norman Settlers, Angevin Kingship: Interactions in Ireland in the Late Twelfth Century* (Oxford: Clarendon Press, 1989)

Flannery, Mary, *John Lydgate and the Poetics of Fame* (Cambridge: Brewer, 2012)

Fontijn, David, 'Epilogue: cultural biographies and itineraries of things: second thoughts', in Hahn and Weiss (eds), *Mobility, Meaning and Transformations of Things*, pp. 183–95

Forni, Kathleen, *The Chaucerian Apocrypha: A Counterfeit Canon* (Gainesville: University Press of Florida, 2001)

Fradenburg, Louise, 'The Manciple's servant tongue: politics and poetry in *The Canterbury Tales*', *ELH: A Journal of English Literary History* 52 (1985), 85–118

Freedgood, Elaine, *The Ideas in Things: Fugitive Meaning in the Victorian Novel* (Chicago, IL: University of Chicago Press, 2006)

Furrow, Melissa, *Expectations of Romance: The Reception of a Genre in Medieval England* (Cambridge: Brewer, 2009)

Galloway, Andrew, 'The making of a social ethic in late-medieval England: from *gratitudo* to "kyndnesse"', *Journal of the History of Ideas* 55 (1994), 365–83

Gasper, Giles E.M., 'Contemplating money and wealth in monastic writing c.1060–c.1160', in Giles E.M. Gasper and Svein H. Gullbekk (eds), *Money and the Church in Medieval Europe, 1000–1200: Practice, Morality and Thought* (Farnham: Ashgate, 2015), pp. 39–77

Gayk, Shannon, *Image, Text, and Religious Reform in Fifteenth-Century England* (Cambridge: Cambridge University Press, 2010)

Gaylord, Alan T., 'The promises in the *Franklin's Tale*', *ELH: A Journal of English Literary History* 31 (1964), 331–65

Geary, Patrick J., 'Exchange and interaction between the living and the dead in early medieval society', in Geary, *Living with the Dead in the Middle Ages* (Ithaca, NY: Cornell University Press, 1994), pp. 77–92

——, 'Gift exchange and social science modelling: the limitations of a construct', in Algazi et al. (eds), *Negotiating the Gift*, pp. 129–40

Gell, Alfred, *Wrapping in Images: Tattooing in Polynesia* (Oxford: Clarendon Press, 1993)

——, *Art and Agency: An Anthropological Theory* (Oxford: Clarendon Press, 1998)

Gerrard, Christopher, 'Not all archaeology is rubbish: the elusive life histories of three artefacts from Shapwick, Somerset', in Michael Costen (ed.), *People and Places: Essays in Honour of Mick Aston* (Oxford: Oxbow, 2007), pp. 166–80

Giancarlo, Matthew, 'Speculative genealogies', in Paul Strohm (ed.), *Middle English* (Oxford: Oxford University Press, 2007), pp. 352–68

Gibson, James J., *The Ecological Approach to Visual Perception* (Boston, MA: Houghton Mifflin, 1979)

Gilchrist, Roberta, 'The materiality of medieval heirlooms: from biographical to sacred objects', in Hahn and Weiss (eds), *Mobility, Meaning and Transformations of Things*, pp. 170–82

Gillingham, John, *The English in the Twelfth Century: Imperialism, National Identity, and Political Values* (Woodbridge: Boydell Press, 2000)

——, 'The cultivation of history, legend, and courtesy and the court of Henry II', in Ruth Kennedy and Simon Meecham-Jones (eds), *Writers of the Reign of Henry II: Twelve Essays* (Basingstoke: Palgrave Macmillan, 2006), pp. 25–52

Given-Wilson, Chris, and Françoise Bériac, 'Edward III's prisoners of war: the Battle of Poitiers and its context', *English Historical Review* 116 (2001), 802–33

Godelier, Maurice, *The Enigma of the Gift*, trans. Nora Scott (Cambridge: Polity Press, 1999)

Gosden, Chris, and Yvonne Marshall, 'The cultural biography of objects', *World Archaeology* 31 (1999), 169–78

Goux, Jean-Joseph, *Symbolic Economies: After Marx and Freud* (Ithaca, NY: Cornell University Press, 1990)

——, *The Coiners of Language* (Norman: University of Oklahoma Press, 1994)

Graeber, David, *Toward an Anthropological Theory of Value: The False Coin of Our Own Dreams* (New York: Palgrave, 2001)

——, *Debt: The First 5,000 Years*, rev. edn (Brooklyn, NY: Melville House, 2014)

Green, Mitchell, 'Speech Acts', Oxford Bibliographies Online, www.oxfordbibliographies.com/view/document/obo-9780195396577/obo-9780195396577-0300.xml

Green, Richard F., 'Hearts, minds, and some English poems of Charles d'Orléans', *English Studies in Canada* 9 (1983), 136–50

Green, Richard Firth, *A Crisis of Truth: Literature and Law in Ricardian England* (Philadelphia: University of Pennsylvania Press, 1999)

Greenfield, Stanley B., 'The authenticating voice in *Beowulf*', *Anglo-Saxon England* 5 (1976), 51–62

Gregory, Chris, *Gifts and Commodities* (New York: Academic Press, 1982)

Groebner, Valentin, *Liquid Assets, Dangerous Gifts: Presents and Politics at the end of the Middle Ages*, trans. Pamela E. Selwyn (Philadelphia: University of Pennsylvania Press, 2002)

Grudin, Michaela Paasche, *Chaucer and the Politics of Discourse* (Columbia: University of South Carolina Press, 1996)

Hahn, Hans Peter, and Hadas Weiss (eds), *Mobility, Meaning and Transformations of Things* (Oxford: Oxbow, 2013)

Hahn, Hans Peter and Hadas Weiss, 'Introduction: biographies, travels and itineraries of things', in Hahn and Weiss (eds), *Mobility, Meaning and Transformations of Things*, pp. 1–18

Hahn, Thomas, 'Gawain and popular chivalric romance in Britain', in Roberta L. Krueger (ed.), *The Cambridge Companion to Medieval Romance* (Cambridge: Cambridge University Press, 2000), pp. 218–34

Hanawalt, Barbara A. and Kathryn Reyerson (eds), *City and Spectacle in Medieval Europe* (Minneapolis: University of Minnesota Press, 1994)

Hanning, Robert W., 'Chaucer and the dangers of poetry', *CEA Critic* 46 (1984), 17–26

Haraway, Donna, 'A cyborg manifesto: science, technology, and socialist-feminism in the late twentieth century', in Donna Haraway, *Simians, Cyborgs and Women: The Reinvention of Nature* (New York: Routledge, 1991), pp. 149–81

Hardman, Phillipa, 'Lydgate's "uneasy" syntax', in Scanlon and Simpson (eds), *John Lydgate*, pp. 12–35

——, 'The true romance of *Tristrem and Ysonde*', in Corinne Saunders (ed.), *Cultural Encounters in the Romance of Medieval England* (Cambridge: Brewer, 2005), pp. 85–100

Harman, Graham, *Tool-Being: Heidegger and the Metaphysics of Objects* (Chicago, IL: Open Court, 2002)

——, 'The well-wrought broken hammer: object-oriented literary criticism', *New Literary History* 43 (2012), 183–203

Harriss, Gerald, *Shaping the Nation: England 1360–1461* (Oxford: Clarendon Press, 2005)

Hart, Keith, 'Marcel Mauss: in pursuit of the whole. A review essay', *Comparative Studies in Society and History* 49 (2007), 473–85

Harwood, Britton J., 'Language and the real: Chaucer's Manciple', *Chaucer Review* 6 (1972), 268–79

——, '*Gawain* and the gift', *PMLA* 106 (1991), 483–99

——, 'Chaucer and the gift (if there is any)', *Studies in Philology* 103 (2006), 26–46

Haught, Leah, 'In pursuit of "trewth": ambiguity and meaning in *Amis and Amiloun*', *Journal of English and German Philology* 114 (2015), 240–60

Hawkes, David, 'Against materialism in literary theory', in Paul Cefalu and Bryan Reynolds (eds), *The Return of Theory in Early Modern English Studies: Tarrying with the Subjunctive* (Basingstoke: Palgrave Macmillan, 2011), pp. 237–57

Hazelton, Richard, 'The *Manciple's Tale*: parody and critique', *Journal of English and German Philology* 62 (1963), 1–31

Heal, Felicity, 'Reciprocity and exchange in the late medieval household', in Barbara A. Hanawalt and David Wallace (eds), *Bodies and Disciplines: Intersections of Literature and History in Fifteenth-Century England* (Minneapolis: University of Minnesota Press, 1996), pp. 179–98

——, *The Power of Gifts: Gift Exchange in Early Modern England* (Oxford: Oxford University Press, 2014)

Heng, Geraldine, *Empire of Magic: Medieval Romance and the Politics of Cultural Fantasy* (New York: Columbia University Press, 2003)

Hicks, Dan, 'The material-cultural turn: event and effect', in Hicks and Beaudry (eds), *Oxford Handbook of Material Culture Studies*, pp. 25–98

——, and Mary C. Beaudry (eds), *The Oxford Handbook of Material Culture Studies* (Oxford: Oxford University Press, 2010)

Hill, John M., 'Beowulf and the Danish succession: gift giving as the occasion for complex gesture', *Medievalia et Humanistica new series* 11 (1982), 177–97

Holford, Matthew, 'History and politics in *Horn Child and Maiden Rimnild*', *Review of English Studies* 57 (2006), 149–68

Holsinger, Bruce, 'Object-oriented mythography', *minnesota review* 80 (2013), 119–30

Horobin, Simon, 'Thomas Hoccleve: Chaucer's first editor?', *Chaucer Review* 50 (2015), 228–50

Hoskins, Janet, 'Agency, biography and objects', in Christopher Tilley et al. (eds), *Handbook of Material Culture* (London: SAGE Publications, 2006), pp. 74–84

Howell, Martha C., *Commerce before Capitalism in Europe, 1300–1600* (Cambridge: Cambridge University Press, 2010)

Hsy, Jonathan, *Trading Tongues: Merchants, Multilingualism, and Medieval Literature* (Columbus: Ohio State University Press, 2013)

Hu, Hsin-Yu, 'Delineating the *Gawain*-Poet: Myth, Desire and Visuality' (doctoral dissertation, University of Oxford, 2015)

Huizinga, Johan, *The Waning of the Middle Ages: A Study of the Forms of Life, Thought and Art in France and the Netherlands in the XIVth and XVth Centuries*, trans. F. Hopman (London: Edward Arnold, 1924)

Hult, David F., 'Words and deeds: Jean de Meun's *Romance of the Rose* and the hermeneutics of censorship', *New Literary History* 28 (1997), 345–66

Hyde, Lewis, *The Gift: How the Creative Spirit Transforms the World* (Edinburgh: Canongate, 2012)

Ingham, Patricia Clare, *Sovereign Fantasies: Arthurian Romance and the Making of Britain* (Philadelphia: University of Pennsylvania Press, 2001)

Jamison, Carol Parrish, 'Traffic of women in Germanic literature: the role of the peace pledge in marital exchanges', *Women in German Yearbook* 20 (2004), 13–36

Jarvis, Simon, 'The gift in theory', *Dionysius* 17 (1999), 201–22

Johnston, Michael, *Romance and the Gentry in Late Medieval England* (Oxford: Oxford University Press, 2014)

Jones, Andrew M., and Nicole Boivin, 'The malice of inanimate objects: material agency', in Hicks and Beaudry (eds), *Handbook of Material Culture Studies*, pp. 333–51

Jost, Jean E., 'Chaucer's vows and how they break: transgression in the *Manciple's Tale*', in Albrecht Classen (ed.), *Discourses on Love, Marriage and Transgression in Medieval and Early Modern Literature* (Tempe: Arizona Centre for Medieval and Renaissance Studies, 2004), pp. 267–87

Jussen, Bernhard, 'Religious discourses of the gift in the Middle Ages: semantic evidences (second to twelfth centuries)', in Algazi et al. (eds), *Negotiating the Gift*, pp. 173–92

Kabir, Ananya Jahanara, 'Analogy in translation: imperial Rome, medieval England, and British India', in Ananya Jahanara Kabir and Deanne Williams (eds), *Postcolonial Approaches to the European Middle Ages:*

Translating Cultures (Cambridge: Cambridge University Press, 2005), pp. 183–204

Kaeuper, Richard, *Chivalry and Violence in Medieval Europe* (Oxford: Oxford University Press, 1999)

——, 'The societal role of chivalry in romance: northwestern Europe', in Roberta L. Krueger (ed.), *The Cambridge Companion to Medieval Romance* (Cambridge: Cambridge University Press, 2000), pp. 97–114

Karras, Ruth Mazo, '"This skill in a woman is by no means to be despised": weaving and the gender division of labour in the Middle Ages', in Burns (ed.), *Medieval Fabrications*, pp. 89–104

Kay, Sarah, *The 'Chansons de geste' in the Age of Romance: Political Fictions* (Oxford: Clarendon Press, 1995)

——, 'Le donne nella società feudale: la dama e il dono', in Piero Boitani, M. Mancini and Alberto Vàrvaro (eds), *Lo spazio letterario del Medioevo. 2: Il Medioevo volgare, vol. 4: L'attualizzazione del testo* (Rome: Salerno, 2004), pp. 545–72

Keane, Webb, 'Signs are not the garb of meaning: on the social analysis of material things', in Miller (ed.), *Materiality*, pp. 182–205

Keiper, Hugo, Christoph Bode and Richard J. Utz (eds), *Nominalism and Literary Discourse: New Perspectives* (Amsterdam: Rodopi, 1997)

Kendall, Elliot, *Lordship and Literature: John Gower and the Politics of the Great Household* (Oxford: Oxford University Press, 2008)

Kightly, Charles, 'Lollard knights', *ODNB*, https://doi.org/10.1093/ref:odnb/50540

Knox, Philip, '*The Romance of the Rose* in Fourteenth-Century England' (doctoral dissertation, University of Oxford, 2015)

Kolve, V.A., *Chaucer and the Imagery of Narrative: The First Five Canterbury Tales* (Stanford, CA: Stanford University Press, 1984)

Komter, Aafke E., *The Gift: An Interdisciplinary Perspective* (Amsterdam: Amsterdam University Press, 1996)

Ladd, Roger A., 'Gower's Gifts', in Ana Sáez-Hidalgo and R.F. Yeager (eds), *John Gower in England and Iberia: Manuscripts, Influences, Reception* (Cambridge: Brewer), pp. 229–39

Latour, Bruno, *Science in Action: How to Follow Scientists and Engineers through Society*, trans. Catherine Porter (Cambridge, MA: Harvard University Press, 1987)

——, *We Have Never Been Modern*, trans. Catherine Porter (Cambridge, MA: Harvard University Press, 1993)

——, *Reassembling the Social: An Introduction to Actor-Network-Theory* (Oxford: Oxford University Press, 2005)

Lawton, David, 'Dullness and the fifteenth century', *ELH: A Journal of English Literary History* 54 (1987), 761–99

Lawton, Lesley, 'The illustration of late medieval secular texts, with special reference to Lydgate's "Troy Book"', in Derek Pearsall (ed.), *Manuscripts and Readers in Fifteenth-Century England: The Literary Implications of Manuscript Study* (Cambridge: Brewer, 1983), pp. 41–71

Legge, M. Dominica, *Anglo-Norman Literature and its Background* (Oxford: Clarendon Press, 1963)

Lerer, Seth, 'Artifice and artistry in *Sir Orfeo*', *Speculum* 60 (1985), 92–109

——, *Chaucer and His Readers: Imagining the Author in Late-Medieval England* (Princeton, NJ: Princeton University Press, 1993)

——, *Courtly Letters in the Age of Henry VIII: Literary Culture and the Arts of Deceit* (Cambridge: Cambridge University Press, 1997)

Lester, Anne E., and Katherine C. Little, 'Introduction: medieval materiality', *English Language Notes* 53 (2015), 1–8

Lévi-Strauss, Claude, *The Elementary Structures of Kinship*, trans. James Harle Bell, John Richard von Sturmer and Rodney Needham (London: Eyre & Spottiswoode, 1969)

——, 'Introduction à l'oeuvre de Marcel Mauss', in Marcel Mauss, *Sociologie et anthropologie*, 11th edn (Paris: Presses Universitaires de France, 2004), pp. 9–52

Lipset, David, 'What makes a man? Rereading *Naven* and *The Gender of the Gift*, 2004', *Anthropological Theory* 8 (2008), 219–32

Liuzza, Roy Michael, '*Sir Orfeo*: Sources, traditions, and the poetics of performance', *Journal of Medieval and Renaissance Studies* 21 (1991), 269–84

Lynch, Andrew, '"With a face pale": melancholy violence in John Lydgate's Troy and Thebes', in Joanna Bellis and Laura Slater (eds), *Representing War and Violence, 1250–1600* (Woodbridge: Boydell Press, 2016), pp. 79–94

Maddox, Donald, 'Specular stories, family romance, and the fictions of courtly culture', *Exemplaria* 3 (1991), 299–326

Mahowald, Kyle, '"It may nat be": Chaucer, Derrida, and the impossibility of the gift', *SAC* 32 (2010), 129–50

Malafouris, Lambros, 'At the potter's wheel: an argument *for* material agency', in Carl Knappett and Lambros Malafouris (eds), *Material Agency: Towards a Non-Anthropocentric Approach* (New York: Springer, 2008), pp. 19–36

——, and Colin Renfrew, 'The cognitive life of things: archaeology, material engagement and the extended mind', in Lambros Malafouris and Colin Renfrew (eds), *The Cognitive Life of Things: Recasting the Boundaries of the Mind* (Cambridge: McDonald Institute, 2010), pp. 1–12

Malinowski, Bronislaw, *Argonauts of the Western Pacific: An Account of the Native Enterprise and Adventure in the Archipelagoes of Melanesian New Guinea* (London: Routledge, 1922, reprinted 2002)

Mann, Jill, 'Chaucerian themes and style in the *Franklin's Tale*', in Boris Ford (ed.), *Medieval Literature: Chaucer and the Alliterative Tradition*, New Pelican Guide to English Literature, vol. 1, part 1, rev. edn (Harmondsworth: Penguin, 1982), pp. 133–53

——, 'Price and value in *Sir Gawain and the Green Knight*', *Essays in Criticism* 36 (1986), 294–318

——, 'Anger and "glosynge" in *The Canterbury Tales*', *Proceedings of the British Academy* 76 (1991), 203–23

——, *Feminizing Chaucer* (Woodbridge: Brewer, 2002)

——, 'Chance and destiny in *Troilus and Criseyde* and the *Knight's Tale*', in Boitani and Mann (eds), *The Cambridge Companion to Chaucer*, pp. 93–111

——, 'Messianic chivalry in *Amis and Amiloun*', *New Medieval Literatures* 10 (2008), 137–59

Marks, Richard, and Paul Williamson (eds), *Gothic: Art for England, 1400–1547* (London: V&A Publications, 2003)

Martin, Jean-Pierre, 'Les offres de présents dans les chansons de geste: structures rhétoriques et conditions d'énonciation', *Romania* 107 (1986), 183–207

Massey, Jeff, '"The double bind of Troilus to tellen": the time of the gift in Chaucer's *Troilus and Criseyde*', *Chaucer Review* 38 (2003), 16–35

Mauss, Marcel, *The Gift: The Form and Reason for Exchange in Archaic Societies*, trans. W.D. Halls (London: Routledge, 1990).

——, *Essai sur le don: Forme et raison de l'échange dans les sociétés archaïques* (Paris: Quadrige/Presses Universitaires de France, 2007)

——, *The Gift: Expanded Edition*, trans. Jane I. Guyer (Chicago, IL: Hau Books, 2016)

McDonald, Nicola, '*The Seege of Troye*: "ffor wham was wakened al this wo"?', in Putter and Gilbert (eds), *Popular Romance*, pp. 181–99

——, 'A polemical introduction', in McDonald (ed.), *Pulp Fictions*, pp. 1–21

——, (ed.), *Pulp Fictions of Medieval England: Essays in Popular Romance* (Manchester: Manchester University Press, 2004)

McGrady, Deborah, *The Writer's Gift or the Patron's Pleasure? The Literary Economy in Late Medieval France* (Toronto: University of Toronto Press, 2019)

Meyer-Lee, Robert J., *Poets and Power from Chaucer to Wyatt* (Cambridge: Cambridge University Press, 2007)

Miller, Daniel, 'Materiality: an introduction', in Miller (ed.), *Materiality*, pp. 1–50

——, *Stuff* (Cambridge: Polity Press, 2010)

——, (ed.), *Materiality* (Durham, NC: Duke University Press, 2005)

Miller, J. Hillis, *The Ethics of Reading: Kant, de Man, Eliot, Trollope, James, and Benjamin* (New York: Columbia University Press, 1987)

——, 'Character', in J. Hillis Miller, *Ariadne's Thread* (New Haven, CT: Yale University Press, 1992), pp. 28–143

——, *Speech Acts in Literature* (Stanford, CA: Stanford University Press, 2001)

Minnis, A.J., *Chaucer and Pagan Antiquity* (Cambridge: Brewer, 1982).

——, *Magister Amoris: The 'Roman de la Rose' and Vernacular Hermeneutics* (Oxford: Oxford University Press, 2001)

Mitchell, W.J.T., *Iconology: Image, Text, Ideology* (Chicago, IL: University of Chicago Press, 1986)

——, 'Word and image', in Robert S. Nelson and Richard Shiff (eds), *Critical Terms for Art History* (Chicago, IL: University of Chicago Press, 1996), pp. 51–61

——, 'Romanticism and the life of things: fossils, totems, and images', *Critical Inquiry* 28 (2001), 167–84

Miyazaki, Hirokazu, 'Gifts and exchange', in Hicks and Beaudry (eds), *Oxford Handbook of Material Culture Studies*, pp. 246–64

Monson, Don A., *Andreas Capellanus, Scholasticism, and the Courtly Tradition* (Washington, DC: Catholic University of America Press, 2005)

Morgan, Gerald, 'Experience and the judgement of poetry: a reconsideration of the *Franklin's Tale*', *Medium Aevum* 70 (2001), 204–25

Munn, Nancy, *The Fame of Gawa: A Symbolic Study of Value Transformation in a Massim (Papua New Guinea) Society* (Cambridge: Cambridge University Press, 1986)

Myles, Robert, *Chaucerian Realism* (Woodbridge: Boydell & Brewer, 1994)

Nagel, Sidney R., 'Shadows and ephemera', *Critical Inquiry* 28 (2001), 23–39

Nall, Catherine, *Reading and War in Fifteenth-Century England: From Lydgate to Malory* (Cambridge: Brewer, 2012)

Newman, Karen, 'Directing traffic: subjects, objects, and the politics of exchange', *differences* 2.2 (Summer 1990), 41–54

Niles, John D., 'Myth and history', in Robert E. Bjork and John D. Niles (eds), *A 'Beowulf' Handbook* (Exeter: Exeter University Press, 1997), pp. 213–32

Offer, Avner, *Between the Gift and the Market: The Economy of Regard* (University of Oxford, 1996)

Oliver, Martin, 'The problem with affordance', *E-Learning* 2 (2005), 402–13

Pakkala-Weckström, Mari, '"No botmeles bihestes": various ways of making binding promises in Middle English', in Andreas H. Jucker and Irma Taavitsainen (eds), *Speech Acts in the History of English* (Amsterdam: John Benjamins, 2008), pp. 133–62

Parry, Jonathan, '*The Gift*, the Indian gift and the "Indian gift"', *Man new series* 21 (1986), 453–73

——, 'On the moral perils of exchange', in Jonathan Parry and Maurice Bloch (eds), *Money and the Morality of Exchange* (Cambridge: Cambridge University Press, 1989), pp. 64–93

Parry, Jonathan, and Maurice Bloch, 'Introduction: money and the morality of exchange', in Parry and Bloch (eds), *Money and the Morality of Exchange*, pp. 1–32

Patterson, Lee, *Chaucer and the Subject of History* (London: Routledge, 1991)

Pearsall, Derek, *The Life of Geoffrey Chaucer: A Critical Biography* (Oxford: Blackwell, 1992)

Pelen, Marc M., 'The Manciple's "cosyn" to the "dede"', *Chaucer Review* 25 (1991), 343–54

——, 'Chaucer's "cosyn to the dede": further considerations', *Florilegium* 19 (2002), 91–107

Perkins, Nicholas, *Hoccleve's 'Regiment of Princes': Counsel and Constraint* (Cambridge: Brewer, 2001)

——, 'Representing advice in Lydgate', in Jenny Stratford (ed.), *The Lancastrian Court (Donington: Tyas, 2003)*, pp. 173–91

——, 'Haunted Hoccleve? *The Regiment of Princes*, the Troilean intertext, and conversations with the dead', *Chaucer Review* 43 (2008), 103–39

——, 'Ekphrasis and narrative in *Emaré* and *Sir Eglamour of Artois*', in Rhiannon Purdie and Michael Cichon (eds), *Medieval Romance, Medieval Contexts* (Cambridge: Brewer, 2011), pp. 47–60

——, 'Introduction: the materiality of medieval romance and *The Erle of Tolous*', in Nicholas Perkins (ed.), *Medieval Romance and Material Culture* (Cambridge: Brewer, 2015), pp. 1–22

——, and Alison Wiggins, *The Romance of the Middle Ages* (Oxford: Bodleian Library, 2012)

Petrey, Sandy, *Speech Acts and Literary Theory* (London: Routledge, 1990)

Pickering, Andrew, 'Material culture and the dance of agency', in Hicks and Beaudry (eds), *Oxford Handbook of Material Culture Studies*, pp. 191–208

Pinney, Christopher, 'Things happen: or, from which moment does that object come?', in Miller (ed.), *Materiality*, pp. 256–72

Price, Leah, *How to Do Things with Books in Victorian Britain* (Princeton, NJ: Princeton University Press, 2012)

Propp, Vladimir, *Morphology of the Folktale*, trans. Laurence Scott, ed. Louis A. Wagner, 2nd edn (Austin: University of Texas Press, 1968)

Prown, Jules David, 'Mind in matter: an introduction to material culture theory and method', *Winterthur Portfolio* 17 (1982), 1–19

Pulham, Carol A., 'Promises, promises: Dorigen's dilemma revisited', *Chaucer Review* 31 (1996), 76–86

Putter, Ad, *An Introduction to the 'Gawain'-Poet* (London: Longman, 1996)

——, 'Gifts and commodities in *Sir Amadace*', *Review of English Studies* 51 (2000), 371–94

——, 'Story line and story shape in *Sir Percyvell of Gales* and Chrétien de Troyes' *Conte du Graal*', in McDonald (ed.), *Pulp Fictions*, pp. 171–96

——, 'The narrative logic of *Emaré*', in Putter and Gilbert (eds), *Popular Romance*, pp. 157–80

——, and Jane Gilbert (eds), *The Spirit of Medieval English Popular Romance* (Harlow: Longman, 2000)

Renfrew, Colin, 'Archaeology and commodification: the role of things in societal transformation', in van Binsbergen and Geschiere (eds), *Commodification*, pp. 85–97

Ricœur, Paul, *Time and Narrative*, 3 vols (Chicago, IL: University of Chicago Press, 1984–88)

Riddy, Felicity, 'Giving and receiving: exchange in the *Roman van Walewein* and *Sir Gawain and the Green Knight*', *Tijdschrift voor Nederlandse Taal- en Letterkunde* 112 (1996), 18–29

Robertson, Kellie, 'Medieval things: materiality, historicism, and the premodern object', *Literature Compass* 5/6 (2008), 1060–80

——, 'Medieval materialism: a manifesto', *Exemplaria* 22 (2010), 99–118

Rubin, Gayle, 'The traffic in women: notes on the "political economy" of sex', in Rayna R. Reiter (ed.), *Toward an Anthropology of Women* (New York: Monthly Review Press, 1975), pp. 157–210

Rust, Martha, 'Blood and tears as ink: writing the pictorial sense of the text', *Chaucer Review* 47 (2013), 390–415

Sahlins, Marshall, 'The spirit of the gift', in Schrift (ed.), *The Logic of the Gift*, pp. 70–99

——, *Stone Age Economics* (London: Routledge, 2017)

Salter, Elizabeth, *English and International: Studies in the Literature, Art and Patronage of Medieval England*, ed. Derek Pearsall and Nicolette Zeeman (Cambridge: Cambridge University Press, 1988)

Sansi-Roca, Roger, *Art, Anthropology and the Gift* (London: Bloomsbury, 2015)

Saul, Nigel, *Lordship and Faith: The English Gentry and the Parish Church in the Middle Ages* (Oxford: Oxford University Press, 2017)

Saunders, Corinne, 'Medieval warfare', in Kate McLoughlin (ed.), *The Cambridge Companion to War Writing* (Cambridge: Cambridge University Press, 2009), pp. 83–97

Scanlon, Larry, and James Simpson (eds), *John Lydgate: Poetry, Culture and Lancastrian England* (Notre Dame, IN: Notre Dame University Press, 2006).

Scattergood, V.J., 'The Manciple's manner of speaking', *Essays in Criticism* 24 (1974), 124–46

Schlauch, Margaret, *Chaucer's Constance and Accused Queens* (New York: New York University Press, 1927)

Schleif, Corine, 'Gifts and givers that keep on giving: pictured presentations in early medieval manuscripts', in Georgiana Donavin and Anita Obermeier (eds), *Romance and Rhetoric: Essays in Honour of Dhira B. Mahoney* (Turnhout: Brepols, 2010), pp. 51–71

Schrift, Alan D., 'Introduction: why gift?', in Schrift (ed.), *The Logic of the Gift*, pp. 1–22

——, (ed.), *The Logic of the Gift: Toward an Ethic of Generosity* (New York: Routledge, 1997)

Scott, Anne, '"Do na ase þu sedes": Word and Deed in *King Horn*, *Havelok the Dane*, and the *Franklin's Tale*' (doctoral dissertation, Brown University, 1988)

Scott, Kathleen L., *Later Gothic Manuscripts, 1390–1490*, 2 vols (London: Harvey Miller, 1996)

Scott-Warren, Jason, *Sir John Harington and the Book as Gift* (Oxford: Oxford University Press, 2001)

Shalem, Avinoam, 'The second life of objects: ivory horns in medieval church treasuries', in Gudrun Bühl, Anthony Cutler and Arne Effenberger (eds), *Spätantike und byzantinische Elfenbeinbildwerke im Diskurs* (Wiesbaden: Reichert Verlag, 2008), pp. 225–36

——, and Maria Glaser, *Die Mittelalterlichen Olifante* (Berlin: Deutscher Verlag für Kunstwissenschaft, 2014)

Shoaf, R.A., *Dante, Chaucer, and the Currency of the Word: Money, Images, and Reference in Late Medieval Poetry* (Norman, OK: Pilgrim Books, 1983)
——, *The Poem as Green Girdle: Commercium in 'Sir Gawain and the Green Knight'* (Gainesville: University Presses of Florida, 1984)
Shonk, Timothy A., 'A study of the Auchinleck Manuscript: bookmen and bookmaking in the early fourteenth century', *Speculum* 60 (1985), 71–91
Short, Ian, 'Language and literature', in Christopher Harper-Bill and Elisabeth van Houts (eds), *A Companion to the Anglo-Norman World* (Woodbridge: Boydell Press, 2003), pp. 191–213
Silber, Ilana F., 'Gift-giving in the great traditions: the case of donations to monasteries in the medieval West', *Archives européennes de sociologie* 36 (1995), 209–43
Simpson, James, 'Spirituality and economics in passus 1–7 of the B text', *Yearbook of Langland Studies* 1 (1987), 83–103
——, 'Chaucer's presence and absence, 1400–1550', in Boitani and Mann (eds), *The Cambridge Companion to Chaucer*, pp. 251–69
——, 'Violence, narrative and proper name: *Sir Degare*, 'The Tale of Sir Gareth of Orkney', and the *Folie Tristan d'Oxford*', in Putter and Gilbert (eds), *Popular Romance*, pp. 122–41
——, *'Piers Plowman': An Introduction*, rev. edn (Exeter: University of Exeter Press, 2007)
——, *Under the Hammer: Iconoclasm in the Anglo-American Tradition* (Oxford: Oxford University Press, 2010)
——, 'Derek Brewer's romance', in Charlotte Brewer and Barry Windeatt (eds), *Traditions and Innovations in the Study of Medieval English Literature: The Influence of Derek Brewer* (Cambridge: Brewer, 2013), pp. 154–72
——, 'Human prudence versus the emotion of the cosmos: war, deliberations and destruction in the late-medieval Statian tradition', in Stephanie Downes, Andrew Lynch and Katrina O'Loughlin (eds), *Emotions and War: Medieval to Romantic Literature* (Basingstoke: Palgrave Macmillan, 2015), pp. 98–116
——, 'Unthinking thought: romance's wisdom', in Katherine C. Little and Nicola McDonald (eds), *Thinking Medieval Romance* (Oxford: Oxford University Press, 2018), pp. 36–51
Smith, D. Vance, *Arts of Possession: The Middle English Household Imaginary* (Minneapolis: University of Minnesota Press, 2003)
Smith, Karl, 'From dividual and individual selves to porous subjects', *Australian Journal of Anthropology* 23 (2012), pp. 50–64
Smyth, Karen Elaine, *Imaginings of Time in Lydgate and Hoccleve's Verse* (Farnham: Ashgate, 2011)
Spearing, A.C., *Medieval to Renaissance in English Poetry* (Cambridge: Cambridge University Press, 1985)
——, *Readings in Medieval Poetry* (Cambridge: Cambridge University Press, 1987)

——, *Textual Subjectivity: The Encoding of Subjectivity in Medieval Narratives and Lyrics* (Oxford: Oxford University Press, 2005)

——, 'What is a narrator?', *Digital Philology* 4 (2015), 59–105

Sponsler, Claire, 'Text and Textile: Lydgate's Tapestry Poems', in Burns (ed.), *Medieval Fabrications*, pp. 19–34

Spufford, Peter, Wendy Wilkinson, and Sarah Tolley, *Handbook of Medieval Exchange* (London: Offices of the Royal Historical Society, 1986)

Stanbury, Sarah, *Seeing the 'Gawain'-Poet: Description and the Act of Perception* (Philadelphia: University of Pennsylvania Press, 1991)

Standley, Eleanor, *Trinkets and Charms: The Use, Meaning and Significance of Dress Accessories, AD 1300–1700* (Oxford: Institute of Archaeology, 2013)

Straker, Scott-Morgan, 'Deference and difference: Lydgate, Chaucer, and the *Siege of Thebes*', *Review of English Studies* 52 (2001), 1–21

——, 'Propaganda, intentionality, and the Lancastrian Lydgate', in Scanlon and Simpson (eds), *John Lydgate*, pp. 98–128

Stratford, Jenny, 'Royal Books', in Richard Marks and Paul Williamson (eds), *Gothic: Art for England, 1400–1547* (London: V&A Publications, 2003), pp. 180–6

Strathern, Andrew J., and Pamela J. Stewart, 'Personhood: embodiment and personhood', in Frances E. Mascia-Lees (ed.), *A Companion to the Anthropology of the Body and Embodiment* (Chichester: Wiley-Blackwell, 2011), pp. 388–402

Strathern, Marilyn, *The Gender of the Gift: Problems with Women and Problems with Society in Melanesia* (Berkeley, CA: University of California Press, 1988)

——, 'Partners and consumers: making relations visible', in Schrift (ed.), *The Logic of the Gift*, pp. 292–311

——, 'Gifts money cannot buy', *Social Anthropology* 20 (2012), 397–410

——, 'Artifacts of history: events and the interpretation of images', in Marilyn Strathern, *Learning to See in Melanesia* (Chicago, IL: Hau Books/Society for Ethnographic Theory, 2013), pp. 157–78, https://haubooks.org/learning-to-see-in-melanesia

——, *Before and After Gender: Sexual Mythologies of Everyday Life* (Chicago, IL: Hau Books, 2016), https://haubooks.org/before-and-after-gender

Strohm, Paul, '*Storie, spelle, geste, romaunce, tragedie*: generic distinctions in the Middle English Troy narratives', *Speculum* 46 (1971), 348–59

——, *Social Chaucer* (Cambridge, MA: Harvard University Press, 1989)

——, 'The textual environment of Chaucer's "Lak of Stedfastness"', in Paul Strohm, *Hochon's Arrow: The Social Imagination of Fourteenth-Century Texts* (Princeton, NJ: Princeton University Press, 1992), pp. 57–74

——, *Theory and the Premodern Text* (Minneapolis: University of Minnesota Press, 2000)

——, 'Sovereignty and sewage', in Lisa H. Cooper and Andrea Denny-Brown (eds), *Lydgate Matters: Poetry and Material Culture in the Fifteenth Century* (New York: Palgrave Macmillan, 2008), pp. 57–70

Summit, Jennifer, 'William Caxton, Margaret Beaufort and the romance of female patronage', in Lesley Smith and Jane H.M. Taylor (eds), *Women, the Book, and the Godly: Selected Proceedings of the St Hilda's Conference, 1993* (Cambridge: Brewer, 1995), pp. 151–65

Sykes, Karen, *Arguing with Anthropology: An Introduction to Critical Theories of the Gift* (London: Routledge, 2005)

Symons, Dana M., 'Does Tristan think, or doesn't he?: The pleasures of the Middle English *Sir Tristrem*', *Arthuriana* 11 (2001), 3–22

Taylor, Paul B., 'Chaucer's *cosyn to the dede*', *Speculum* 57 (1982), 315–27

Treharne, Elaine, *Living through Conquest: The Politics of Early English, 1020–1220* (Oxford: Oxford University Press, 2012)

Trigg, Stephanie, 'The rhetoric of excess in *Winner and Waster*', *Yearbook of Langland Studies* 3 (1989), 91–108

——, 'The romance of exchange: *Sir Gawain and the Green Knight*', *Viator* 22 (1991), 251–66

——, 'The traffic in medieval women: Alice Perrers, feminist criticism and *Piers Plowman*', *Yearbook of Langland Studies* 12 (1998), 5–29

——, '"Shamed be…": historicizing shame in medieval and early modern courtly ritual', *Exemplaria* 19 (2007), 67–89

Turner, Marion, *Chaucerian Conflict: Languages of Antagonism in Late Fourteenth-Century London* (Oxford: Clarendon Press, 2007)

——, *Chaucer: A European Life* (Princeton, NJ: Princeton University Press, 2019)

van Binsbergen, Wim, 'Commodification: Things, Agency, and Identities: Introduction', in van Binsbergen and Geschiere (eds), *Commodification*, pp. 9–54

——, and Peter Geschiere (eds), *Commodification: Things, Agency, and Identities; 'The Social Life of Things' Revisited* (Münster: LIT Verlag, 2005)

van der Veen, Marijke, 'The Materiality of Plants: Plant–People Entanglements', *World Archaeology* 46 (2014), 799–812

van Dijk, Rijk, 'Questions of (in-)dividuality and (in-)alienability in transcultural reciprocal relations', in van Binsbergen and Geschiere (eds), *Commodification*, pp. 201–26

Vestergaard, Elisabeth, 'Gift-giving, hoarding, and outdoings', in Ross Samson (ed.), *Social Approaches to Viking Studies* (Glasgow: Cruithne Press, 1991), pp. 97–104

Wadiak, Walter, *Savage Economy: The Returns of Middle English Romance* (Notre Dame, IN: University of Notre Dame Press, 2017)

Wallace, David (ed.), *The Cambridge History of Medieval English Literature* (Cambridge: Cambridge University Press, 1999)

Walter, Katie L., 'Fragments for a medieval theory of prosthesis', *Textual Practice* 30 (2016), 1345–63

Warner, Kathryn, 'The provenance and early ownership of John Rylands MS English 1', *Bulletin of the John Rylands Library* 81 (1999), 141–54

Weiner, Annette B., *Inalienable Possessions: The Paradox of Keeping-While-Giving* (Berkeley: University of California Press, 1992)

Weiner, Annette B., and Jane Schneider (eds), *Cloth and Human Experience* (Washington, DC: Smithsonian Books, 1991)

Weiss, Judith, 'The wooing woman in Anglo-Norman romance', in Maldwyn Mills, Jennifer Fellows and Carol M. Meale (eds), *Romance in Medieval England* (Cambridge: Brewer, 1991), pp. 149–61

——, 'The power and weakness of women in Anglo-Norman romance', in Carol M. Meale (ed.), *Women and Literature in Britain, 1150–1500*, 2nd edn (Cambridge: Cambridge University Press, 1996), pp. 7–23

——, 'Thomas and the Earl: literary and historical contexts for the *Romance of Horn*', in Rosalind Field (ed.), *Tradition and Transformation in Medieval Romance* (Cambridge: Brewer, 1999), pp. 1–14

Whetter, K.S., *Understanding Genre and Medieval Romance* (Aldershot: Ashgate, 2008)

White, Stephen D., *Custom, Kinship, and Gifts to Saints: The 'Laudatio Parentum' in Western France, 1050–1150* (Chapel Hill: University of North Carolina Press, 1988)

Wilcockson, Colin, 'Thou and tears: the advice of Arveragus to Dorigen in Chaucer's "Franklin's Tale"', *Review of English Studies* 54 (2003), 308–12

Windeatt, Barry, '*Troilus* and the disenchantment of romance', in Derek Brewer (ed.), *Studies in Medieval English Romances: Some New Approaches* (Cambridge: Boydell and Brewer, 1988), pp. 129–47

Wogan-Browne, Jocelyn, *Saints' Lives and Women's Literary Culture, c.1150–1300: Virginity and its Authorizations* (Oxford: Oxford University Press, 2001)

Wogan-Browne, Jocelyn, et al. (eds), *Language and Culture in Medieval Britain: The French of England, c.1100–c.1500* (Woodbridge: Boydell & Brewer, 2009)

——, 'General introduction: what's in a name: the "French" of "England"', in Wogan-Browne et al. (eds), *Language and Culture in Medieval Britain*, pp. 1–13

Wood, Diana, *Medieval Economic Thought* (Cambridge: Cambridge University Press, 2002)

Woolgar, C.M., *Household Accounts from Medieval England*, 2 vols (Oxford: Oxford University Press, 1992)

——, *The Senses in Late Medieval England* (New Haven, CT: Yale University Press, 2006)

——, 'Gifts of food in late medieval England', *Journal of Medieval History* 37 (2011), 6–18

Worth, Liliana, 'Exile-and-Return in Medieval Vernacular Texts of England and Spain, c.1170–1250' (doctoral dissertation, University of Oxford, 2015)

Wright, Monica, *Weaving Narrative: Clothing in Twelfth-Century French Romance* (University Park, PA: Penn State University Press, 2009)

Index

Note: scholars and critics are only indexed where substantive discussion of their ideas is included in the text.

Lightning Source UK Ltd.
Milton Keynes UK
UKHW022245040321
379802UK00004B/174